ADVANCE PRAISE FOR THE GLOBAL FOURTH WAY: THE QUEST FOR EDUCATIONAL EXCELLENCE

By **Andy Hargreaves and Dennis Shirley**

"Andy Hargreaves's and Dennis Shirley's fascinating and powerful new book outlines new paths that can be forged by the profession, its organizations, and our schools. I hope everyone interested in the futures of young people takes the opportunity to read The Global Fourth Way.*"*

–Fred Van Leeuwen
General Secretary
Education International

"Inspiring, informative, and irresistible, The Global Fourth Way *is a book we cannot afford to ignore. Armed with extensive research and sound analysis of high-achieving schools and systems around the world, Shirley and Hargreaves present a powerful vision and a clear plan of action. They invite us to dream big when education is reduced to test scores. They ask us to personalize learning when standardization and homogenization are gaining silver-bullet status. They remind us of the human nature of education when teaching is rendered a mechanical process of knowledge transmission.* The Global Fourth Way *is indeed THE way to educational excellence!"*

–Yong Zhao
Presidential Chair and Associate Dean
for Global Education
University of Oregon

"Anyone looking for sage advice on how to improve schools and school systems could do no better than this book. Hargreaves and Shirley provide thoughtful ideas about schooling in ways that reignite our sense of what public schools can and should be, for all children."

–Ben Levin
Professor and Canada Research Chair, OISE
University of Toronto
Author, *More High School Graduates*

"The Fourth Way *inspired our national organization of school leaders to advocate and strategize successfully for a significant reduction in national standardized testing in England and for a better assessment alternative that benefits pupils and teachers alike."*

—Chris Harrison
President of the NAHT
National Association of Head Teachers

THE GLOBAL FOURTH WAY

ANDY HARGREAVES • DENNIS SHIRLEY

THE GLOBAL FOURTH WAY

The Quest for Educational Excellence

A JOINT PUBLICATION

FOR INFORMATION:

Corwin
A SAGE Company
2455 Teller Road
Thousand Oaks, California 91320
(800) 233-9936
www.corwin.com

SAGE Publications Ltd.
1 Oliver's Yard
55 City Road
London EC1Y 1SP
United Kingdom

SAGE Publications India Pvt. Ltd.
B 1/I 1 Mohan Cooperative Industrial Area
Mathura Road, New Delhi 110 044
India

SAGE Publications Asia-Pacific Pte. Ltd.
3 Church Street
#10-04 Samsung Hub
Singapore 049483

Acquisitions Editor: Arnis Burvikovs
Associate Editor: Desirée A. Bartlett
Editorial Assistant: Kimberly Greenberg
Permissions Editor: Karen Ehrmann
Project Editor: Veronica Stapleton
Copy Editor: Gretchen Treadwell
Typesetter: C&M Digitals (P) Ltd.
Proofreader: Dennis W. Webb
Indexer: Gloria Tierney
Cover Designer: Scott Van Atta

Printed in the United States of America

A catalog record of this book is available from the Library of Congress.

978-1-4129-8786-8

This book is printed on acid-free paper.

SFI label applies to text stock

12 13 14 15 16 10 9 8 7 6 5 4 3 2 1

CONTENTS

PREFACE

These are the dog days of public education and large-scale reform. At least that's how most teachers and many school leaders see it. It's easy to sympathize with them. In most of the Anglo-American group of nations, public education, as we have known it for over half a century, is under increasing attack. The idea of public education for the common good is being replaced by the insistence that anyone can provide public education, even at a profit, so long as it improves tested outcomes for individual students. Local democratic control of schools is being eroded and eradicated in favor of individual free schools, charter schools, and academies that are separated from each other but funded and regulated by a distant, centralized government bureaucracy. Things are changing quickly, and not always for the better.

> The idea of public education for the common good is being replaced by the insistence that anyone can provide public education, even at a profit, so long as it improves tested outcomes for individual students.

> The joys and triumphs of teaching are found in things like hearing children read their first words, introducing students to interests that stay with them for the rest of their lives, and finding ways to connect children's learning to their languages and cultures.

One of the most serious new developments is the escalating assault on teachers. What teachers do is constantly demeaned. The inspiring purposes that brought teachers into teaching and that keep children engaged with their learning are no longer officially respected. The joys and triumphs of teaching are found in things like hearing children read their first words, introducing students to interests that stay with them for the rest of their lives, and finding ways to connect children's learning to their languages and cultures. When teachers introduce young people to the wonders of nature; when they answer children's questions about fairness, death or God; when they are able to turn a bully into a protector of weaker children, then they know they picked the right profession, and that their work has been well done. But these things are being squeezed aside by demands to drive up test scores, to compete with other schools and teachers, to deliver a centralized curriculum, and to hammer away at the basics week after week until the heads of the nation's children are flattened and blunt!

And if it is not enough for teachers to be attacked for what they do, they are increasingly insulted for who they are and what they make. In the age of austerity, hard-earned retirement benefits are portrayed as expensive indulgences that should be cut down to size or eliminated altogether. The communications coup following the global economic collapse has brilliantly turned public anger away from bankers and on to public sector workers and particularly teachers. Based on unreliable and unstable test-score data, teachers are compared with one another in order to reward and punish them on the basis of these narrow measures of performance. A profession that once was—and in the highest-performing countries, still is—dignified as the achievement of years of long and rigorous training, is now being recast as something that can be picked up in a few quick weeks of preparation over the summer holidays.

These reform measures have more than two decades of a track record behind them and they are making teachers weary. The results of the 2012 *MetLife Survey of the American Teacher* confirm the depressing decline of the teaching profession in the United States. In the previous two years, the percentage of teachers surveyed who reported being very satisfied in their jobs declined sharply, from 59% to 44%. The number who indicated they were thinking of leaving the profession jumped from 17% to 29%.[1] Imagine being a student knowing that the teachers you encounter are becoming less satisfied, and close to one in three would rather be somewhere else.

The dog days of reform also apply to the reforms themselves. After being tried time after time, in place after place, the repeated failure of the reforms does not deter their advocates from driving them through with even greater ferocity. The reforms are defied by the evidence and contradicted by the experience of high performance in other countries and systems. Stubbornly, too many reformers in Anglo-American nations refuse to change horses in midstream.

Consider the contrary evidence. First, while many U.S. systems have turned public schools in entire urban areas over to charter management organizations, charter schools, as an aggregate, perform worse than conventional public schools.[2] Although some academies in England perform well, many demonstrate no consistent advantage over conventional state schools.[3] Second, although schools have invested heavily in educational technology while cutting teacher positions, it turns out that often students *do* want to be taught by teachers after all, and their academic achievement results show it.[4] Third, despite all the efforts to link teachers' salaries to test-score results, pay for tested performance has little or no evidence of prior success in the teaching profession, and external incentives do not raise performance in other complex professions either.[5] To make matters worse, these ineffective policies are exported to developing nations, with even fewer resources as well.[6]

All of these different change forces—marketplace models of school improvement, technology as a replacement for teachers, and pay for performance—are redefining the teaching profession as one where teachers are being trained faster, with careers that are shorter, even though most teachers do not hit peak periods of performance until at least four and often eight years into the job.[7]

And then there are the lessons of international experience. The world's highest-performing systems—Finland, Singapore, and Canada among them—are also strong *public* systems. They engage people in their schools locally. They use testing prudently, not pervasively. They favor innovation, not detailed standardization. Teachers' performance rewards are not based on student test-score data. Teaching is a lifelong career requiring rigorous training, not a short-term engagement that can be prepared for fast.

There is a better way forward with abundant evidence to support it. We first outlined it in our previous book—*The Fourth Way: The Inspiring Future for Educational Change.*[8] This drew upon our research to articulate a new change architecture for school improvement. We stated that to be high achieving, educators in school systems need the right kind of purpose that inspires them, a strengthened professionalism that propels them forward, and a cultural and structural coherence that holds them together.

To be high achieving, educators in school systems need the right kind of purpose that inspires them, a strengthened professionalism that propels them forward, and a cultural and structural coherence that holds them together.

We showed that three previous ways of change have all had some strengths, but also real limitations that prevented schools from reaching their full potential. The *First Way,* from the 1960s, gave educators unprecedented professional freedom in their classrooms but no way to spread what they learned or to bring it together. *Second Way* reforms that began in the 1980s created a push for standards and greater academic rigor, combined with the stimulus of market competition. But standards turned into standardization, and instead of innovating more, schools found themselves struggling to outdo each other at the same game instead. *Third Way* reforms, which were launched most successfully in England and parts of Canada but only got partial traction in the United States, gave teachers opportunities to learn from one another through new lateral networks, but mainly according to data-driven testing processes that limited the depth and scope of their professional conversations.

On top of this retrospective account, we drew upon international evidence of high achievement that we investigated in a network of 300 high schools, a high-performing country, a turned-around district, and an oppositional movement to bring about positive change despite prevailing policies. Our book sketched out a broad route for the Fourth Way, but it needed to be mapped in more detail and had to be laid out in practice to be truly useful.

The Global Fourth Way therefore fills out, refines, and sometimes redefines the features that characterize high achievement. It is organized around, and springs from, a new international research agenda of investigating high performance in different schools and systems across the world that we have developed over several years.

We lay down the foundations of this argument in the first two chapters. We begin by asking what *kind* of change we want. Do we want to improve what already exists or transform it into something fundamentally new? We explore and explain the dynamic combination of improvement with innovation. The point, we argue, is not just to continue with incremental change, but also to push for deeper, disruptive transformations of schools and systems.

The following six chapters set out the evidence for our argument. They consist of six cases of successful innovation and improvement. Two are high-performing nations. Two are large-scale systems that have hybrid properties of and, in different ways, are transitional between the Third and Fourth Ways. The final two cases depict schools and systems that strive and struggle to establish the Fourth Way within contrary systems of market competitiveness, standardization, and extensive testing.

Chapters 3 and 4 describe two high-performing national systems that exemplify many Fourth Way principles: Finland and Singapore. Although very different from each other geographically, politically, and culturally, they have transformed themselves and their educational systems within a generation or so. Despite and even because of their differences, the two nations are both defined by the possession of a compelling and coherent moral purpose, an emphasis on the civic necessity of strong public education, clear commitments to high-quality teachers and teaching, and ways of securing system integration that are more about cultural coherence in beliefs and communication than about bureaucratic alignment on paper.

Chapters 5 and 6 describe two systems poised between the Third and the Fourth Ways: the Canadian provinces of Alberta and Ontario. In educational results, as in its quality of life and government policies, Canada is a global leader. Officially bilingual and multicultural, Canada possesses many features that are similar to its U.S. neighbor, but some decisive differences as well. Its provincial education systems point to the importance of public investment and professional quality and stability as platforms for educational success. Canada also shows that educational excellence does not require centralization of federal power and authority. This authority, it shows, can be dispersed effectively across provinces (the equivalent of U.S. or Australian states), where local school districts have considerable influence too.

The next two chapters examine a Fourth Way school and network of schools that have established themselves within and against wider systems that operate on Second Way principles of markets and standardization, and on Third Way policies of data-driven improvement. Chapter 7 examines a turned-around high school in an impoverished cultural minority community in the North of England. Like a number of similar peers, this school courageously adopted a highly innovative change strategy that based the curriculum on how its students learned best. It galvanized its teachers through inspiring and distributed leadership and worked closely with local parents and the community. This was all achieved within and occasionally against a national system of intense pressures for meeting the demands of data-driven improvement and standardized testing.

Chapter 8 sets out a successful case of bottom-up, union-driven reform in California that shows how, on a considerable scale, and even when the larger policy environment is unsupportive and obstructive, meaningful and measurable academic gains are still possible. This chapter shows how Fourth Way unions along with a range of partners can be in the forefront of changes that benefit students and uplift teachers. It also illustrates how and why governments and system administrators in Second Way systems especially sometimes have to be circumvented or even challenged because they resist changes that benefit students. The point made in all these chapters is that Fourth Way thinking and acting can and do occur everywhere—even in systems that are uncongenial to them.

> We certainly need great urgency for change in many schools and systems, but we cannot do this without generating professional energy as well.

The six case studies pinpoint essential change principles that enable and inspire a school or a system to innovate and improve. The final chapter addresses the nitty-gritty, and potentially galvanizing practical issues that change leaders must confront and conquer in order to take charge of the profession and release its dynamic potential. Educational change, we say, doesn't need just levers or drivers to make it happen. It also needs professional dynamos who generate and transform people's energy for change. We certainly need great urgency for change in many schools and systems, but we cannot do this without generating professional energy as well.

The dynamos of educational change can and should be a system's thousands of teachers and its school leaders. Governments can provide an inspiring sense of direction and the resources and constant messaging to match it. The public can lift its sights not only to raise expectations for individual parents' own children, but also to embrace aspirations for all the nation's children. But, in the end, nothing of value will occur without the commitment and capability of thousands of classroom teachers and their leaders who have ultimate control over how they teach their own students every day.

This is the call of the Fourth Way—a call that is not abstract or academic, but that is practical and palpable because it already exists in the highest-performing schools and systems in the world. It is a call that requires us to reflect on and return to our most deeply held principles about high-quality teaching and learning, to learn from the successes of others that can help us advance, and to redouble our efforts to provide an outstanding education for all young people.

ACKNOWLEDGMENTS

We are grateful to our co-investigators, to the support and stimulation of our research teams and graduate students inside and outside of Boston College, and to the organizations that believed in our mission of identifying and spreading the lessons of outstanding performance and funded our work accordingly. We would like to thank the teachers, schools, and educational officials who have openly engaged with our questions and given freely of their time and energy during our visits to their schools and jurisdictions.

We thank the people who worked on the following projects on which the thinking and work in this book draws extensively:

Performing Beyond Expectations. Codirected by Andy Hargreaves and Alma Harris (at the London Institute of Education). Research team: Alan Boyle, Michelle De La Rosa, Kathryn Ghent, Janet Goodall, Alex Gurn, Corrie Stone Johnson, and Lori McEwen. Funded by the National College for School Leadership and the Specialist Schools and Academies Trust in England.

Review of Essential for Some, Good for All in Ontario. Codirected by Andy Hargreaves and Henry Braun. Research team: Maureen Hughes, Matt Welch, Karen Lam, Beth Morgan, Kathryn Sallis, Lauren Chapman, Alex Gurn, Adam Steiner, and Yu Jin Lee. Funded by the Council of Directors in Education, in Ontario, Canada.

Teachers Union Reform Network (TURN). Directed by Dennis Shirley. Research team: Carrie Fuller and Lyda Peters. Funded by the Ford Foundation.

OECD Review of School Leadership and School Improvement in Finland. Research Team with Andy Hargreaves, Beatrice Pont of the Organization for Economic Cooperation and Development (OECD), and Gabor Halasz—formerly director general of the Hungarian National Institute for Public Education.

Review of the Alberta Initiative for School Improvement. Conducted by Andy Hargreaves, Dennis Shirley, Robert Crocker (Memorial University, Newfoundland), Pasi Sahlberg (Centre for Immigration and Mobility Organization, Helsinki), Brent Davis (University of Calgary), and Dennis Sumara (University of Calgary), with the support of Maureen Hughes and Lori McEwen, Boston College. Funded by the Alberta Ministry of Education.

OECD Review of Lower Secondary Schools in Norway. Research team with Dennis Shirley, Nancy Hoffman, Kirsti Klette, Pasi Sahlberg, as well as Beatriz Pont and Diane Toledo Figueroa of the OECD.

Review of Singapore Educational System. Codirected by Andy Hargreaves and Pak Tee Ng (National Institute of Education, Singapore). Funding support from the National Institute of Education, Singapore.

The Finland-Alberta School Partnership Project. Conducted by Dennis Shirley, Andy Hargreaves, and Karen Lam. Funded by the Alberta Teachers' Association and the Centre for Immigration and Mobility Organization (Finland).

Adam Steiner and Brad Kershner provided excellent support in preparing this manuscript at several stages of the editing process. Kristie Thayer provided valuable support with proofreading. Arnis Burvikovs at Corwin Press has always been a true believer in what we try to do, and a patient, persistent supporter of our efforts to bring all this work to fruition. He is not only a great publishing colleague, but he has become a very great friend to us as well.

Finally, we express our heartfelt gratitude to our wives, Pauline Hargreaves and Shelley Cochran. We have the incredible good fortune to be married to two outstanding educators in the field, who have given us the forthright feedback we have needed to sharpen up our arguments, and all the loving support we could ever have wanted on the occasions we have started to falter in our personal quests for educational excellence. It's not been easy for them, or for us, staying up all hours, week after week, and month after month. We owe a great debt to both of them for sticking with us through these years.

ABOUT THE AUTHORS

Andy Hargreaves is the Thomas More Brennan Chair in the Lynch School of Education at Boston College. The mission of the chair is to promote social justice and connect theory and practice in education. Before moving to Boston, he taught primary school and lectured in several English universities, including Oxford. Prior to coming to Boston College, he was co-founder and director of the International Center for Educational Change at the Ontario Institute for Studies in Education in Toronto. He has been awarded visiting professorships in the United States, Canada, the United Kingdom, Hong Kong, Sweden, Japan, and Singapore and holds an honorary doctorate from Scandinavia's oldest university, Uppsala in Sweden. He has received the Whitworth Award for outstanding contributions to educational research in Canada.

Andy was founding editor in chief of the *Journal of Educational Change* and is lead editor of the first and second *International Handbook of Educational Change.* He has authored or edited more than 30 books, several of which have received outstanding writing awards. His most recent books are *Professional Capital* (with Michael Fullan, 2012), *The Fourth Way* (with Dennis Shirley, 2009), and *Sustainable Leadership* (with Dean Fink, 2006). For more information, see www.andyhargreaves.com.

Dennis Shirley is Professor of Education at the Lynch School of Education at Boston College. His pathbreaking scholarship on community organizing and educational change has led to speaking engagements in many countries. Dennis's recent articles have appeared in *Educational Leadership,* the *Phi Delta Kappan, Teachers College Record,* and *The Journal of Educational*

Change. His research has been translated into many languages, and he speaks German and Spanish. He has provided expert testimony to the Education Committee of the California State Assembly, to the Education Committee of the Commonwealth of Massachusetts, and on Capitol Hill, in Washington, D.C.

Dennis recently concluded a grant from the Ford Foundation aimed at increasing the regional satellites of the Teachers Union Reform Network (TURN) in the United States. He is currently the principal investigator on an academic technology innovation grant at Boston College, in which he is exploring the potential of new technologies not to distract and interrupt, but rather to focus and concentrate attention. This research builds on his book with Elizabeth MacDonald titled *The Mindful Teacher.* For more information, visit www.mindfulteacher.com.

Dennis has been a traveling scholar for the Australian Council for Educational Leaders and a visiting professor at Harvard University, the National Institute of Education in Singapore, and the University of Barcelona. He is chair of the Educational Change Special Interest Group of the American Education Research Association. Dennis holds a doctoral degree from Harvard University. For more information, visit www.dennisshirley.com.

Chapter One

THE CRISIS OF EDUCATIONAL CHANGE

We are at a pivotal moment of world history. An immense crisis has come upon us, and our lives are being turned upside down. We are in the midst of the greatest economic turmoil in half a century. The technological changes of the digital age are rampant and relentless. Political unrest and instability is erupting everywhere—some of it promising; much of it perilous. Climate change is unabating. And the movement of people and ideas around the world is greater than ever before.

When we wrote *The Fourth Way,* we saw a lot of this coming, and we spelled out the implications it had and the options it offered for the future of public education. All these change forces still apply. Many are even more intense in their impact and effects. But the biggest change since our last diagnosis is not in something that affects education from the outside; it is in the global transformation of education itself. It's not just the world that's changing education now. An orchestrated shake-up of every aspect of education is starting to change the world.

It's not just the world that's changing education now. An orchestrated shake-up of every aspect of education is starting to change the world.

A GLOBAL EDUCATION MARKET

Education, including public education, is a massive new market for global capital investment that is worth tens of billions of dollars.[1] The financial debt bubble has burst. The property bubble has too. Capital investment has to find new markets to gravitate toward. For many investors and venture capitalists, one big new answer is education.[2]

Markets are not new to public education, of course. As long ago as 1776, in *The Wealth of Nations,* Scottish economist Adam Smith argued for the importance of markets in education. A century later, Victorian capitalists and philanthropists supported and inaugurated a public educational system that would produce people with the skills required for a growing industrial economy. In the second half of the 20th century, the human capital argument positioned public education as an investment in economic returns that would come from a more educated and skilled generation in the future.[3] And in the past few decades, a multimillion dollar "school improvement industry" of textbook and testing companies, providers of staff development services, and research and development consultants has mushroomed.[4]

But the most recent impact of markets on public education represents a step-change. This is because of what Diane Ravitch calls "venture philanthropy," where the leaders of vast foundations "converged in support of reform strategies that mirrored their own experience in acquiring huge fortunes, such as competition, choice, deregulation, incentives, and other market-based approaches."[5] This recent shift is also due to the direct influence of large publishing, testing, and technology conglomerates in the delivery of services for the public sector and in convening international meetings of political leaders, corporate executives, and academic consultants that shape and shift the national and international conversation about global educational reform. What are the effects?

The most obvious development is that more and more schools are being turned over to private control. In England, the Coalition Government is converting locally controlled schools into independent academies, sometimes by raising the floor for what counts as failure in order to legitimize these conversions. In the United States, the No Child Left Behind Act plowed millions of dollars into "supplemental educational services," including for-profit companies, even though, by comparison, traditional school districts have demonstrated superior student learning gains.[6]

In England, the spread of academies is weakening local authorities to the extent that many can no longer run their school improvement and support services. Academy staff and the "chains" of schools for which they work must, in the words of one newspaper, be "rubbing their hands together with glee" at the prospect of taking over private control of these services instead.[7] Meanwhile, in the United States, almost entire school districts, such as New Orleans and Detroit, have been transferred to charter management organizations.[8]

These entrepreneurial interventions are being made easier as school system leaders implement Common Core State Standards in the United States, a detailed national curriculum in England, and common standards elsewhere. Some districts are being consolidated to the point where they are no longer the guardians of local democracy, but more like regional line managers of central government policy.

Then there is the influence of the private sector through educational technology. Despite the very real potential of "personalized learning" for offering students more flexible ways to access and process their learning, in too many instances, schools are being cajoled and coerced into uncritical adoption of digital technology products and services. For example, an increasing number of U.S. states are now legislating that all high school students must take at least one course through online platforms in order to graduate, even though there is no evidence this improves learning.[9]

Meanwhile, publishing and testing companies are reaping huge returns from designing, marketing, and sometimes operating the burgeoning products of standardized testing. One single testing contract alone with New York State in 2012 cost taxpayers all of $32 million.[10] New certification requirements for U.S. teachers include filming themselves teaching and sending copies of their films to private corporations that charge these young recruits hundreds of dollars for the privilege of rating their teaching for them. The corporations also retain exclusive copyright of the films, allegedly for research purposes.[11]

One way to increase profits is to reduce costs. The greatest cost in public education is teachers' salaries. Profits from public education can therefore increase if the immediate costs of teaching can be kept low. This is already occurring on many fronts. These include attacks on teachers' pensions and tenure in the United States and the imposition of local bargaining in England so that teachers working in poorer parts of the country will be awarded less rather than more pay. The introduction of performance-related pay can also be employed to remove more experienced and therefore more costly teachers if they have low value-added scores, and replace them with young, flexible, and temporary teachers at less cost to the system. Indeed, some U.S states are using performance measures to grade their teachers on a bell curve—ensuring that 7% or so of them will fail every year. The modal (most commonly occurring) number of years experience in teaching in the United States is now just *one year*.[12] Imagine if the modal number was the same for doctors. What an outcry there would be!

All these profit-oriented policies and strategies that yield short-term economic returns from education are controversial. *None* of them are practiced in high-achieving nations described in this book. These nations have very tiny or nonexistent private sectors. Because they want to encourage their teachers to work with the most challenging students and understand that teaching is an altruistic profession where most motivation is intrinsic, not one of them assesses teachers' performance in relation to student test scores. All of them invest high authority in local control. Every one of them attracts high-quality teachers and then retains them until they perform at their best. High performers also invest more of their resources in learning and teaching because they are not diverting funds into things like transportation or centralized administration. Last, not one of the governments of these high performers tests all their children on almost all of the curriculum, year after year.

Market-oriented reforms that are designed to yield short-term economic returns are clearly the wrong strategy, headed in the wrong direction.

Private education has a legitimate role in educational provision. It can offer options that the public system may not be providing, and it can stimulate the public system to change by spearheading innovations and alternatives. But market-oriented reforms that are designed to yield short-term economic returns are clearly the wrong strategy, headed in the wrong direction. Another kind of change is urgently needed in those countries like the United States and England that are currently underperforming. What might that be?

THEORIES OF CHANGE IN ACTION

All reforms have theories of change. They have a *purpose* that has to be achieved, *tools* to achieve that purpose, and *practices* to arrange those elements in a particular way. They entail *processes* to adjust and refine the design over time as problems surface and the reality of the environment becomes better understood. These theories of change can be explicit or implicit, intentional or assumed.

In the world of educational change, theories of what to change and how to change abound. Market-oriented reforms emphasize competition, comparison, survival of the fittest, consumer choice, and performance-based pay. Standardized reforms encompass common standards and curricula, high-stakes testing, and a range of mechanisms to ensure fidelity and compliance. Some changes try to balance pressure with support, using targets and transparency to exert pressure and providing training and professional interaction to offer all the necessary support. Meanwhile, those who want to innovate, rather than merely improve, try to create platforms of resources and support—increasingly, though not necessarily, of a digital nature—so that people can make changes for themselves in creating curriculum, accessing people who can teach them, or constructing professional learning networks, for example.

All theories of change are also premised on assumptions or beliefs about how people change as individuals, and how to bring about change altogether. Psychotherapists believe that people will find insight and experience personal growth when they explore their feelings and release their repressions. Alcoholics Anonymous puts its faith in peer support and the organization's famous twelve steps of recovery. Weight Watchers grounds its principles in peer pressure, self-set targets, transparency of outcomes, and a bit of televised celebrity role modeling as well. Market-based changes assume that a competitive instinct and the lure of external rewards drive people. Opposing theories are premised on the idea that people can be drawn into change through inspirational leadership, professionally engaging interactions, success at their work, and support to perform it well.

In the end, theories of educational change must be judged not by their ideological or philosophical underpinnings, but by their outcomes and effects on students. For this reason this book provides six examples of educational change from around the world that have achieved excellent results. These are drawn from our firsthand studies of successful practice. We look at high-performing schools and systems in detail and then map backward to determine the theories of change in action that hold them coherently together. The design principles of these theories of change are in many cases startlingly simple and, with suitable adaptation, surprisingly applicable to quite different contexts. This book invites readers to explore these high-performing systems and schools to see how their underlying principles of change can be put to work in other institutions and systems—including, we hope you will discover, your own.

But before looking at the best systems around us, it's important to engage with the change models that prevail in the present and the ones that have inscribed themselves in our memories and practices before. These models form the mainstream assumptions and memory-laden backdrops against which alternative models have to assert their claims to success.

THREE WAYS OF CHANGE

In *The Fourth Way,* we began by analyzing three approaches to educational change that have taken place across the world over the past four decades. We unpacked the assumptions each way of change contained, and then examined each of these Ways in terms of their impact and effects. These distinct Ways of change emerged from our research on the experiences of more than 200 educators in eight U.S. and Canadian high schools over 30 years.[13] The idea of *The Fourth Way* then began to evolve through our subsequent investigations of high-performing countries, networks, and school districts that we happened to be investigating in different parts of the world.

The First Way of educational change, which characterized the late 1960s and then the 1970s, was an age of strong investment in public education, high professional autonomy and discretion in selecting and designing the curriculum, passive trust from parents who left teachers alone to get on with the job, and encouragement of innovation in group-based and open-plan methods along with child-centered approaches to learning. The First Way was also a period when a lot of innovation was not understood in any real depth, much of it did not spread, and there was great inconsistency among schools. As a movement, the First Way is now no longer with us, but it lives on in the nostalgic memories of some boomer generation teachers and union leaders who still defend principles of individual professional autonomy against the political forces that threaten to intrude upon them. Memories of past innovations also influence how older educators interpret and respond to innovations today.

After the first oil crisis of the 1970s, a *Second Way* of educational change followed the First during the Reagan and Thatcher eras in the United States and United Kingdom, respectively. In an environment of declining resources and rising teachers' salaries, the Second Way was an age of growing austerity in salaries and resources, and of centralized prescriptions of curriculum and instruction. Educators experienced unprecedented and orchestrated attacks on the competence and privileges of public school teachers. Declining confidence in the ability and financial capacity of the welfare state to serve the public good led to a new model of market competition in education, as well as public rankings of school performance, and eventually of individual teacher performance too.

The Second Way of educational change, with intense top-down pressure and little support, characterized England, Chile, the United States, and parts of Australia and Canada through the 1990s. The Second Way is still very present in the Race to the Top (RTTT) legislation of current U.S. educational policy, with its aggressive support for charter schools and individualized performance-based pay for teachers based in large part on student test scores. In many U.S. states, these trends also accompany attacks on the allegedly unjustified privileges of teachers' benefits and tenure compared to private sector workers.

The Second Way's stringent and unsupportive measures led to a widespread crisis of teacher recruitment and retention. Governments responded by searching for reform solutions that were pitched somewhere between and beyond the First Way and the Second. In the United States, President Bill Clinton hosted a summit in 1998 with Tony Blair of the United Kingdom to explore new "Third Way" policies that would combine the security of a reformed welfare state, along with a renewed respect for professions and professionalism, with the entrepreneurial energy and innovative spirit of markets. Anthony Giddens, former director of the London School of Economics, served as the thought leader who gave this new Third Way its intellectual bearings and legitimacy.[14]

In U.S. education, the Third Way was apparent in how magnet schools emerged as a legitimate alternative to regular public schools in the 1990s. The Comprehensive School Reform Program enabled teachers to make First Way–like choices in reform options for their schools, but only within the imposed parameters of officially approved, evidence-based alternatives. Award-winning districts like Norfolk, Virginia, and Boston, Massachusetts, supported a more participatory professional climate within schools by providing teachers with opportunities to coach and learn from one another.

In the end, though, the Third Way never achieved the high impact and political visibility in the United States that it did in other nations. American policy leaders persisted with Second Way strategies of systemwide testing and increasing private alternatives that had already started to take hold in many states, through the federal legislation of No Child Left Behind. This approach intensified under the RTTT strategy of the Obama administration.

In contrast to the United States, Third Way strategies were pursued more fully in England and parts of Canada where top-down pressure was retained and even increased. This occurred in the form of system targets in literacy and mathematics achievement. Increased support was also provided in terms of training, materials, and extra coaching and assistance. The Third Way invested in peer-to-peer interactions to enable teachers to deliver the targeted results by forming data teams to identify gaps and make interventions, by developing new strategies in professional learning communities, and by moving ideas and instructional strategies around schools through clusters and networks. Data teams and professional learning communities were two aspects of the Third Way that did have an impact in the United States as a supplement to policy makers' persistence with Second Way priorities in market competition and standardization.

Some real gains were made in Third Way systems in terms of student achievement and teacher morale. However, we also criticized the Third Way for the narrowness of its focus on literacy and mathematics to the exclusion of other curriculum areas, and for its preoccupation with imposed achievement targets that, as we will see in Chapter 2, sometimes led teachers to "game the system" and use inauthentic strategies to produce the appearance of improved results.

Finnish education expert Pasi Sahlberg argues that combinations of developments now comprise what he calls a "global education reform movement" or GERM.[15] GERM, according to Sahlberg, consists of

- standardization of teaching and learning;
- focus on literacy and mathematics achievement;
- teaching for predetermined results;
- test-based accountability;
- increasing bureaucratic control;
- merit-based pay for teachers; and
- renting of other countries' premade reform models, rather than creating and owning one's own.

We would make two additions to these developments that point to a kind of "Third Way Plus":

- the use of data to drive decisions and discussions about student learning and achievement; and
- the spread of digital technology into the everyday life of classrooms and schools.

In the Second and Third Ways, the metaphors of global educational change are often quite mechanical. Within GERM, change doesn't grow, adapt, emerge, or evolve as it does in natural or complex systems. It is "driven" and "delivered" as in the industrial world of commodity production and distribution. This blue-collar model of teaching fails to produce the innovation and creativity in children's learning that are essential for 21st century knowledge economies.[16]

THE FOURTH WAY ALTERNATIVE

There are alternative theories of change. These have different design principles and assumptions that produce the economic and social outcomes that are essential for economic dynamism, social cohesion, and democratic ways of life. The Fourth Way of change leads to different end points of education that encompass yet also extend beyond high standards and individual achievement. At the same time, the Fourth Way reaches these end points through particular processes of change that have their own distinctive design principles as well. It approaches the purposes and outcomes of education on its own deliberately designed paths. This book is about these pathways to educational excellence.

The Fourth Way set out an alternative vision to the first three Ways of change, based on the countries, districts, and networks of schools we had been studying in different parts of the world. In this Fourth Way of educational change, we argued the following points in our earlier book:

- System targets for securing achievement gains by raising the bar and narrowing the gap in measured student performance are replaced by inspiring and shared moral purposes to transform learning and achievement for all, with any targets remaining being collectively decided, not politically imposed.
- Teaching and learning include but also extend beyond the basics of literacy and mathematics to encompass and engage a broader range of learning for all kinds of learners.
- Data are used to inform teacher inquiry and decision making in professional learning communities, rather than to drive it.
- Testing is employed to sample the progress of a system without distorting the way it operates, compared to the Third Way's combination of high-stakes testing coupled with imposed system targets that can produce widespread gaming of that system in order to produce the required results.
- Teachers engage in developing curriculum together within and across their schools, rather than just delivering the curriculum on behalf of others.
- Leadership is not about individuals managing the delivery of imposed reforms, but about developing distributed and sustainable responsibility for innovating and changing together. It is about collective responsibility rather than vertical accountability.

Figure 1.1 provides a comprehensive overview of the different components of Fourth Way theories of change in relationship to the three previous Ways of change, as outlined in our previous book.

Figure 1.1 A Framework of the Four Ways of Educational Change

		The First Way	*The Second Way*	*The Third Way*	*The Fourth Way*
Pillars of Purpose and Partnership	**Purpose**	Innovative; inconsistent	Markets and standardization	Performance targets: raise the bar, narrow the gap	Inspiring, inclusive, innovative mission
	Community	Little or no engagement	Parent choice	Parent choice and community service delivery	Public engagement and community development
	Investment	State investment	Austerity	Renewal	Moral economy
	Corporate influence	Minimal	Extensive - charters and academies, technology, testing products	Pragmatic partnerships with government	Ethical partnerships with civil society
	Students	Happenstance involvement	Recipients of change	Targets of service delivery	Engagement and voice
	Learning	Eclectic and uneven	Direct instuction to standards and test requirements	Customized learning pathways	Truly personalized; mindful teaching and learning
Principles of Professionalism	**Teachers**	Variable training quality	Flexible, alternate recruitment	High qualification, varying retention	High qualification, high retention.
	Associations	Autonomous	Deprofessionalized	Reprofessionalized	Change-makers
	Learning Communities	Discretionary	Contrived	Data-driven	Evidence-informed
Catalysts of Coherence	**Leadership**	Individualistic; variable	Line managed	Pipelines for delivering individuals	Systemic and sustainable
	Networks	Voluntary	Competitive	Dispersed	Community focused
	Responsibility	Local and little accountability	High-stakes targets; testing by census	Escalating targets, self-monitoring, and testing by census	Responsibility first, testing by sample, ambitious and shared targets
	Differentiation and Diversity	Underdeveloped	Mandated and standardized	Narrowed achievement gaps and data-driven interventions	Demanding and responsive teaching

This book now concentrates attention on this quest for excellence by examining six deliberately selected examples of high performance in school systems and schools across the world. This is a means to flesh out the Fourth Way in action, to focus on some of its core elements, and to refine what we can learn about it through the hard test of evidence and comparative experience.

One thing this new work has taught us is that few systems are purely Fourth Way, Second Way, or any other Way in character. Fourth Way principles often coexist alongside those of the Third Way, or even the Second Way, in emerging policy hybrids of change. The four Ways are more like what German sociologist Max Weber described as "ideal types." Ideal types, Weber said, are categories that exist nowhere in their entirety yet can still be classified as having certain traits because they help us explain the main properties of cultures or systems.[17] In the real world of schools and school systems, a wide array of teaching styles can bump up against one another, even among teachers who might be on the same grade-level team or who have been teaching in the same subject department for years. Likewise, what happens to "pure" policy directives is often determined by how these directives relate to, overlap with, or conflict with preceding policies from a different era. In this sense, it's not unusual to find First Way teaching in a Second Way system with a Third Way school principal or superintendent, for example.

Our book explores six examples of educational excellence and the theories of change that underpin them, on a global scale, across five countries. Each of them has been a unique educational project, yet all of them possess and express common purposes and principles of design and development. They are all part of one broad path or way of achieving educational success that draws on yet also transcends previous traditions of educational change and reform.

BENCHMARKING OR BENCH-PRESSING

One way to determine whether the Fourth Way or any other way is the best way, and to discern what this best way or these best ways might look like in practice, is to compare different countries and systems with one another. However, comparing high-performing countries does not, by itself, lead to a better way. A lot depends on how people draw these comparisons and what kinds of purposes they have in mind. In general, the process of comparing systems with one another and of learning from these comparisons is known as *international benchmarking*—something that is now a big feature of international educational policy discussions and directions. International benchmarking, we will see, has immense benefits in helping people understand how to achieve excellence—but the process is often misdirected and misunderstood. If we return to the origins and evolution of benchmarking, we are more likely to be clearer about how to use the benchmarking process to best effect.[18]

One of our grandfathers was a cobbler. He repaired people's shoes for a living. In the 19th century, part of the practice of shoemaking for particular customers was to place the foot of the person who would be wearing the shoe on a "bench" so they could "mark" out the pattern of the shoe to get a better fit. And so emerged the practice that we now call *benchmarking.*

One of the cobbler's grandsons (who is also a coauthor of this book) spent several summers helping to finance his way through university by working on a survey of the town's municipal sewer system. While one surveyor operated an instrument to calculate angles, his partner would balance a calibrated metal staff on a chiseled notch or mark that had, decades earlier, and as far back as the 1800s in some cases, been cut into the corner of a nearby stone building. These notches or benchmarks had figures for altitude recorded in a printed local and national database. The height of benchmarks was calculated in relation to surrounding benchmarks. The joint task of the sewer survey was to determine the height or level of a particular sewer in relation to the premeasured benchmark in the nearby building.

It wasn't until the 1980s that benchmarks and benchmarking migrated from being used as ways to measure and *guide* existing practice in shoemaking or surveying, to being deployed as a tool to *improve* other kinds of practice elsewhere. In the early 1980s, the new chief executive officer of Xerox, David Kearns, sent teams of his executives to visit the sites of high-performing Japanese competitors in order to figure out the processes that led to the outstanding results, learn from what had been seen, and apply what had been learned to improve practice within Xerox itself. This was one of the first known uses of what is now called *industrial benchmarking.*[19]

The president of the U.S. National Center for Education and the Economy (NCEE), Marc Tucker, believes that educators can learn a lot from industrial benchmarking. This, he says, is not a strategy to replicate or merely copy what other people are doing, because the likely outcome would be merely an inferior version of something that already exists. Instead, when comparing U.S. factories with Japanese higher performers, for example, the point is "to sort out those strategies that worked because of conditions that could be duplicated in the United States from those conditions that we could not hope to duplicate, and then identify those things that would be much easier for us to do, than it was for them to do."[20]

Industrial benchmarking is not a simple or solely technical process. It involves establishing teams who assemble a wide range of data, including those gathered during a site visit, to look at the processes that competitors use in order to produce their superior results. The teams then apply what they have learned to their own unique settings in order to streamline or revise their organization's production processes.

In recent years, these processes of industrial benchmarking have been adopted in the practice of making international comparisons of educational performance. Measures of student achievement such as the Organization for Economic Cooperation and Development's (OECD) Program for International Student Assessment (PISA), and Trends in International Math and Science Studies (TIMSS) have been used to identify superior performers or those who are "best in class" in relation to people's own systems. International organizations with links to policy and business strategy—such as the OECD, McKinsey & Company, and the NCEE—send teams of researchers, practitioners, and other experts to the top performers overall or in a particular class in order to elicit the processes that seem to explain successful outcomes.[21] They then endeavor to determine what lessons can be learned from all of this that might benefit other countries that are doing less well. Within education, this widely used and influential strategy has become known as *international benchmarking*.

The chief designers and users of international educational benchmarking intend that it should be at least as sophisticated as its industrial counterpart, if not more so. For them, benchmarking of one country's achievement against another is not a ploy to induce anxiety or bring about a competitive drive to increase performance in any way, at any cost. It is not about whether one country can leapfrog another by one or two positions or by a few points in achievement scores. The main purpose of benchmarking is to prompt *learning* about and *inquiry into* one's own performance as a result of comparing it with a thorough and authentic review of the performance of those who do even better.[22] The immediate goal of educational benchmarking, then, shouldn't be increased competitiveness, but "policy learning" within and across systems.[23]

Unfortunately, while the publication of and publicity given to international test results have directed needed attention toward international benchmarking, they have also led to some distortions of the benchmarking process.

1. *Bench-Pressing.* Benchmarking is often converted into pointlessly competitive bench-pressing as country after country tries to prove it can push harder and higher than its peers. Irish politicians say they want to get into the top five of PISA. The Netherlands laments its fall from seventh to tenth on PISA, even though three jurisdictions that entered PISA for the first time in 2009 are now placed above it—this means that, compared to its former peers, the Netherlands actually sustained its high performance. The Norwegians say that at least they can do better than the Swedes, and the Swedes say the opposite!

2. *Teleported Models.* Systems can be tempted to gravitate toward some countries and jurisdictions rather than others among benchmarked high performers because they seem to have a reform package that looks politically plausible, technically intelligible, easily transportable, and able to deliver short-term results. This may be one of the reasons that various nations are drawn more to Ontario than other equally high-performing Canadian provinces as a model of educational change. Ontario has a clear and well-articulated policy design that emphasizes a tight focus on literacy and numeracy in relation to targets of tested achievement under firm central guidance. The Ministry of Education in Ontario provides persistent and relentless pressure along with ample supplies of human and financial resource support. The more sparsely populated province of Alberta in western Canada, however, has so far had much more difficulty providing a compelling explanation for its equally high performance that others might see as easy to replicate.

3. *Inconvenient Truths.* Some of the features that define or explain high-performing countries may not be easily transportable by or even seem desirable to many governments, so they are deemphasized or neglected, even though they may be a critical part of those countries' success. Finland and Singapore, for example, have compulsory military service or its equivalent for men, which may play a role in supporting student achievement in schools as part of an overall ethic of disciplined patriotism. Most Asian high performers are not conventional

Western-style democracies and this can aid strength of coordination and speed of implementation in a way that international agencies reporting on comparative educational achievement tend to overlook. Finland's high-tax Scandinavian democracy and its abundant investment in public services may explain why, in the international reports of McKinsey & Company, Finland has been increasingly positioned as an extreme and, by implication, easily discounted case.[24]

4. *Restricted Range of Indicators.* Industrial benchmarking uses a wide a range of indicators to judge the success of competitors and the strategies they use to secure that success. So when *international* benchmarking in education refers only to comparisons in student standardized achievement scores, it departs from the original richness and spirit of *industrial* benchmarking. For example, the fact that the culturally diverse Netherlands is at the top of UNICEF's indicators of child well-being is just as important as that country's seventh and then tenth placed ranking on PISA in recent years.

The point of international benchmarking should *not* be to rank and rate people against one another to induce international status anxiety and panic-driven competitiveness. It should *not* be to cherry-pick this or that policy because it is ideologically compatible with one's own current political ambitions or priorities, while neglecting other equally influential ones that are not. Entire models of change should *not* be taken out of their original context that may be quite alien to one's own. And inconvenient but influential items such as high taxation levels, military service requirements, or forms of political control should *not* be overlooked because they may spoil a good change story or be politically difficult to transplant.

The most significant contribution of international benchmarking is to *inquire into* and to *learn from* the exemplary performance of others. This sort of learning is not only advanced by transnational advocacy and consulting groups who use comparative achievement data to help promote improvement and innovation around the world. It is also practiced by all of the high-performing nations themselves. These nations eagerly and aggressively benchmark themselves against and are constantly learning from fellow high performers, in order to keep on

The most significant contribution of international benchmarking is to *inquire into* and to *learn from* the exemplary performance of others.

improving and innovating. In some cases, this benchmarking process includes innovative partnerships that link principals, teachers, and students directly with one another across nations.

The OECD notes that the world's highest performers such as Finland, Singapore, Ontario, and Shanghai (China) are also all "most determined international benchmarkers." These systems are open-minded and eager to learn from one another. "A strong and consistent effort . . . to do disciplined international benchmarking and to incorporate the results of that benchmarking into policy and practice is a common characteristic of the highest-performing countries," the OECD says.[25]

This book uses international benchmarking to promote learning about six systems that exemplify exceptional practice in widely varying contexts with quite different cultures and political systems. Some of the practices are produced by governments together with the education profession and some are produced by the profession in at least partial opposition to the government. The book is about what we can learn from these exemplars, individually and together. Much of this kind of work has already been undertaken by impressively large and influential national and transnational economic and policy organizations such as the OECD, McKinsey & Company, and the NCEE. What can this book offer that adds value to the significant body of work that they have already set out?

CORNERSTONES AND CORNER STORES

In recent years, national and transnational policy organizations have harnessed their considerable resources to raise important questions about educational policy that generally support improved status, conditions, and compensation for teachers; increased equity in student outcomes; and strong investments in the development of public education. They collect impressive bodies of data to inform cross-country comparisons in student achievement. They dispatch expert teams to the highest performers or the more dramatic improvers to undertake the difficult international benchmarking work of determining the policies and other processes that are responsible for these countries' results. We have been privileged to be part of these teams. We appreciate just how rigorous their work is—and some of their results are represented in this book. More than this, two of the reviews we undertook for this book, in California and Singapore, are modeled on the procedures these organizations pioneered.

The international benchmarking undertaken by these organizations has become a *cornerstone* feature of how countries now examine and reflect on their own policies. Through publication of country-by-country case studies; compilations of cross-country comparisons around particular issues like leadership, school improvement, and teacher quality; and conferences and seminars that convene ministers, policy advisors, and researchers, nations are prompted to inquire more deeply into the effectiveness of their own policies. They exchange information and insights with comparable peers who seem to be performing better. They also start to develop an international consensus about the directions that countries should aspire to if they want to attain greater educational excellence and equity.

The more publicly visible and transparent national and transnational cornerstones of international educational change today are the OECD, McKinsey & Company, and the NCEE. The OECD consists of 34 predominantly western European nations dedicated to markets and democracy. Founded in 1948 to help administer the U.S. Marshall Plan to coordinate the reconstruction of Europe and Japan in the aftermath of the Second World War, the OECD has now developed a diverse portfolio addressing virtually all social policy matters of significance. In education, the OECD administers PISA, one of the most important benchmarking tests. In its latest administration, PISA went far beyond the OECD members to encompass 65 nations and territories, giving it a truly global reach.

Compared to the OECD, McKinsey & Company is one of the world's leading consulting firms. More than 70 chief executive officers in Fortune 500 companies have worked for McKinsey & Company previously. In the past dozen years, McKinsey & Company has become increasingly involved in the education sector, studying and making recommendations to policy makers on better ways to improve teacher quality, reduce achievement gaps, and deploy resources.

The third cornerstone group, the NCEE, focuses its efforts primarily on the United States. The NCEE has, from time to time, convened influential blue ribbon committees of chief executives, former White House educational leaders, and outstanding school district superintendents to provide state of the nation reports on public education and its future. Examples include *A Nation Prepared: Teachers for the 21st Century,* published in 1986, and in 2006, *Tough Choices or Tough Times* that criticized America's obsession with standardization and proposed a stronger focus on flexible and creative problem solving.[26] The NCEE's president, Marc Tucker, has been an outspoken advocate for international benchmarking as a way to study and improve school systems. In *Standing on the Shoulders of Giants: An American Agenda for Educational Reform,* published in 2011, he used international data to make a blistering denunciation of recent U.S. policies and urged the nation to learn from and start to adapt successful practices from high-performing countries.[27]

As cornerstones of international educational change, these organizations play crucial roles in collecting, publishing, and interpreting the data that are the basis of international benchmarking. They convene high-level meetings of ministers and other political and bureaucratic leaders to discuss the implications of this benchmarking, and make their own statements and summaries on the implications of their research and interpretations for future educational policy. These organizations' status as advocacy bodies as well as disseminators of research results gives them leverage over future policy strategies, often in a progressive and socially just way. For instance, they support increased teacher professionalism, the adoption of equity measures such as de-tracking schools for early adolescents, and the provision of increased support rather than merely the exertion of external pressure to stimulate school improvement.

But as policy advisory and agenda setting organizations, each of these three bodies also serves particular stakeholders such as government ministers and other policy makers or is guided by predominantly economic interests and agendas. These affiliations affect the kinds of explanations and recommendations they provide as well as what is omitted from them. These limitations occur not because these organizations are partisan, but because of the nature of their mandates. None of these organizations, for example, provides advice about ways that community organizing can be used to improve schools or how to place pressure on policy makers to reconsider ill-advised educational reforms. Nor do they advise how teachers in low-performing systems could develop their collective voice to achieve the same kinds of status and support that their colleagues enjoy in high-performing ones. This is why it is important to have complementary narratives of high performance and educational change that have different sources of support and that embrace other examples, evidence bases, and outlooks.

Our corner store perspective in this book concurs with much of what the OECD, McKinsey & Company, and the NCEE have already established. But for the reasons previously described, there are also some key differences. Compared to the cornerstone perspective, our own corner store explanations point to the equivalent impact of local control, local development, and local authority in educational decision making in Finland, Canada, and even in Singapore—a tiny, compact country where what is national is also inevitably very local too.

Second, while cornerstone and our own corner store perspectives both recognize how teachers and school leaders can be more than deliverers and implementers of other people's curricula, the independent evidence of our own corner store studies is that teachers can be designers and developers of good curricula and effective innovation themselves.

Last, just like the OECD, McKinsey & Company, and the NCEE, our own corner store analysis concentrates a lot of attention on Canada, but whereas all three cornerstone organizations have focused almost exclusively on the Canadian province of Ontario as being interchangeable with the whole of Canada, our own corner store analysis also examines an equally high-performing province—Alberta—with a quite distinct cultural and political identity of its own and a rather different set of educational policies.

It is also worth pointing out that, like McKinsey & Company, our understanding of high performance is grounded in analyzing outliers of success. One of these, in our case, is a high-performing school serving a large cultural minority population in the North of England. Another is a significant movement to undertake successful turnarounds in the lowest performing schools in California. The California case in particular demonstrates what can be achieved when political and professional capital work together to renew public education and the achievement outcomes of students by opposing government policies that are inequitable and that are directed toward extraneous political purposes.

So as well as politically and economically based *cornerstones* in education and public life, we need independent *corner stores* to offer products that sometimes produce something different from the mainstream. This is the purpose of our book.

THE ORGANIZATION OF THE BOOK

This book is an analysis of educational high performance from one corner store perspective. It is based on our firsthand studies of six jurisdictions in ways that, we believe, get to a deeper level of complexity and detail in understanding teachers and schools, as well as government officials and leading stakeholders, than is usually possible in the more leadership and policy-focused accounts of cornerstone organizations. *The Global Fourth Way* sets out six examples of high performance.

1. *Finland,* the highest performing country outside Asia on PISA, the highest performer of all for the PISA cycles before the most recent one, and an outstanding achiever in the World Economic Forum's rating of economic competitiveness;

2. *Singapore,* the highest performing country in the world on PISA in mathematics, and among the top three in literacy and science, where per capita income and life expectancy now exceed that of the United States, and where citizens have leapt from third- to first-world status in the course of a single generation;
3. *Alberta,* the highest performing English- and French-speaking jurisdiction on PISA that shares many cultural similarities with western, oil-rich U.S. states like Texas but that posts achievement gains far above them;
4. *Ontario,* that performs almost identically to Alberta and that has become a living laboratory of successful educational reform for leaders around the globe;
5. *England,* where a failing secondary school in a low-income immigrant community turned itself around through inspirational leadership and culturally responsive pedagogy by swimming against the tide of prevailing government policy;
6. *California,* where the California Teachers' Association fought its governor and launched an ambitious initiative to raise student achievement in one-third of the state's most disadvantaged and academically challenged communities, with early results indicating significant gains.

The final chapter draws together what we have learned from these very different but compelling cases to draw out the key implications for teachers, principals (or headteachers), and school system leaders. It presents pointers for practice for moving beyond the unimaginative and often deadening grip of excessive testing on children and beyond the micromanagement of professionals by top-heavy bureaucracies.

Before delving into these six cases, the next chapter raises a prior question about the nature of high performance and the kind of high performance that schools, systems, and entire nations should want to pursue. Should they get better or improve at their current game, we ask? Or should they innovate and change the game altogether? How is this question addressed through the three existing ways of educational change? How should it be addressed in the future? This is one of the key challenges of all educational change today, to which we give our imminent attention.

Chapter Two

THE PARADOX OF INNOVATION AND IMPROVEMENT

What kinds of excellence are we looking for? What sorts of success or high performance should we value? What kinds of change are we trying to achieve? Knowing what to change comes before knowing how to change. These are the essential issues we address in this chapter.

Shaped as it was by the evidence of the samples we had already been studying, the Fourth Way was our first stab at a new idea. Despite the idea's potential, it also had gaps and omissions. One of the criticisms made of it was that it did not address the spread of new digital and media technologies into schools. What does the Fourth Way have to say about mobile phones, laptops, SMART boards, online learning, and all the digital media that are an integral part of young people's lives today, and increasingly also a part of their schools? This book therefore includes an examination of the role of these new technologies in high-performing systems.

The significance and impact of new technologies form part of an even larger question. What is the role of schools and educational systems in relation to educational change in the 21st century? Should they be *improving* what they already do, and undertake everything in their power to make it better, and more effective? Or should they be embracing *innovation* in terms of new ideas, outcomes, and practices—not merely making their existing practice more effective, but transforming that practice and perhaps even the nature of their institutions altogether? This chapter addresses the goals and merits of educational innovation and improvement respectively, preparing the way for their key roles in the six case study chapters that follow.

THE IRONY OF INNOVATION AND IMPROVEMENT

One of the most unexpected successes in the business literature in recent decades was a book by a hitherto little-known Harvard Business School professor on the unlikely topic of the history of disk drives. In *The Innovator's Dilemma,* Clayton Christensen used this seemingly arcane topic to make a key distinction between "incremental innovations," or refinements and improvements in existing products on the one hand, and "disruptive innovations" that completely change the game of what a product looks like in order to deliver the same outcome with a far superior result.[1]

Christensen's examples include the diesel shovel that replaced the mechanical steam shovel and the compact steel mini-mill that took over from the large iron and steel foundries. It is Christensen's research on the creation of smaller and smaller disk drives that is most telling, though. Often, he shows, when innovators in an established market leader create a smaller disk drive, this leads to a minor incremental adjustment in the existing technology—a more efficient, sleek, or attractive version of what existed before. But once in a while, the creation of a smaller disk drive leads to a step-change in computer technology—a leap from the desktop to the laptop or from the laptop to the palmtop or tablet. The result is no longer evolution for the parent company but an impending revolution that eliminates previous forms of consumer demand and creates enormous new ones instead.

What happens next is fascinating. With great excitement, innovators take their breakthrough product to their corporate bosses. These corporate leaders express interest in this new development and test out the innovation on their customers. Against expectations, the customers turn out to be quite conservative. They like the new product, they say, but don't want to lose the memory that this smaller machine entails. Consequently, "the leading firms were held captive by their customers."[2]

As a result, corporate leaders tend to stick with their existing products and brands. And the innovators? They become frustrated, and start up somewhere else by themselves. At first, the quirky new products of these exiled innovators pose no threat to the powerful hosts who could not accommodate them. The first diesel shovels could only dig tiny trenches for pipe-laying work in people's gardens. The first battery operated vehicles only seemed usable on golf courses or in relation to parking enforcement. These products had low status applications in niche markets of limited scope.

But innovators like the ones Christensen studied are disciplined and relentless. Their developments and refinements do not stop. Car battery technology advances, diesel excavation shovels develop larger and larger capacity, and the palmtop and the laptop accommodate ever-increasing memory and start to oust the older models to which the corporate giants are still wedded. Over time, innovation moves upward in the status of its applications and customers, and outward in terms of its market reach. One innovation builds on another, leaving the older products manufactured by long-established business leaders increasingly outdated and unprofitable. Eventually the upstart innovators overtake the parent company that abandoned them. Ironically, the underestimated and ostracized children return to kill off their parents! Upstart and out-stretched innovation overtakes incremental improvement.

Christensen's subsequent book, coauthored with Michael Horn and Curtis Johnson, argues that the same process is afoot in education today. In *Disrupting Class: How Disruptive Innovation Will Change the Way the World Learns,* the book's authors argue that innovations such as homeschooling, online courses, and online tutoring services are threatening the 150-year supremacy of public schools.[3] Furthermore, as public schools become more standardized, more and more students and their parents will exit from the schools, seeking opportunities for individual attention and tailored learning online or through other private options that public schools do not offer. Every visual arts, music, and foreign language class that is cut in the name of tough-minded accountability, the authors argue, drives students into "nonconsumption opportunities" outside existing schools such as online credit recovery and Advanced Placement courses. From these apparently unthreatening beginnings, alternative and innovative provision expands to the point where, the authors note, if current trends continue, by 2019 over 50% of high school courses in the United States will be taught online.[4]

Christensen, Horn, and Johnson aren't especially concerned about the impending collapse of public education in the light of new technologies and emerging markets. From their perspective, even though public schools are better than most people believe, and have been getting steadily better over time, comparing current to past performance is irrelevant. Just as no one cared when improved electronic typewriters in the 1980s were wiped out along with the entire typewriting industry by personal computers, public schools, they propose, should be afforded no special protection when better learning platforms become available.

Christensen and his colleagues' arguments present a huge challenge to public education as we know it. Their theory of disruptive innovation predicts that a vast wave of innovation will start sweeping our schools and that public education will be transformed and perhaps even terminated as a result. Internet-driven innovations and alternative providers will move in from the margins and become the overwhelming mainstream instead. Unless public education can adapt and embrace some of these innovations, then, like its sector leaders in business, it may fail to survive.

THE TRAGEDY OF EDUCATIONAL INNOVATION

In contrast to Christensen's dramatic scenario of technological transformation, historians David Tyack and William Tobin have compellingly shown how one innovation after another in public education has been rejected for more than century. The reason, they say, is because these innovations ultimately threatened the clients' and the public's existing understandings of schooling.[5] Despite every effort, innovations in technology, curriculum, and pedagogy were unable to disturb or disrupt the existing grammar of schooling—its segregation into age-based cohorts, classroom-based instruction, standard curriculum subjects, and paper-and-pencil testing to which almost everyone had become deeply attached. Over time, this grammar of school became what Mary Metz called "real school"—the kind of school parents remembered from their schooldays and wanted to preserve—a school that looked like a normal institution rather than something eccentric that might turn their children into experimental guinea pigs.[6]

The history of school subjects and of efforts at curriculum integration offers other reasons to be skeptical about educators' capacities to reinvent school. Historically, high status knowledge in traditional subjects (such as science and mathematics) will always prevail when it competes with lower status alternatives (such as the performing and visual arts). People might allow courses to be integrated, subjects to be blended, and students to be more self-directed when the children are younger, or when they are lower status underachievers in lower tracks, vocational programs, second language learning groups, or programs of special educational needs, for example.[7] But once these integrations and innovations threaten the purity and hierarchy of mainstream school subjects among higher-achieving students who prosper and profit from them—once they move upward and outward in Christensen's terms—or when they get close to the life-determining point of selection for higher education, then the innovations are challenged, and a revolt of the elites brings a backlash in its wake.

The history of attempts to establish innovative schools is another largely tragic narrative of early radicalism that is then followed by regression to the institutional norm. Although innovative schools typically offer a fresh start with new facilities, leadership, and staff in order to challenge the ingrained assumptions that make up the traditional grammar of schooling, longitudinal studies of a number of innovative schools indicate that, after an initial golden age, they suffer a predictable "attrition of change" over time.[8] Charismatic founding leaders prove hard to replace; staff become exhausted by the constant workload of innovation and begin to leave; the mission of the school is not renewed when teacher replacements arrive; nearby schools become envious of the favored-child status that innovative schools attain within the system and start to undermine it; and the discretion these schools initially enjoyed to break some of the rules within the system is lost when system leadership turns over and the school's original benefactors are replaced. More than this, with the movement of educational reform paradigms toward large-scale reform and increased external accountability, it becomes more and more difficult for existing innovative schools to retain their identities, or for newly arrived innovators to gain any kind of foothold at all.[9]

And what about educators' ability to make optimal use of new technologies? Even in this promising area, teachers have been slow to adopt new practices. In *Teachers and Machines: The Classroom Use of Technology Since 1920,* Stanford historian Larry Cuban found that much of teachers' reluctance to endorse new technologies in the 1960s and 1970s had to do with their core understanding of teaching as a vocation. Even when they were granted easy access to television and movies, promised reduced workloads, and reminded of how popular media were used by the young, teachers generally avoided new technologies. This was "because teachers believe that interpersonal relations are essential in student learning." In addition, "The use of technologies that either displace, interrupt, or minimize that relationship between teacher and child is viewed in a negative light."[10]

Cuban found that teachers tended to integrate more technology into their instruction in the afternoon when they were tired and when they and their students welcomed a break. Elementary school teachers especially used more television and film in their classes because this gave them a much-appreciated break from the demands of managing one large group of the same children all day. Television turned into a custodial child-minder rather than a developer of new skills.

Parents' demands for "real schools," educators' insistence on the sacrosanct hierarchy of curriculum categories, and technology's easy employment for classroom management and entertainment rather than pedagogically sound purposes are just three reasons why it is so hard to change the grammar of schooling. The same is true for charter schools. These schools began with all kinds of radical aspirations, but many of them now display orthodox ways of teaching that are indistinguishable from and sometimes even caricatures of those that are found in traditional public schools.[11]

Despite the predictions of business gurus and of the prophets of technological revolution in education, the record of history suggests that innovation in education faces a steep uphill climb. Inertia and resistance repeatedly pull schools back to the norm of practices that were established to serve societies with very different needs than those of today. Yet without continual innovation from within, what chances do schools have not only to survive but also to prosper in a world where students' lives and everyday experiences and interactions are undergoing profound and not always positive transformations?

INNOVATING AND IMPROVING TOGETHER

It is hard to change traditional schools when they are familiar to everyone—even if they seem inefficient and outdated. Since the onset and onward march of large-scale reform models of improvement dedicated to raising test scores in basic literacy and mathematics, it is even harder to convince policy makers and system leaders to change to a new approach if they have experienced educational and political success with the existing one.

So is the world of innovation and improvement an *either/or* universe where we must go one way or the other? Do we *either* have to opt for effective but rather ordinary incremental improvements in educational basics that may nonetheless provide continuing and sustainable gains for large numbers of people; *or* should we choose more exciting innovations that initially benefit a few people but that have a high risk of eventual failure when efforts are made to scale them up? Are improvement and innovation mutually exclusive? Or can the instrumental bureaucrats and the intellectual boffins work together side by side?

Our current challenge is to find ways to develop innovation within our schools while continuously improving them. We need to harmonize incremental improvements and disruptive innovations.

Our current challenge, whatever our school system, is to find ways to develop innovation within our schools while continuously improving them. We need to harmonize incremental improvements and disruptive innovations for three reasons.

1. *The Sigmoid Curve.* Adapted from mathematics by leading organizational experts such as Charles Handy and Peter Senge, the Sigmoid curve describes how people and organizations start off slowly and often falteringly, ascend up a steepening curve of improvement and then begin to level off before embarking on a gradual then precipitous decline.[12] It is before, not right at, the peak of your performance that the dynamics of decline already occur. This brings us back to Christensen. It is before, not after, an organization has improved its existing product as much as it has been able, that it needs to be inventing new ones. And it is before a school's or system's existing way of producing results has reached its zenith that it needs to be rethinking what kinds of results it wants and how to get them in the future. This is the paradox of improvement—knowing you have to quit when you still look like you're ahead!

2. *Disciplined Innovation.* In *Great by Choice,* Jim Collins and Morten Hansen examine the features of companies that lasted despite the turbulence all around them.[13] The point in highly

successful companies, they write, is to be able to innovate and also to deliver "with high reliability and great consistency."[14] "The great task, rarely achieved, is to blend creative intensity with relentless discipline so as to amplify the creativity rather than destroy it."[15] Discipline requires relentless perseverance and complete indefatigability to ensure that a good idea comes to fruition in practice. But it's also important, Collins and Hansen emphasize, to understand what discipline is not:

> Discipline is not the same as regimentation. Discipline is not the same as measurement. Discipline is not the same as hierarchical obedience or adherence to bureaucratic rules. True discipline requires the independence of mind to reject pressures to conform in ways incompatible with values, performance standards, and long-term aspirations.[16]

So the sort of discipline you need for conventional improvement that involves top-down control and bureaucratic alignment is not the kind of collective self-discipline of sheer determination that disciplined innovation requires.

3. *Platforms, not Pipelines.* In 2004, innovation guru Charles Leadbeater undertook an analysis of what would be required to move health services from responding to existing problems by, for example, prescribing more statins for people with high cholesterol—to supporting and disseminating more healthy lifestyles that would result in things like lowered cholesterol levels.[17] Leadbeater described five radical solutions for addressing this issue through personalizing public services more for the people who used them:

   - Provide *more customer friendly* access to existing services.
   - Make it *easier for users to navigate* a wider variety of options.
   - Move the money that is involved in public services from providers to *users* so they *exercise greater control* over how it is spent.
   - *Involve users* in local program design.
   - *Establish platforms* that enable users to self-organize their own lives and behaviors more effectively.

Leadbeater's work indicates that in public services, promoting innovation is not only a question of relaxing or releasing control and responsibility. It is about a shift in approach to build platforms where people are increasingly able to design learning supports and lifestyle options for themselves.

Leadbeater's analysis raises important questions for educators. For example, what platforms do governments need to create so teachers can develop their own curriculum together, instead of delivering curriculum designed by government with the backing of intensive training and support to ensure fidelity and effectiveness? What systems can be created and how can resources be reallocated so that peer-to-peer networks of schools can raise achievement and remedy failure, instead of expensive central intervention teams imposing turnaround and improvement efforts from the top?

Innovation in public services is not about governments withdrawing from public life. It is about shifting from the government driving and delivering services, to a position where it creates platforms so that people can support themselves.

So now we have some ideas about how to reconcile innovation and improvement, and some reminders about why we should. We need to innovate before our improvement efforts flatten and before increasing results stop. Effective innovation is disciplined and not dissipated in its organization. Many of the dispositions of the relentless improver belong to the resilient innovator too (although this is no excuse for perpetuating the bad habits of top-down bureaucracy). Innovation in public services is not about governments withdrawing from public life. It is about shifting from the government driving and delivering services, to a position where it creates platforms so that people can support themselves.

This is not, however, the way that the relationship between innovation and improvement often works out in practice. To understand why, we next explain different kinds of relationships between these two orientations to change.

THE SECOND WAY: NEITHER IMPROVEMENT NOR INNOVATION

In many respects, recent United States national education reform strategies have turned into failures to either innovate or improve in relation to educational change. Reading scores have been flat for fourth and eighth graders measured by the National Assessment for Educational Progress (NAEP) for years.[18] This is unaltered by more than a decade of U.S. reforms, despite the enormous effort and expense they have entailed. Although mathematics scores have improved, this trend predates recent reforms that are therefore unlikely to have caused the gains.[19] On the OECD's PISA test, the United States is 17th in reading, 31st in mathematics, and 23rd in science, out of a total of 65 systems.[20]

When U.S. President Barack Obama was elected in 2008 he entrusted education strategy largely to his secretary of education, Arne Duncan who, to the disappointment of the education profession, continued with the No Child Left Behind (NCLB) legislation of the Bush administration. This perpetuated a relentless and unimaginative emphasis on standardized testing and continued and even increased government advocacy of charter schools and individual school choice.

Just as Tony Blair had done in his first term of office in the United Kingdom, Secretary Duncan and his team played the existing reform game with even greater ferocity than their predecessors. The largely Second Way policy strategy of markets and standardization, introduced in Chapter 1, was given the bench-pressing title of "Race to the Top" (RTTT).

RTTT built on NCLB's focus on test-score gains and market incentives with the following strands:

- *Reward* states that endorse new Common Core State Standards by assigning them increased points on their RTTT funding applications—even though high-achieving systems elsewhere have slimmed down their centralized curriculum requirements in order to empower local schools and their teachers to be high-quality curriculum developers and classroom innovators.[21]
- *Award* extra points to states that promise to fire principals in struggling schools and displace teachers from the same schools despite the fact that repetitive turnaround efforts of this kind add instabilities to people's lives in poor communities that have far too much instability already.[22]
- *Use* value-added measures of tested student achievement and teacher performance to identify and reward teachers with high test-score gains and to reprimand or remove those whose students have struggled—even though a century of performance-based pay efforts have failed and despite the research evidence

that the measures have no lasting impact on improving student achievement.[23]

- *Provide* funding for states that endorse a variety of prescribed "turnaround" models, even though efforts at instant turnaround in a year or less have a poor record of success in education and business alike.[24]
- *Increase* the numbers of permissible charter schools despite the fact that, overall, charters show lower achievement outcomes than traditional public schools.[25]
- *Invest in and improve upon* data systems for tracking student progress, even though the trust and openness necessary to analyze these data intelligently and effectively together do not flourish in high-threat environments.[26]
- *Promote* the recruitment and retention of excellent teachers by opening up alternative training routes to traditional university-based systems—which flies in the face of the fact that none of the world's highest performing systems prepare their professionals in this way.[27]

While there are some positive dimensions to RTTT—especially its efforts to support teacher retention and to create a sense of urgency about the most chronically underperforming schools—we anticipate that, like NCLB, many of its components are destined to disappoint in practice. They do not align with the international benchmarks of high performance, and they are not supported by research on similar initiatives in the past or the present.

> The charter schools that were meant to revolutionize public schools have often become schools that reinforce and recycle practices that are caricatures of the old-style factory school.

One of the greatest ironies in all this is that the charter schools that were meant to revolutionize public schools have often turned out to do the opposite. They have become schools that reinforce and recycle practices that are almost caricatures of the old-style factory school, such as the prohibition of talking during lunch or when students move between classes.[28]

The reason for this tragic irony where innovation turns into traditionalism is an unholy alliance of three forces. *Market forces* make competition and choice the prime drivers of reform. Parents' *nostalgia* for something coherent and predictable in times of insecurity then leads them and the schools that have to appeal to them to reinforce old *institutional* understandings of traditional grammars of schooling.

Like the conservative customers in Christensen's business examples, parents don't want to break away from the existing product they know until they are sure that innovation will have a payoff. And many charter schools as well as growing numbers of public schools are more than willing to cater to this pattern if it brings in the customers, raises the results, and can be mastered relatively quickly by an inexperienced and undertrained teaching force.

Not all schools in the United States represent these recent reforms. Yong Zhao points out that in many U.S. schools there still is plenty of entrepreneurial spirit that is the reputational hallmark of U.S. culture and technological innovation worldwide.[29] Affluent suburban schools in particular continue to graduate students with excellent ratings on Advanced Placement courses who go on to excel in the world's most competitive research universities. Indeed, White and Asian-American students in U.S. schools perform on a par with students in high-performing nations elsewhere.[30]

At the same time, Zhao cautions that policy models of command and control incur the opposite of innovation in U.S. urban systems. This may mark the beginning of a new educational era of school segregation in America where private schools or schools in wealthy white suburbs, along with a few charters, attract and retain high-performing professionals who have the professional flexibility to teach their students the 21st century skills that prepare them for the knowledge economy. Meanwhile, underqualified, underprepared, and transient young teachers in urban systems that deal with the poor and students of color follow a prescribed and standardized curriculum, confined to the basics that is the opposite of what knowledge economies require. This may or may not narrow tested achievement gaps, but at the expense of widening the learning gap in the kinds of knowledge children acquire in richer and poorer communities respectively.

Given the evidence of history, of high performance in other countries, and of the impact of NCLB in America itself, the prospects for RTTT look grim. In many ways, current U.S. reforms have promulgated unsustainable change. The impulse is to circumvent the profession, refer to markets whenever possible, and grab unproven approaches that hold the chimerical allure of new technology as an answer to existing educational ills. U.S.-style reforms may look bold and decisive on paper, but they are proving exhausting and demotivating for educators and are turning out to be thin on results for students.

THE THIRD WAY: IMPROVEMENT WITHOUT INNOVATION

Some schools and systems have become excellent at what they already do. They are always moving forward, always improving. One of the finest examples of this kind of educational change is the province of Ontario in Canada. Ontario is one of four high-performing provinces on the OECD's PISA test at age 15, and Canada is the sixth highest-performing jurisdiction on that test in the world. Ontario has also attracted attention as a successful reformer because of the introduction of specific policies since 2003 to concentrate on raising achievement in elementary students' literacy and numeracy performance and on improving high school graduation rates.[31] There has been gradual, if uneven, progress toward reaching the provincial target that was set at 75% of students attaining Level 3 proficiency in Grade 6 on the provincial standardized test administered by the Educational Quality and Accountability Office (EQAO). Although this "Drive to 75," as it has been colloquially called, has not yet reached the stated target, significant gains have been made nonetheless. Proficiency levels stood at around 70% in 2011—up from 54% at the beginning of the drive in 2004. At the same time, high school graduation rates have climbed upward from 68% in 2004 to 82% in 2011.

Ontario's strategy has been represented in ways that make it highly consistent with the *high pressure-high support* strategy of the Third Way. Firm targets linked to strong accountability measures, a clear focus on literacy and numeracy achievement as well as high school graduation rates, and a determined system of delivery from the province, through the districts and down to the schools, exert the kind of pressure that is typical of Third Way strategies and that are strong carryovers from the Second Way. At the same time, strong support has been evident in the establishment of labor peace with the teacher unions, significant increases in budgetary investment, and abundant provision of quality materials, training, and coaching. Lateral peer-to-peer networks—another distinguishing Third Way feature—have been established where schools can connect with and receive support from similarly placed but higher-performing partner schools. A nonpunitive emotional and political climate assumes that shortfalls in achievement are due to insufficient understanding and capacity among teachers and leaders, rather than deficits of competence or commitment. What are the effects of this high-pressure, high-support change design?

One of us has codirected a project in collaboration with our Boston College colleague Henry Braun and a team of graduate researchers on a seventh of Ontario's school districts in order to determine the architecture and impact of the province's special education strategy.[32] Designed to help those students who have a wide variety of learning challenges, the special education strategy has significant connections with and therefore offers important insights into the province's broader policies to improve literacy and numeracy as well as raise test scores in relation to that achievement. As part of our study, we compiled detailed reports for each of the ten districts studied and also collected survey data from classroom and special education resource teachers in all but one of the districts.

The data indicate that educators saw strong and positive connections between the special education strategy and the province's focus on literacy and numeracy achievement. They felt the project had been associated with improvements in their literacy practice over time that had benefitted not just students with special learning needs, but all students. One educator wrote that "the various initiatives have strongly complemented each other [and] worked to better teaching practices and focus on the varied learning profiles of students."[33] This complementary approach encouraged "teachers to engage in practices that benefit students," which has "translated into better results in testing. Also, there is a more collaborative atmosphere amongst teachers which, in turn, benefits students."

At the same time, the data revealed more ambivalent results about the benefits of Third Way uses of standardized testing. On the one hand, system administrators tended to be highly supportive of the EQAO because this was a way for them to understand progress in their system and to exert leverage over their schools. Many principals saw some benefits to EQAO and so too did special education resource teachers. They felt that it often pushed classroom teachers in a positive way to take responsibility for all their students and to raise their own expectations for those who had been formally identified as having learning disabilities, rather than transferring responsibility for these students to the resource teachers.

The EQAO and other data-driven assessments of a more diagnostic nature had other benefits as well. They built momentum in the districts to understand where children were currently in their academic coursework, and then to move them forward. The focus for student achievement was that all students would learn and that teachers would take students from their current level to a higher one. In the best case scenarios, and in the views of administrative staff especially, the assessments raised expectations for all students, enabled teachers to set more specific goals for each student, prompted teachers to listen to each other's ideas more, created a common language for them to talk about their students' achievement, and developed a sense of collective responsibility for all students' success.

Many districts developed data walls that enabled them to visualize and track the literacy progress of each student toward the provincial benchmarks. These data walls listed the various reading levels (emergent, early readers, transitional readers, and extending readers) and represented individual students and their current levels of achievement and progress by letters and numbers according to diagnostic assessments undertaken in October, February, and May. A coloring system highlighted the progress of each student: red representing students falling below provincial benchmarks, yellow indicating ones who were at risk of falling below, and green showing students who had met the benchmarks. As students' progressed, their marker moved along the continuum to the next level.

Teachers consulted these data walls weekly. Students who were below provincial benchmarks as well as those just under the benchmarks were flagged, and tailored interventions were constructed to boost proficiency. Teachers were trained to differentiate instruction to help these students and monitor their improvement. Teachers also challenged students to move to the next level by giving them small, achievable short-term goals.

This technology for tracking progress did increase the likelihood that students' problems would be picked up in real time, that interventions would be timely, that improvement goals would not be too vague, and that everyone would take responsibility for all students together. These are significant Third Way accomplishments. At the same time, the connection of this tracking system to the Drive to 75 and the particular importance it attached to Level 3 proficiency over all other levels, could lead to calculative concentration on meeting these targets, and on various ways of gaming the system in order to do so.

Teachers in one district, for example, reported that they were under constant pressure to move students to the 3.0 mark of measured proficiency and to concentrate especially on those students hovering around the 2.7 to 2.9 mark.[34] These students whose results are right below the cut score mark are those who are most likely to advance over the designated achievement barrier to help the school meet its test goals. Educators reported that system leaders told them "they need to push [these students] over to the next level."[35] One interviewee recalled being instructed: "Keep doing [the special education project] thing. But for those groups of children [near the threshold], we need to do something different, a different skills set to work with those kids, more differentiating for that group."[36] While educators recognized that they must be "more precise in their teaching,"[37] these borderline students clearly took priority over all their other students—including those whose academic performance was lowest and arguably in need of the greatest attention.

A chart hanging in one principal's office represented this hyperfocus on those students at the 2.7 to 2.9 levels whose advancement was critical for a school to meet its established targets in the Drive to 75 on the EQAO.[38] On the chart, the number of students who fell into this category was circled in order to stimulate focused interventions that could possibly move more students to a 3.0. These students were not the ones whose performance was the weakest.

Teachers' efforts were drawn toward concentrating on and intervening with students near the borderline of measured proficiency while their efforts were drawn away from other students whose own achievement needs may have been just as great or greater. "That's been a thrust in low performing districts. You need to look at results. You need to look at 2.7 to 2.9 and figure out how to get them over the 3.0 hump. There was no consideration for all the school has done to get kids into Level 1."[39] In another district where principals reported tensions between differentiated instruction (DI) and standardized testing that reflected larger tensions between inclusion and accountability, one elementary teacher described the tension this way:

> I do think DI and the EQAO tests are dramatically different in the fact that in DI we want kids to think and talk and compare answers and contrast and debate and all those kinds of things. And then EQAO is three days where you sit and you do not speak to anyone and you write. They're two foreign worlds from each other.[40]

Another educator pointed out that "the students are being groomed to take part in this assessment whether or not it is anywhere near the level they are working at. It puts pressure on these students as well as the teachers and principal."[41]

One senior Ministry of Education official was keen to recognize the progress that had been made throughout the system in "kids moving from Level 1 to Level 2," as well as those who had moved to Level 3. However, he continued,

> It's not part of the public domain from a perspective of how we are doing as a province because the provincial standard is Level 3 and that's what's deemed to be the standard. Externally it's up to the government to determine what it chooses to promote on behalf of the government. And when you have already established targets and that's a significant part of the present government's mantra, I'm speculating that they don't want to be perceived to be changing the nature of those targets.[42]

This does not mean there was an official policy or strategy to have teachers concentrating all their attention on these students.

Indeed, one high-level official was emphatic that they "never wanted the motivation to be about the test scores. It was always about the skills and the fact that the kids have more potential than we actualize."[43] There was, he said, no plan to focus all the system's energy on students just below the Level 3 threshold either as a desirable goal in itself or even as a necessary evil to achieve a greater end. At the same time, the existence of practices in some schools that concentrated disproportionate effort on borderline students did not come as a surprise to him.

> It saddens me because I think it's completely unnecessary and inconsistent with what we wanted but obviously did not successfully communicate in those cases. Our communication and substance was never about the 2.7s. That doesn't mean that [the Literacy and Numeracy Secretariat] may not have had some people who didn't communicate that because they had 80 people involved. Messages can get twisted. One of the things I always communicated to people about EQAO is that our results are weakest in higher order skills. We are not going to get to 75% by drilling kids because they already know that stuff. They need reading comprehension. They need rich literacy environments. That's how we're going to get to 75. So it's not about doing the test prep. We told people not to do test prep. That doesn't mean people didn't do it. I'm sure they did at some schools.[44]

What process was operating to produce these professional distortions, despite official stipulations to the contrary? In the literature on statistical issues in educational testing, there is a famous principle called Campbell's law, named after Dartmouth College professor Donald T. Campbell: "The more any quantitative social indicator is used for social decision-making, the more subject it will be to corruption pressures and the more apt it will be to distort and corrupt the social processes it is intended to monitor."[45]

> Once high-stakes targets with arbitrary numbers are inserted into a system, the system will then organize itself to produce the required result by creating a set of "perverse incentives" to manufacture the numerical outcome.

In Ontario, as elsewhere, even if the consequences are not punitive, once high-stakes targets with arbitrary numbers are inserted into a system, the system will then organize itself to produce the required result by creating a set of "perverse incentives" to manufacture the numerical outcome.[46] This does not only occur in schools. It also happens in crime statistics (for instance by redefining what count as crimes), in hospital waiting time targets (by leaving patients outside the waiting room, in the ambulance, or a corridor to delay when the waiting time will officially start) and in educational test results too.[47]

So what can we conclude from this? Ontario has produced definable achievement gains in the core skill areas of literacy and mathematics. Many of the system's educators see great advantages in how this has been achieved by sharpening the system's focus on priority areas, bolstering teachers' sense of professionalism, and increasing their levels of support. Provincial educational strategies have produced precision-like systems of tracking and monitoring that concentrate people's attention on intervening in real time whenever there is a difficulty, and on developing shared professional learning, common language, and collective responsibility among teachers in responding to the needs of all their students. In Chapter 6, we will see in more detail how the great strengths of Ontario's performance include but also extend well beyond these strategies typically associated with the Third Way.

But especially as they mature, even very strong improvers can develop Achilles' heels. The major weakness of Third Way strategies in general, and of Ontario reform in particular, is not the concentration on developing improved literacy and numeracy skills. Ontario educators consistently compliment these foundational elements of the province's reform. The system's weaknesses, rather, are caused by pushing its strengths to excess. The EQAO's links to threshold targets within the system lead, in more than one or two cases, to gaming of the system to produce required results.

Even when broader diagnostic assessments are used rather than just being restricted to the standardized tests of EQAO, constant attention to quantitative data and measurement can still have ironic side effects:

> The diagnostic assessments, although very beneficial in tracking students' success and need for assistance, have taken over as the main focus. Our district has now mandated the use of these assessments with set timelines for administration of these tests. Now rather than using them when we feel it would be most useful, we have to interrupt the flow of learning to complete the tests, mark and input the data. The students' abilities often change within a short period, making the data invalid.[48]

The emphasis on incremental annual gains in publicly measurable improvement also inhibits innovation outside the areas of literacy and numeracy. However, we will see in Chapter 6 that, outside the province's publicly known narrative of educational change that has concentrated on the gains in these foundational areas, parallel efforts at innovation alongside existing improvement efforts are already underway and are demonstrating signs of success.

THE THIRD WAY PLUS: INNOVATION WITHOUT IMPROVEMENT

We live in a brave new "Age of Techne" today, when new information and communication technologies give us hitherto unimaginable power to shape our world for better or for worse.[49] New technologies promise dramatic transformations in teaching and learning that can be highly engaging for many students who have had limited access to rich curricula in the past. But just as in the original First Way of uncoordinated innovation, new technologies in education can rapidly become overextended, distracting, and self-defeating. Overinvestment in educational technology as an answer to the challenge of educational change replays some of the excess optimism of unbridled innovation in the First Way. It can also exacerbate an already excessive belief in or dependence on data as a way to drive forward improvement in the Third Way. This combined investment in data and digital media amounts to a kind of "Third Way Plus" of educational change—a Third Way that is supercharged with elaborate data systems and technological innovations.

Like everything else in education, technology has undergone different ways of change. In the First Way, as we have seen, it was used occasionally and expediently as an entertaining extra, like television, filmstrips, and color slide shows.[50] In the Second Way, technology took the form of computer laboratories installed at some central location in the school—an extra resource allocated separate time as a supplement to the existing curriculum.[51]

In the Third Way, technology has been infused throughout the curriculum, mainly to provide more flexible access to it, through iPods, laptops, and cell phones. This Third Way Plus of ubiquity and speed offers greater technological integration and flexibility in curriculum delivery, but it also risks overreaching. Technology products and budgets are thrust upon schools, external mandates impose online courses, and classroom interactions are vulnerable to becoming superficial and distracted rather than reflective and mindful.

Educators adopt a variety of orientations to new technology. In our view, there are four strategic positions that educators often assume: (1) to *embrace* technology, (2) to *challenge* it, (3) to *protect* children from it, or (4) to *harmonize* it with other interests. All have an element of validity, but it is the last that holds the greatest potential for the future.

1. *Embrace.* Some educational change advocates are exhilarated about unleashing the potential of new technologies in schools. Young people now send an average of over 3,000 text messages a month and use various devices, from iPads to cell phones to laptops, incessantly, throughout the day. If students find these tools useful and gratifying, what's wrong with them taking out an iPhone to confirm a sequence of historical events during a debate in social studies class? Why can't students interacting in small groups use handheld devices to tweet questions on a SMART board while they solve quadratic equations? Isn't it empowering for students who find an error on a Wikipedia website to be able to correct it, and then receive extra credit for doing so?

In line with Christensen's theory of disruptive innovation, new technology already gives students more flexible access to learning opportunities that the system doesn't currently provide. This might be a foreign language that is not already offered, an Advanced Placement course that is not available in the local high school, or a technology provided at home that can reverse the colors of print and background to make text more readable for the visually impaired. These options outside school are already morphing into more flexible kinds of delivery within schools, again in line with Christensen's theory, where flexible access and delivery offer a more modularized student-centered approach that is now termed *personalized learning.* This is learning that, in the words of Alberta's Ministry of Education in Canada, can and should be accessed any time, any place, anywhere—faster or slower, in school or out of school, online or offline—just in time, exactly as needed, in ways that suit everyone's own learning style.[52] The unmoderated embracement of new technology is the Third Way Plus stance of educational change.

Embracing new technology in education means more than advocating for more flexible access to the existing curriculum, though. Flexible access is not true personalization in our view, but merely customization—tweaking a standardized offering to suit individual tastes, without changing the offering. As we will see in later chapters, the most disruptive uses of new technology in education transform the curriculum and the nature of teaching and learning themselves. This is the promise of embracement.

2. *Challenge.* Those who enthusiastically and sometimes excessively embrace the educational adoption of digital technologies are often naive about or neglectful of their distracting and addictive nature. The problems are evident throughout society, and not just in schools.

- On the day this section of our book was being written, a 17-year-old youth in Massachusetts was sentenced to a year in prison and a 15-year driving ban for texting while driving, and killing a 56-year-old male as a consequence.[53]
- "Multitasking" turns out not to be simultaneous tasking—it is performing this task and then that one, minute after minute—in an attitude of *continuous partial attention* that has redefined the ways we interact.[54]
- Corporations' surveys show that a digital interruption—an e-mail, a visit to another site in a window that is already opened, a check on the weather or the sports results, or just a quick tweet—means that it takes at least 10 minutes to regain the concentration that had been lost.[55]

As we become more and more connected by our electronic umbilical cords to our iPods and iPhones, it is easy for these new media to become foregrounded and for the rest of our lives to fade into the background. Dinner conversations lose their spirit of shared conviviality and become mere backdrops for the next awaited tweet or text message on a device that is forever furtively lurking just beneath the tabletop. Students seem less and less willing to read whole books where an argument is set out and supported in depth. DVDs, video games, and iPhone apps are the new babysitting devices that entertain children with games turned on and off in random places, while parents attend to their own needs as adults elsewhere—foregoing the rich uses of language and conversation with their children that are essential for educational success.[56]

Sherry Turkle is a Professor of Social Studies of Science and Technology at the Massachusetts Institute of Technology, who is surrounded by colleagues promoting what she calls "the triumphalist narrative of the web."[57] In *Alone Together: Why We Expect More From Technology and Less From Each Other,* Turkle explains how "with constant connection" come "new anxieties of disconnection."[58] Instead of being connected by personal intimacy, Turkle observes, people become "tethered" to their devices.[59]

In addition to the negative influences of technology on moral responsibility and human interaction, there also is a lack of evidence on any scale that computer technology in particular has been improving learning in schools.[60] U.S. states like Michigan, Maine, and Texas that instituted one-to-one laptop programs for students found that they received little in return for their investment, with mixed results at best showing rising scores in some subjects and schools, no differences in others, and declines in the rest.[61] In the final analysis, the mediating role of the school district, school principal, or individual classroom teacher—of real people, in other words—seemed to matter more than the technological tools themselves.

3. *Protect.* Protectors go further than challengers. They believe their responsibility is to shelter young people from new technology. They want to protect children and teens from Internet predators and online bullies, of course. But they also want to shelter young people from the worst impulses within themselves. In *Virtually You: The Dangerous Powers of the E-Personality,* Elias Aboujaoude, a Stanford University psychiatrist who treats patients with impulse control and obsessive compulsive disorders, describes people who live out most of their waking hours fixated on fictional selves that they've created online.[62] In extreme cases, depressed individuals disappear into their two-dimensional screens for the majority of their waking hours, scarcely interacting any more with other people face-to-face. "Sticky" online opportunities draw young people more and more into short-term activities with instant rewards. Children need to be shielded from these influences, protectors believe, by inculcating habits of self-control, discipline, listening, civility, perseverance, and delayed gratification that are the foundations of adult responsibility and educational success.

4. *Harmonize.* Too many issues in education are polarized—direct instruction versus group-based methods, process over product, unstructured play against structured literacy, and whole language in opposition to phonics. It is important not to fall into this trap and divide into manic technophiles or morose technophobes who are unable to communicate or work with each other. All the positions on educational technology we have listed have their virtues, but none of them hold the answer all by themselves. How can we embrace the benefits of technology, yet also protect our children against its very

real drawbacks and dangers while being critical of its worst effects? This is the more thoughtful and also practical way to proceed.

In his unusually titled but remarkably insightful book, *Hamlet's Blackberry: A Practical Philosophy for Building a Good Life in the Digital Age,* William Powers asks what an optimal mixture of an online and off-line, connected and disconnected lifestyle might look like.[63] Powers asks us to step back and reflect on our relationship to technology, as we might reflect on any major aspect of our lives. He wants us to consider through philosophical contemplation how technology can enhance our lives by placing us in more frequent contact with our parents or children, for example; or how it impinges less positively on our lives by undermining our interactions and relationships. He devotes each chapter of his book to different thinkers—from the ancient Greeks to Benjamin Franklin—and asks what guidance their philosophical approach might provide for rethinking our relationship to technology.

Toward the end of his book, Powers brings us to Henry David Thoreau, whose introspective masterpiece, *Walden,* exhorted readers to pursue lives of voluntary simplicity that would allow them abundant time for meditation and communion with nature. Thoreau's expeditions into the most remote parts of the Maine woods on foot and by canoe exemplified a life of purposeful and continuous exploration of his interior self and of the external, wild, and natural world around him. But his most legendary act was to spend two years, two weeks, and two days in a rustic cabin on Walden Pond near his birthplace in Concord, Massachusetts, where he cut himself off from "the lives of quiet desperation" that people lived in the cities, to engage with the unfolding of the seasons and the stillness of his natural environment.

Powers doesn't advise us to live like hermits and to give up all our modern hi-tech possessions before decamping to a switched-off rural cabin. Admirers of Thoreau often forget that he earned his living as a surveyor and thereby played a part in the economic development of Concord. The wages that he earned gave him the money he needed to travel by train to Maine, Minnesota, and Cape Cod to undertake his explorations of nature and to have the time to write his enormous journals from which his books are extracted. But Powers does encourage us to take Thoreau's praise of quiet contemplation in nature to heart by developing what he calls "Walden Zones" that are places of "inner simplicity and peace."[64]

Harmonizers like Powers remind us that new technologies are just *one* resource that should be drawn upon to enhance the education of children—like a dictionary, an abacus, a periodic table, or a map.

Teachers need to reflect upon how their instructional technologies are selected, for what purpose, and with what adjustments. Digital resources might be advantageous in some classes but inappropriate for one in which students are memorizing and acting out parts from a play. Having students watch a chemical reaction on YouTube can pale in significance when compared to creating the reaction with a classmate in a hands-on experiment. Engaging with trigonometry to measure the heights of objects can be enhanced by computer simulation and rotation, but equally well by making a measuring apparatus out of a hockey stick.

It is time to be neither an educational technophile nor a technophobe, but simply a mindful teacher who has a comfortable yet contemplative relationship to the medium.

Sometimes we need hi-tech, and sometimes we want hi-touch. Sometimes you need online communication and simulation. And sometimes, for reasons of physical and mental health and for just connecting with that Walden sense of awe and wonder, we need to step outside and "anchor some of the curriculum in Mother Nature."[65] And when the curriculum becomes too obsessed with technology and testing, the answer is not to squeeze back in half an hour of organized physical activity here and there. The answer is to change the frame altogether for a few hours or days. In Canada, Mennonite children are healthier than their peers because they participate in walking, cycling, and farm chores, rather than the organized sports activities that are popular in the larger society.[66] There is a lot that the rest of us can learn from this.

Turn off and tune out for a few hours. Leave only a couple of extra windows open on your laptop, rather than clicking frantically between many of them. Set times that have clear online and off-line engagement. Don't text when it is better to talk. Stay balanced. It is time to be neither an educational technophile nor a technophobe, but simply a mindful teacher who has a comfortable yet contemplative relationship to the medium, that should sometimes be embraced, sometimes be critiqued, and sometimes be set aside altogether.[67]

The harmonizing challenge is to engage with the possibilities of technology but not to become so attracted to and dependent on technology that we imagine we are smarter and better than anyone or anything else. At the point where we are inclined to indulge an Olympian moment of technological triumph and self-gratification, this is the time we are liable to fail and to fall.

TOWARD THE FOURTH WAY: INNOVATION WITH IMPROVEMENT

The rest of this book is dedicated to an exploration of six examples of high performance in educational change. They provide a case-by-case study of high-performing schools and systems that have innovated *and* improved—that have developed new models of educational change that can inspire others to learn from them and adapt their finest features. The six cases are not the only occupants of their class, and they are not without their flaws either. But they are some of the leading and most instructive instances of innovation and improvement combined in the world today. They show how to bring improvement together *with* innovation, instead of forcing a choice between the two. We now turn to these 21st century exemplars of exceptional educational change and transformation, beginning with the country that has been one of the world's top educational performers for more than a decade: Finland.

LAPPI
Rovaniemi
Oulu
POHJOIS-SUOMI
Kajaani
Finland
Vaasa
Kuopio
LÄNSI- JA SISÄ-SUOMI
Joensuu
Jyväskylä
ITÄ-SUOMI
Pori
Tampere
Lahti
Lappeenranta
LOUNAIS-SUOMI
ETELÄ-SUOMI
Turku
Vantaa
ÅLAND
Espoo
Helsinki

Chapter Three

FINLAND

Professionalism, Participation, and Persistence

There are all sorts of ways to size up a culture, but as many travelers will tell you, one of the quickest and by no means the least effective, is to turn on the TV. In the United States, a big part of prime time viewing is reality television. Among U.S. reality TV shows are programs where groups of young women compete for the romantic or marital attentions of a hunky millionaire or famous rap star. Every young American woman's fantasy, the programmers seem to assume, must be to marry a man of wealth and fame.

If a parallel program were to be aired across the Atlantic in the northern European nation of Finland, it would likely involve a group of eager young men (Finland is, after all, a world leader on indicators of gender equity) competing for the lofty attentions of an ultra-smart female teacher of the year. If this sounds too strange to be true, consider this. The status of teachers in Finland is so high that teaching is one of the top two preferred occupations for a future spouse—right up with medicine, and higher than business or law.[1] When you go to a party in Finland and say you are a teacher, the nonteachers in the room don't ignore you, use you as a sounding board to complain about their children's education, or even admire you because of the sacrifices you must have made to pursue such a worthy calling. They admire you all right—but because you must be impressively qualified and incredibly smart.

Since the turn of the century, Finland has been rated the world's most competitive economy by the World Economic Forum.[2] For 10 years, it has also been at or very close to the top of the world educationally in reading, mathematics, and science in OECD's PISA results while also displaying the lowest variance (or narrowest achievement gaps) between schools—just one-tenth of the OECD average.[3]

Finland's remarkable performance has given it iconic status as an international leader in educational change. National and international policy advocates and analysts such as the OECD, McKinsey & Company, and the NCEE have given Finland the highest of educational profiles.[4] Publishing giants and Ivy League scholars have produced films and videos celebrating the country's achievements.[5] National newspapers and magazines have also engaged a wider public readership with its surprising success.[6]

Before much was known about Finland's phenomenal accomplishments, one of us worked in a team with OECD expert Beatriz Pont, and former director general of the Hungarian National Institute for Public Education, Gabor Halasz, to undertake the first external review of Finland's high performance and the reasons for it.[7] Since that time, we have returned to Finland on multiple occasions and supported as well as studied partnerships between schools in Finland and other systems that are keen to benchmark themselves, in the best sense, in relation to each other's practice. In many ways, Finland provides clear proof that another way exists other than that pursued by policy makers in the Anglo-American sphere who have insisted on forcing through Second Way and sometimes Third Way reforms against an increasingly resistant profession.

Our research shows that Finland exemplifies and also continues to inspire a Fourth Way philosophy of learning, education, and the purpose of life in Finnish society. This draws good people into teaching, keeps them there, and supports them to do their work well. It builds strong professional capital among the nation's highly regarded teaching force. Finland's Fourth Way philosophy also engages teachers and the wider community in taking responsibility for their own local municipalities. In Finland, democracy, collective responsibility, and public life extend beyond abstract principles and occasional elections to the ways that people participate in and contribute to their local communities.

This chapter looks at Finland's success through these windows of understanding and engagement—the *professional capital* of the nation's teachers, and the way that its citizens support and exercise *collective autonomy* and responsibility in their thriving *local democracies.*

PROFESSIONAL CAPITAL

Across all the reports and commentaries of international organizations, there is consensus that much of Finland's success is attributable to the high quality of the nation's teachers. There is also broad agreement about why Finnish teachers are so strong. Their selection is stringent. Finnish teachers come from the very top tiers of the secondary school graduation range.[8] They are interviewed and tested for their emotional intelligence and their moral commitment to young people's learning, and only one in ten applicants actually succeeds.[9] Their training is long and rigorous. It is based in universities as well as connected to extensive practice in schools, and it incorporates an extended project in educational research—rightfully bestowing on all successful graduates the professional qualification of a master's degree.

Finnish teachers are thoroughly prepared in the cognitive science of how children learn, and at least half the teachers in primary schools have mathematics or science as their major or minor subject in university. In their jobs, teachers in Finland take a cooperative approach toward much of their work. The conditions in which they do this are good in all schools, wherever they are located. In short, well-qualified and highly respected teachers do interesting work with trusted colleagues in conditions that support and do not constantly interfere with their efforts.

Our research with the OECD found things that many others have echoed since, and that have been reinforced in subsequent research about the importance of teachers and teaching in Finland, and the central part they play in their country's educational success. What we found is a national teaching force that is rich in what we now call *professional capital.*[10]

Professional capital refers to the assets among teachers and in teaching that are developed, invested, accumulated, and circulated in order to produce a high yield or return in the quality of teaching and student learning. Professional capital is made up of five other kinds of capital—human, social, moral, symbolic, and decisional.

1. *Human capital* consists of the individual knowledge, skills, capabilities, qualifications, and training that contribute to a person's talent.
2. *Social capital* is to be found in the collaborative patterns of interaction and levels of trust that contribute to the mutual learning and degrees of support that people enjoy as they seek to become more competent and confident in their work.

3. *Moral capital* is about the power and the pull of performing a service for others or even fulfilling a calling towards them.
4. *Symbolic capital* is seen in the signs of status and regard throughout a society that attract people to particular kinds of work or activity.
5. *Decisional capital* is the capacity to make good decisions or judgments in complex situations over sustained periods of time.

The perspective of *professional capital* highlights how getting good teaching for all learners requires teachers to be highly committed, thoroughly prepared, and continuously developed. Finnish teachers are well regarded, properly paid, effectively networked with each other to maximize their own improvement, and able as well as allowed to make effective judgments using all their knowledge, capabilities, and experience. Finland may have few natural resources other than timber and fresh water, but it is rich in the professional capital of its people, and especially its teachers.

HUMAN CAPITAL

Finnish teachers know about learning. They are thoroughly educated in cognitive science and child development. They know their subjects—especially the core subjects of reading literacy, science, and mathematics, which are prime elements of their university preparation. They know how to undertake research and inquiry because this is an integral element of their master's degree qualification, and a professional expectation throughout their careers. Finnish teachers are not just intellectual eggheads, even though they come from the very top tier of the university graduation range. They also have high emotional intelligence in which they must excel as a condition of entry into the profession.

Teachers in Finland also know the curriculum that they teach. This is because they create much of the curriculum together within the broadest directions that are steered by the state. Finnish teachers aren't obsessed with interpreting and integrating hundreds of national standards or with implementing a detailed national curriculum that a distant government department concocted. Finland doesn't *deliver* curriculum to its teachers through detailed plans that are tightly aligned in a bureaucratic system, and that teachers then somehow have to master. Rather, a set of common values and beliefs holds everyone together through quiet yet constant interaction so that they can and do develop and interpret the curriculum flexibly within this broad direction in each local municipality.

Part of the reason why Finnish teachers are rich in human capital is the fact that they themselves develop the curriculum that they must deliver. They create handsomely bound texts that are easy for colleagues to share and for students to use. Curriculum and instruction are not separate in Finland. They are the same thing. Teachers invest in what they teach and master what it involves because they engage together in its development. This is where human capital meets social capital.

Part of the reason why Finnish teachers are rich in human capital is the fact that they themselves develop the curriculum that they must deliver.

SOCIAL CAPITAL

Teachers in Finland cooperate as a matter of habit, not just to complete assigned tasks. They feel a sense of collective responsibility for all the children they serve together. Teachers say they feel responsible for children in all grades, not just those in their own classes. Cooperation is not just an add-on when the workday is over. It's not about temporary teamwork or interpreting student achievement data together after busy days at school. Cooperation is about how they create the curriculum and how the work itself gets done. A ministry official explained: "If you give resources to them, they find a way to solve the problem." Vision and goals in Finnish schools are often implicit and shared through daily acts of cooperation, rather than just set out in a printed strategic plan. Cooperation and a sense of collective responsibility extend beyond the school as well as operate among professionals within it. "People in the field don't hate people in this [Ministry of Education] building," we were told. "It's more cooperative. It's an informal way of distributed leadership."[12] To teachers, in other words, the system is their ally, not their overlord.

Through consultation and discussion, the National Board of Education's guidelines stimulate "intensive cooperation all the time," according to its former national director. A director of a local municipality—the equivalent of a North American school district—described how

> we just pick things up, not in a systematic way. These values are easy to find at the national level. We are taking part in many seminars, etc.—working together, managers and directors. [While our] values are quite similar, we have freedom in how we organize.

The social capital of the teaching profession in Finland is to be found in widespread habits of cooperation, in pervasive feelings of trust among teachers as well as between teachers and those who work in the wider system, and in a collective sense of shared moral responsibility.

MORAL CAPITAL

Finnish teachers feel collectively responsible not just toward doing a job well, but also and especially for the children who are in their care. Teachers serve all their students in a spirit of equity, care, and justice for everyone. Professions distinguish themselves from corporations because they are driven not by the profit motive, but by a sense of service toward their clients. Teachers in Finland have the time and take the trouble to know their children so that they can serve them effectively.

Educators at one school explained that Finland performs well not by creating geniuses but by lifting up each child from the bottom. The goal is "no social exclusion, so that nobody is forgotten." In their school, they observed, if a child began to behave differently or unusually, the teacher would immediately ask the child why, talk to the child's parents, and then swiftly converse with other teachers who taught the same child to share perceptions and strategies. There are teams that meet three times each week to discuss how to help children with problems. This somewhat informal but highly insistent pattern of early intervention then extends to a Student Welfare Group, if necessary, where the school's principal, teachers, administrators, nurses, and counselors address individual student problems before they escalate into major crises.[13] Every school also has a special teacher whose brief is to watch over the whole area of special educational needs.

In Finland, every student is special. Special education is not a permanent medical label or an individual legal entitlement that then leads to assigned resources following separate children—often at very great cost. Instead, special education is a response to a learning difficulty that many children might have at one time or another. Because of this broad and flexible definition of special education, by the time they leave upper secondary school, more than half of all young people will at some time have received special tutoring or support services.

The inclusive approach of the Finnish system reduces the stigma that is elsewhere often attached to having special educational needs, and it avoids having to make many expensive and medically based legal interventions later on. Most children with learning difficulties are responded to within relatively small classes of not more than 24. These classes are normally made up of about 8 students if unusual difficulties prevent them from learning properly. In the primary or elementary years, children are often with the same teacher for several years. Specific intervention therefore comes about not as a result of bureaucratic procedures as in some North American processes of tiers of intervention, but as a consequence of individual knowledge, personal care for all students, and focused discussions within learning communities that meet together regularly.

Finnish teachers know their children well. Schools are small, with rarely more than 400 students, so there are not too many children to know. They are known year after year, especially at the primary level, where they often remain with the same teacher to build a sense of community and continuity. They are known by teachers who feel collectively responsible for all students in every grade and who tend to make a lifelong commitment to a single school instead of moving around. The schools provide stability for their young people and communities and they thrive without the fear that policy makers might abruptly remove or reassign their teachers or principals arbitrarily.

> The test scores, spreadsheets, and data warehouses that are increasingly common in other countries are poor proxies for the intense personal and professional knowledge that comes from strong classroom relationships with children and clear senses of collective responsibility among colleagues.

Teachers can also concentrate on their professional calling to serve their children, and thereby build their moral capital. They are not overwhelmed with and overly focused on the test scores, spreadsheets, and data warehouses that are increasingly common in other countries. These systems are poor proxies for the intense personal and professional knowledge that comes from strong classroom relationships with children and clear senses of collective responsibility among colleagues. All this shared personal and professional knowledge promotes a climate of continual improvement and innovation for all children in all schools.

SYMBOLIC CAPITAL

Teachers and learning have high status in Finnish society. An educator at a school in the city of Tampere put it like this:

> The whole society is respecting teaching and schools. People are reading a lot [for instance, through] fairy tales. Mothers [with generous parental leave benefits] can be home for three years. There is a good library system. All teachers are studying in universities, so are highly educated.

Attracting better teachers comes down to more than having stringent selection procedures or awarding master's degrees to all new teachers—although these things are also important because they put teaching on a par with the classic professions of medicine and law. The capacity to attract highly qualified teachers is also a question of how the public, the media, and politicians value lifelong learning as a priority throughout the society in a country where the *average* number of public library withdrawals per year per head of population is as high as 17—a sign of the country's commitment to literacy and learning in family priorities, public funding, and public life, rather than just in the schools.[14]

Finnish teachers feel they have high status and are accorded widespread respect. The attractive conditions of their schools reinforce this, and the critical contribution they are seen to be making to the future of their society underlines it. Teachers in Finland have positive symbolic capital. They are respected and admired in politics and the media, rather than criticized and abused by them.

DECISIONAL CAPITAL

Finnish teachers aren't charismatic superstars. Their pedagogy is rather ordinary. Innovation in Finland has more to do with how teachers work together, how the society organizes its schools, and how children develop creative capacities by engaging with a broad curriculum, than it has to do with technological transformations or constant upheavals in instruction. Interestingly, Finnish teachers have a reputation for "pedagogical conservatism." [15] In the classrooms we have visited, we have seen examples of children listening to their teachers, working individually, and engaging in whole-class question-and-answer sessions. When we have seen cooperative groupwork, it has been quiet and persistent rather than technically complex or dramatic—as in a middle school lesson where small groups of students were calmly and informally cooperating on producing research reports on different Finnish towns and regions. What we have not seen is teachers attending in a self-conscious way to categorizations of students' multiple intelligences or learning styles, or orchestrating technically complicated strategies of U.S.-style cooperative learning where children are allocated precise roles in their groupwork.

Finns favor competent, trustworthy, and calmly assured teaching over the flamboyant, heroic role models featured in Hollywood films that pit the (always young) insurgent against the (always aging) advocate for traditional teaching. Outsiders looking for a Finnish version of Robin Williams in the *Dead Poet's Society* or Michelle Pfeifer in *Dangerous Minds* are in for a disappointment. One educator summed up the pragmatic Finnish position here: "We have many, many good practices but we are not describing it and its theoretical basis. We just do it."[16] Finns don't believe that a few brilliant heroes will save their children and their schools. They trust that a vast critical mass of steadfast, effective teachers will advance their whole society. These teachers patiently improve their practice and solve their professional problems together in a spirit of continuous improvement and collective responsibility. This is the essence of decisional capital.

This capacity to make good judgments is accrued through lots of practice, but not through practice alone. Reflecting on that practice and taking the time to learn from it are indispensable to the quest of improving it over time. Paradoxically, perfecting practice requires being able to step back from it from time to time. Doctors need time to think about their patients. Lawyers need time to consider the facts of their cases. It's no different in teaching.

This is where Finnish teachers have a significant advantage over many of their counterparts in other countries. Finnish teachers have the time—and they use it well—to develop their decisional capital. Finland's leading education expert and international education ambassador, Pasi Sahlberg, summarizes it this way:

> In lower secondary schools, on average, Finnish teachers teach about 600 hours, i.e., 800 lessons of 45 minutes, annually. This corresponds to four teaching lessons daily. In the United States, [by comparison], average annual teaching time in lower secondary grades is 1080 hours, which, in turn, equals six or more daily classroom lessons of 50 minutes. [In the U.S.], teaching six or more lessons daily is a tough job and leaves many teachers too tired to engage in anything professional when teaching is done. Teachers' work is therefore primarily defined as teaching in a classroom. In a typical Finnish lower secondary school, [however], teachers teach, on average, four lessons a day. Although teachers are paid by the number of lessons they teach, there is also time every day to plan, learn, and reflect on teaching with other teachers, as well as assess their students' achievement and overall progress, design their own school curriculum, participate in several school health and well-being issues concerning their students, and provide remedial support to those who may need additional help.[17]

Compared to many Anglo-American countries that try to raise student achievement by doing more things, more often, and with more intensity–teaching more hours, starting school earlier, or lengthening the school day–Finland does precisely the opposite.

Sahlberg's striking insight is that compared to many Anglo-American countries that try to raise student achievement by doing more things, more often, and with more intensity—teaching more hours, starting school earlier, or lengthening the school day—Finland does precisely the opposite. Finnish teachers stop, reflect seriously, take their time, learn the most important lessons, and only then act decisively.

Sometimes, teachers in other countries fall short of achieving stronger results not because they are lazy or incompetent, but because they actually teach too hard and too much.[18] They are so busy teaching—using every strategy possible to try and engage their students—that they have no time to watch and understand how the children are actually learning. As we will see most spectacularly when we look at the performance of Singapore, in order to learn more, teachers may have to teach a bit less. For Sahlberg, this is one of the sublime paradoxes of the Finnish system. In Finland, teachers have the time to step back, inquire, reflect, and learn—not just quick "take-aways" but deeper lessons that could lead to lasting improvements in teaching. This increases their capacity to make effective judgments. It develops their decisional capital.

Teaching in Finland is not a temporary engagement. It is a permanent commitment–a job for life.

This decisional capital accumulates over long periods of time. Teacher retention rates in Finland are very high. For most Finnish teachers, their chosen profession is their lifelong career. They have many years to perfect their practice by putting in all the hours it takes to master their profession. There are no alternate paths to certification. No one senses and certainly no one argues that teaching should be a way station on to something else that is more important and consequential. Like medicine or architecture, teaching is a permanent professional commitment where developing the decisional capital of expert judgment is allotted the proper time to unfold. Teaching in Finland is not a temporary engagement. It is a permanent commitment—a job for life.

SUMMARY

The cornerstone international organizations of OECD, McKinsey & Company, and the NCEE and our own corner store analysis are mainly in agreement about the crucial contribution of Finland's high-quality teachers to the country's educational and also economic success. We concur about Finland's capacity to attract, select, rigorously prepare, appropriately certify, properly support, and dynamically bring together a teaching force that can act capably, without detailed supervision or regulation, in conditions of high autonomy, and collective responsibility.

Finns are supremely able to invest in and develop the strong *professional capital* of their teaching force in terms of the individual human capital of capabilities and commitment, the social capital of collective responsibility, the moral capital of including and caring for all young people, the symbolic capital of assigning high status to teachers by everyone in the society, and the decisional capital of developing shrewd judgment through structured experience, a solid knowledge base, and action research.

What our own analysis adds to that of the cornerstone organizations is a somewhat sharper sense of what all this means for countries outside Finland, for the ways they prepare and develop their teachers, for what they should stop doing, as well as what they should start. Figure 3.1 summarizes some of these contrasts.

If we take this corner store analysis seriously, it poses fundamental questions about how other nations treat their teachers and think about their schools. Can supporters of organizations like Teach for America in the United States and Teach First in the United Kingdom still justify the belief that teachers can prepare quickly and that it is acceptable for many of them to leave the education profession forever after only a few years in the job? How can we ensure that collaboration and cooperation extend beyond teamwork and tasks to include building the basic trust and relationships that are the foundation of strong professional

Figure 3.1 Professional Capital Choices

Human Capital. Teachers are qualified developers of curriculum, not quickly prepared deliverers of standards.

Social Capital. Teachers work in communities of trust, not just in teams undertaking tasks.

Moral Capital. There is inclusion and knowledge of all students, not only identification of some.

Symbolic Capital. Teachers are valued as a high-status investment, not as a disparaged taxpayer cost.

Decisional Capital. Teaching is a long-term career, not a temporary job.

communities? How can special educational needs strategies establish inclusive and caring environments for all students, rather than overemphasizing legal and medical processes to identify, assist, and place particular individuals? What will it take to change entire mind-sets about the status of teaching throughout the whole society?

COMMUNITY AND SOCIETY

How does Finland get such good teachers and support them with such consistency? The pay is only average by the standard of developed countries, so Finnish teachers can't be in it for the money. Finnish teachers can supplement their salaries by up to 50% by taking on additional tasks, but no one claims this is a major reason why young people enter the profession. There is certainly historic traditional respect for teachers in Finnish society that goes back to the high esteem for literacy that was held by Lutheran ministers in the 18th century. But other Nordic nations with lower achievement results share this esteem. We must look to more recent reforms that were deliberately introduced as recently as the 1980s if we want to understand the rigor and status that underpin the modern Finnish profession.

What seem to matter most in the status accorded to Finnish teachers are factors having to do with the fulfilling nature of the work, the important role that teachers play in shaping the future of Finnish society, and the strong and rewarding relationships with children and with adults. Finnish teachers value consistency of support from the system to perform the work and to learn how to improve at it. They cherish the flexibility and freedom to exercise the shared discretionary judgment that is the mark of all true professions.

Overall, Finnish teachers understand and value the importance of their work and they have the collective autonomy and local authority to pursue it without interference or interruption. Sahlberg asked teachers an especially telling question that cut to the heart of these issues. What, he asked, might prompt or push young primary teachers to leave their profession for another line of work?

> Interestingly, practically nobody cites their salary as a reason to quit teaching. Instead, many point out that if they were to lose their professional autonomy in schools and their classrooms, their career choice would be called in question. For example, if an external inspection to judge the quality of their work or a

> merit-based compensation policy influenced by external measures [was introduced], many would change their jobs.
>
> Many Finnish teachers report that if they encountered similar pressure through external standardized measuring and test-based accountability as do their peers in the UK or North America, they would seek other professional challenges. In short, teachers in Finland expect that they will experience professional prestige, respect, and trust in their work, just as medical doctors do. It is, first and foremost, the working conditions and moral professional environment that count as young Finns decide whether they will pursue a teaching career or seek work in another field.[19]

In Finland, it is the definition and role of the profession itself in the society that is decisive. Other systems that adapt only a tiny sliver of Finnish reforms—master's degrees for all teachers, or more inclusive special education, or teachers as curriculum developers—will be unlikely to attain Finnish-level results unless they also promote the high status of their teachers and the indispensable roles they play in serving their society.

With high status comes strong support. In Finland, a number of supportive features beyond the classroom profoundly affect Finnish teachers' commitments and develop their considerable capabilities. Four factors are especially important:

1. the influential role of the local municipality,
2. the unique character of Finnish assessment and accountability,
3. the ability to solve problems through self-correcting assistance, and
4. the overall character and direction of Finland's state and society.

1. LOCAL AUTHORITY

Finland is made up of more than 300 local municipalities. The term *municipalities* can be a bit misleading for English language readers because some Finnish municipalities cover rural areas that are vast and thinly populated. As in many other countries, municipalities are the lowest level of elected government. They correspond to school districts in North America and are the essence of local democracy. They are integral to the success of Finnish schools and public services.

Outside Finland, in England, in the United States, and even in neighboring Sweden, there is an orchestrated assault on and undermining of community engagement and local democracy in public education:

- U.S. legislation on the RTTT has made funding to states contingent on raising restrictions on the number of independent charter schools that can be created—leading in turn to the closure of locally controlled public schools that accept all students and are connected to the public good.
- The United Kingdom's Coalition Government is converting more and more of England's state schools into independent academies that are funded directly by central government. This is rapidly reducing local education authorities to being providers of residual services like special needs identification and bits and pieces of professional development.
- In Sweden, cities like Malmo find themselves being educationally and socially split into two. Wealthier white Swedes on one side of the city send their children to "free schools" that operate independently of overall municipal control, while poor immigrant families on the other side are left to send their children to the shrinking residue of municipal public schools.

This erosion and elimination of local democracy elevates market interests over democratic rights and privileges, and individual choice over the common good. It takes away the opportunity for citizens to engage with local politics through school committees and other branches of municipal government. Once the "inconvenient" interference and opposition of local democracy and community engagement have been eradicated, state and national governments are able to cut their taxes, cut their costs, and cut their deals with educational testing and technology conglomerates for more standardized assessments or more student online learning requirements. More and more schools are run as for-profit enterprises; less and less attention is paid to public issues and local democracy. With local municipal control out of the way, education is up for sale as a market for short-term business capital. This threatens the whole future of participatory democracy and also the health of the long-term economy.

In response to this erosion and eradication of local authority, a number of reform advocates have been highlighting alternative ways to create middle tiers of organization and administration between the individual school and the centralized state.[20] They talk up the value of networks and clusters of schools learning from each other and acting together, but these usually connect schools to peers outside their local authority, district, or municipality, not to neighbors who share the same community together within it.[21] They support the development of chains and brands of schools that are owned and controlled by upstart entrepreneurs or long-established companies—but the danger of these chains is that they can turn schools into little franchises of educational change where people's attachment and loyalty is to the franchise and the brand, not the local community.[22] This includes the hiring of school leaders, for instance, who are often promoted from within other parts of the chain, rather than appointed with a view to strengthening connections to the local community.[23]

Clusters and chains of free schools, charters, and academies may sometimes be prepared to band together to serve the local community, but even in these conditions, they still have no democratic representation or local authority. In Finland, though, the democratically representative local municipality remains the unapologetic foundation of public education, public services, and public life. It is also the basis for curriculum development that serves the needs of local children and that develops the professional capital of high-quality teachers. High-performing and actively democratic Finland thumbs its Nordic nose at the chains and charters of market-driven educational reform. And the consistent excellence of its educational and economic results rubs the noses of its corporate-driven reform competitors into their own lower performing dirt.

Finnish municipal leadership "tries to support every school to be successful."[24] Diverse groups of educators have to work together with urban planners and those who are responsible for developing the local culture and economy within their municipalities. Free health and counseling services as well as free school meals for all children (not just those who have the stigma of poverty) are all provided on the school site. If a country requires its children go to school, it has a responsibility to feed them all as well.

Finnish schools are not only spared from having to compete with each other. They are actively expected to cooperate. In one city, for example, all comprehensive secondary schools follow the common curriculum that has been created through a citywide effort involving hundreds of teachers.

In Finland, local municipalities have great powers that include allocating budgets among education, health, and social services; designing and distributing curriculum that is specific to the schools and the local municipality; determining the appointment criteria for school principals; conducting self-evaluations; and defining a collective vision

In places like England and the United States, districts and local authorities have become inconvenient enemies to be eliminated. In Finland, they are the inalienable engines of educational success, common good, and a democratic way of life.

and direction together. During our OECD review, Helsinki was setting a new five-year vision (with benchmarks after three years) that involved every school discussing what the vision along with desired objectives might mean for them. Again, in contrast to other country's practices, the directions and benchmarks were cooperatively determined, not administratively imposed.

Part of the brilliance of Finland's success is that all this local democratic control of schools is not seen as being opposed to the creative and innovative sides of market forces and competitiveness. Best educational practice aligns with best business practice (rather than short-term commercial opportunism). Municipal educational leaders use ideas and procedures coming from business management, such as the use of purchasers and providers, and the balanced score card approach of multidimensional evaluation that goes far beyond relying on single and simple bottom lines.[25] Finnish educational and social thinking grasps that efficiency and competitiveness are in synergy with educational cooperation and creativity. In places like England and the United States, districts and local authorities have become inconvenient enemies to be eliminated. In Finland, they are the inalienable engines of educational success, common good, and a democratic way of life.

2. ALTERNATIVES TO ACCOUNTABILITY

Accountability is the remainder that is left when responsibility has been subtracted.

One of the most striking differences between Finland's approach to educational accountability and the approaches taken by most of the Anglo-American group of nations is the importance it attaches to responsibility. Finland has no word for accountability. Responsibility (*vastuullisuus*) is the closest thing to it. Collective professional responsibility precedes and supersedes accountability. Indeed, as we said in *The Fourth Way,* "Accountability is the remainder that is left when responsibility has been subtracted."[26]

Finland does not impose standardized testing on a census of all students. It tests samples, in three- or four-year cycles, for confidential monitoring purposes, and to provide feedback to the schools. Sahlberg wryly remarks that when health professionals give us a blood test, they don't extract all the blood from our bodies to do so.[27] There are no public rankings, no competitive hierarchies. The public already has confidence in its high-performing schools and does not need external standardized tests either to underscore that confidence or to undermine it.

There is no need for layers and levels of bureaucracy when the basic teaching force can be trusted and can produce quality learning in each and every locality.

The absence of a national standardized testing system in Finland removes many layers of interference and accountability that would distract teachers from their core tasks. There are only 18 employees in Finland's National Board of Education, for example, compared to hundreds in similar organizations overseas. Within this small National Board, Finland's Education Evaluation Council that oversees the national student assessments in the country has an operating budget of barely more than one million U.S. dollars. There is no need for layers and levels of bureaucracy when the basic teaching force can be trusted and can produce quality learning in each and every locality.

The principle of putting responsibility before accountability, and the practice of testing by sample rather than by census that once made Finland look like a quirky but impractical international outlier, now persuades one jurisdiction after another to review its testing and accountability strategies. The United Kingdom's Coalition Government has severely curtailed all standardized systemwide testing before age 16 because of the "perverse incentives" this creates to place undue attention on students very close to the test threshold, and encourages teaching to the test.[28] The Finnish approach to educational assessment played a significant part in this decision, as did the advocacy and activism of England's National Association of Head Teachers (NAHT). The NAHT drew on our original Fourth Way evidence about educational assessment and responsibility in Finland, and proposed an alternate strategy that was based on Finnish-like assessment of samples for accountability purposes and on the development of more diagnostic assessments to help teachers improve their practice.[29]

Meanwhile, the high-performing province of Alberta that has been Canada's frontrunner in standardized educational assessment for two decades, is reviewing its assessment strategies at the instigation of new Progressive Conservative premier, Alison Redford. This has followed years of persistent advocacy by the Alberta Teachers' Association and other professional organizations that have included exchange visits between Albertan and Finnish educators, as well as public showcasing of the successful approaches that Finland has adopted. These international developments that echo the assessment successes of high-performing

Finland are making the United States and other heavily pro-testing systems look like aging ideological outlaws of outmoded educational change.

3. HIGH TRUST AND SELF-CORRECTION

Twenty years ago, Finland was in the depths of economic despair. The world had been thrilled by the fall of the Berlin Wall in 1989 and by the *glasnost* reforms of the former Soviet Union that followed in its wake. For the Finns, though, the end of the Cold War was an economic catastrophe. Until that moment, their mighty neighbor to the East had been a huge captive export market for lumber and other raw materials. When Russia's market became available to everyone else, Finland's economy collapsed, and by 1992, the nation's unemployment rate had climbed to almost 20%.

Finland hasn't always been top of the world economically or educationally. It has had more than its fair share of setbacks and adversity. So how did the country respond educationally to the adversity and looming austerity of 1992? At moments like this, other countries have imposed severe financial austerity, cut back on programs and professional development, standardized as much practice as possible, and increased levels of oversight, accountability, and intervention to convince the public that it is getting value for money. Finland's first response, by contrast, was actually to *abolish* its external schools inspection service.[30] Having already initiated strategies to improve the training and quality of teachers in the 1980s, and being committed to pushing these much further so as to prepare young people for a creative knowledge society, the Finns believed that better teachers could be trusted to monitor themselves and would no longer be in need of external inspection. The cost savings would also be considerable. A representative of the National Board of Education remarked that

> we trust the expertise of our principals and teachers. We respect that expertise and we try to understand what is happening in the everyday life of schools and what questions have to be worked with, and we try to combine that with issues, interests and needs of the future at the national level.

When a school experiences difficulty, instead of adopting strategies such as removing staff, or imposing sanctions, the local municipality asks:

> How can we help the school? What were the things that went wrong? The knowledge [of how to solve the problem] is in the

> school and we have very capable principals. You have to trust. Trust is the first thing. We try to help rather than count the budget. If there's a problem, we are sitting together and thinking "what can we do?" Principals are highly valued in our society. We don't want to fail.[31]

If principals are not leading well, the strategy is not to fire them but, in the words of one city administrator, to "try to develop them, actually." Finland doesn't perseverate on the extremes of identifying good and bad teachers, leaders, or schools. Indeed, with differences between schools being smaller than in any other developed country, Finns scarcely believe these differences exist. Providers of school leadership training told us that "all schools must be good enough and there is no reason to have elite schools and bad schools." If schools experience difficulty, the government does not intervene punitively but relies on self-correcting systems of assistance and support.

As we will see, more and more high-performing countries believe that when there is a problem, the first presumption must be that people are acting in good faith but need assistance and support to be more effective. More intrusive interventions are only introduced after the assistance and support proves to be insufficient. Finland takes this strategy one step further. Assistance and support are pretty much all of the answer, all of the time. This is possible and effective because of how the Finnish system is organized.

> High-performing countries believe that when there is a problem, the first presumption must be that people are acting in good faith but need assistance and support to be more effective.

The Finnish educational system is self-correcting. This occurs through a process of school self-evaluation that is incorporated into national evaluations, and that is guided by norms of collective professional responsibility. In these ways, the system is able to "build cooperative structures and hear the weak signals."[32] When these "weak signals" are heard, the system responds through training, support, and assistance from the local municipality and from other schools. High quality, high trust, collective commitment, and local responsibility enable Finland's educational system to operate as a self-correcting, complex system. Difficulties are rectified through broad participation and constant interaction rather than through public exposure and top-down intervention.

4. THE FINNISH DREAM

How did the Finns climb out of the depths of economic depression to become one of the most competitive, prosperous, and educationally high-achieving nations in the world? The corporate, political, and intellectual leaders of Finland were able to construct a dream that resonated with the nation's people. This dream featured Finland as a highly successful, creative, and innovative knowledge economy in which Finns, through their education, would be able to outperform international competitors.

They would do this with creative skills that built on the traditional musical and craft accomplishments of their heritage and that would apply to areas of modern innovation, like digital technologies, through strong investment in science and technology. Connecting their technological future to their creative past, Finns would still retain their long-standing social values of equity, inclusion, and a strong welfare state. And Finnish people would continue to bring to life the word that is so often seen as encapsulating Finnish identity: *sisu*—the willingness to persist despite all obstacles.

Finns may dream but Finnish innovation is disciplined, dogged, and determined. The Finns exemplify the "fanatic discipline" that Jim Collins and Morten Hansen, in *Great by Choice,* said was a key characteristic of highly successful organizations.[33] These extremely high performers are "utterly relentless," even "unbending in their focus on their quests."[34]

Finnish philosopher Pekka Himanen, along with his collaborator, Manuel Castells, points to the telling nature of this paradoxical achievement and its implications for differently organized systems elsewhere:

> Finland shows that a fully-fledged welfare state is not incompatible with technological innovation, with the development of the information society, and with a dynamic, competitive new economy. Indeed, it appears to be a decisive contributing factor to the growth of this new economy on a stable basis. Finland stands in sharp contrast to the Silicon Valley model that is entirely driven by market mechanisms, individual entrepreneurialism, and the culture of risk—with considerable social costs, acute social inequality and a deteriorating basis for both locally generated human capital and economic infrastructure.[35]

If the Finnish dream is held together by discipline, it is driven forward by a sense of destiny in the face of enormous historical and political obstacles. Finland is sandwiched between two powerful neighbors—Sweden and Russia—who dominated and colonized it for the best part of 700 years. This legacy has galvanized Finns into asserting and sustaining their own identity, and it explains Finland's combination of former eastern Europe commitments to collective welfare (while shedding the authoritarian elements of Soviet-style communism) on the one hand, and western European, Swedish-style traditions of parliamentary democracy, on the other.

A key part of Finland's success is its cosmopolitan open-mindedness to other countries and their policies—as is evident in a partnership that some Finnish schools have formed with colleagues in the fellow high-performing jurisdiction of Alberta in Canada. This open-mindedness combines with a pragmatic stance where all policies are adapted only after careful consideration of how they might or might not fit the Finnish context.

The Finnish dream is a public and a social dream that has had spectacular economic and educational results. It is a dream that, as Sahlberg says, has "survived opposing political governments and ministries unharmed and intact."[36] One of the inconvenient truths for overseas observers of Finland is that it has almost no private schools—there are only about 75 in the whole country. These independent schools still receive public funding. All the public has been educated in and is invested in the nation's schools, in the education of everyone's children, and in the common future they share together.

Finland has outstanding teachers, who work together in well-supported schools, and serve a common and inspiring moral purpose. This is not the common Anglo-American technical purpose of raising the bar and narrowing the gap in tested achievement. It is a purpose grounded in inclusive, equitable, and innovative social values that animate and elevate its remarkable educational performance.

SUMMARY

When admirers of the Finnish system articulate the inconvenient truths of its educational success, skeptics and critics in other countries produce a range of retorts as to why we should disregard it. With a population of around 5.5 million, they say, Finland is too small to be comparable. But this figure is only slightly less than the average U.S. state where most educational policy is actually decided.[37] Or it's just not racially or culturally diverse, they argue. It is true that there is little evidence of racial diversity in Finland—although we should note that more than a third of American states have less foreign-born residents than

Finland. Some will say that Finnish achievement comes at a price—in high rates of suicide and also male alcoholism, for example. This ignores how Finland, like other northern European societies with low income inequality, fares very well on a wider range of social and health outcomes compared to other countries.[38]

Our own corner store analysis of Finland agrees with international cornerstone organizations in emphasizing the way that Finland values, selects, and develops its teachers. Our analysis adds other elements as well—particularly concerning the strength of Finnish community and local democracy. Much of Finland's societal strength that supports education, we have seen, resides in its local communities—in local districts, municipalities, and authorities that develop true local capacity. These local municipalities become a focal point where teachers can work on curriculum together and enhance their own professional skills and quality. The municipalities also become a place for integrating public and health services, for promoting community engagement, and for expressing local democracy. This evidence on the power of local democracy, within broad steering by the wider state, is a Fourth Way lesson for those parts of the world that are busy eradicating local authorities.

CONCLUSION

Finland tells us a lot about *what to do* to develop a high-quality teaching force that is rich in professional capital: select the best, get them to work together, and take collective responsibility for curriculum development and children's learning; then develop and keep them over many years until they reach the peak of their powers. This is a big enough challenge for most other countries.

As a society, Finland challenges us even more about *how to be* in the way we participate in public life on a local and national level and in our financial commitment to support everyone's schools and everyone's children. The Finns prioritize strategies that enable all children to be in nurturing relationships with their parents in the earliest years of life, ensure that there is health care and shelter for all citizens, and promote values of collective responsibility and the public good. The Finns, in short, build *professional capital,* they develop local community *participation,* and they pursue their goals in society and in life with relentless, disciplined *persistence.*

The Finns build *professional capital,* they develop local community *participation,* and they pursue their goals in society and in life with relentless, disciplined *persistence.*

The cornerstone organization of McKinsey & Company has gradually marginalized Finland from its exemplars of high performance. Either it omits Finland altogether, or it argues that, from the standpoint of other systems, the Finnish combination of strategies can be realized only when every other more centrally directed stage of improvement has been undertaken and completed before it.

Yet the Finnish Fourth Way of professional capital, local participation, and disciplined persistence is not the ornate icing on the stodgier cake of more common and basic improvement that must be baked beforehand. Finland did not first go through the austerity and autocracy of the Second Way or the data-driven hyperactivity of the Third Way before it became a Fourth Way system. It approached the Fourth Way on its own terms with a set of strategies that emerged from its unique history and that was adapted creatively and effectively to its historical challenges. But it is not alone in taking this approach. Indeed, we will see in the next five cases, Finland is not an isolated and eccentric outlier of Fourth Way strategy. It is one of an impressive international group of strikingly high performers.

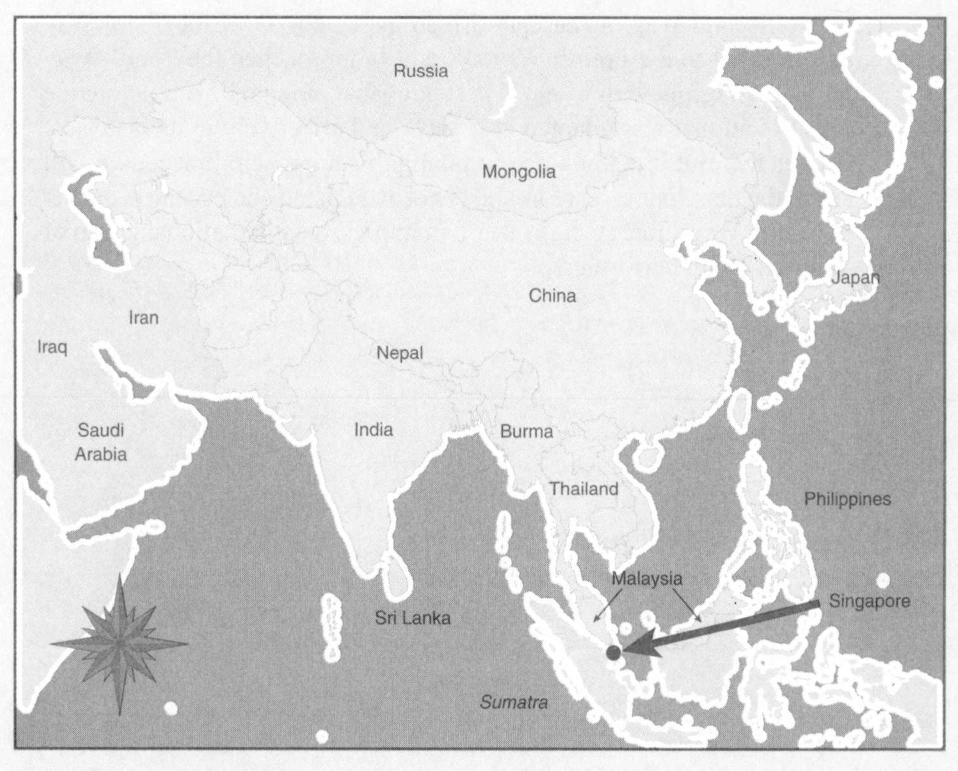
Russia
Mongolia
China
Japan
Iran
Iraq
Nepal
Saudi
Arabia
India
Burma
Thailand
Philippines
Malaysia
Singapore
Sri Lanka
Sumatra

Chapter Four

SINGAPORE

Innovation, Communication, and Paradox

With Pak Tee Ng

For years, Finland held the first place on PISA—attracting attention and acclaim from all over the world. But before PISA even existed, the International Association for the Evaluation of Educational Achievement (IEA) administered the Trends in Maths and Science Studies (TIMSS) examination to students in 28 countries. When the first results were released in 1995, the top achiever in both mathematics and science for 13-year old students was tiny Singapore, a former British colony at the tip of the Malay peninsula.

In February 2011, we were seated in the office of Singapore's then minister of education, Ng Eng Hen. The hot topic that had preoccupied the global media for many weeks was Singapore's international high performance. Together, we were discussing the explanations for this success in the media and among cornerstone international organizations. These had included strong and stable top-level leadership, a competitive school culture committed to hard work and disciplined achievement, recruitment of high-quality teachers, ways of rewarding those among them who demonstrated superior performance, provision of support and capacity-building in the system, and clear plans and processes for the career development of teachers and leaders.

Graciously accepting the legitimacy of many of these components of change, the minister then leaned forward, and with the surgical precision of his former profession, remarked that one thing he had to stress repeatedly to international visitors, but that they sometimes found difficult to understand or accept, was the importance of *culture*—of habits, beliefs, ways of doing things—in families, organizations, and political institutions that were distinctive to Singapore and to its way of doing business as a country. Lee Sing Kong, director of Singapore's prestigious National Institute of Education, reiterated the point with characteristic directness—you just could not "teleport" the items that were successful in one system or country into another, he said. It was how everything fit together within a particular culture that was crucial.

Singapore is an international enigma of high performance in a place where few people would have expected it. This tiny "red dot" (as a former president of Indonesia first called it) is a global powerhouse of impressive economic growth and astonishing educational achievement. Singapore is in the world's top ten in terms of gross domestic product per capita of population; a leading educational achiever; and the source of half the world's perfect scores on the International Baccalaureate.[1]

These are extraordinary accomplishments, given Singapore's history. Barely half a century ago, the tiny island nation of Singapore was, to use the words of British documentary filmmaker David Attenborough, just "a series of small tin sheds."[2] Now it is a towering nation of glass and steel. A third world country in 1960, Singapore ranked as a leading first-world nation on a wide range of indicators by 2010.

Founding prime minister, Lee Kuan Yew, predicted and planned that this transformation would take place within a single generation. In his autobiography, he refers to how, in 1978, China's Deng Xiaoping used his visit to Singapore as a point of departure for transforming the People's Republic of China into the economic powerhouse it is today.[3] Two decades later, the West is waking up to how this nation's educational achievements might be emulated as well.

Singapore's success has been built on improbable foundations. This little island had less than a million people when it gained independence from Britain in 1965, but has now grown to over 5 million—almost the size of Finland, in a fraction of that country's space. Fly in to Singapore, and you will see serried ranks of ships lining up to pass through the world's leading center for high-tech, high-speed containerization in a port that was once little more than a military base in a far flung colonial outpost. Take off from microscopic Singapore and you cannot land again without flying over another country.

How has all this happened in such a relatively short period of time? Following a month-long review of the Singapore education system in February and March 2009, including senior level policy and leadership interviews in the Ministry of Education and the National Institute of Education, as well as site visits to and data collection in some of Singapore's schools, and also just living in the culture and with its people, we have concluded that three key factors explain Singapore's recent success:

1. innovation in technology;
2. intensity of professional interaction; and
3. an ability to live and work with paradox.

Let's start by looking at two of Singapore's schools that are among the more obvious exemplars of Singapore's recent innovation in digital technology, and that also represent much about the strength of this nation's school system.

TEACHING AND TECHNOLOGY

Rulang Primary School has gained a stellar reputation in Singapore for its integrated robotics curriculum. Walk around at the right time of day and you will see small children gathered in groups on the floor, assembling crocodiles out of LEGO, then using the basic ones and zeros of computer programming to make these creatures' amphibian jaws open and shut on command. The robotics program is the brainchild of the principal, Cheryl Lim, who has been at the school since 2005. She envisioned it would be a way to integrate core subjects such as language, mathematics, and science. Binary codes, oral interaction, basic mechanics and electronics, as well as the power of play—these are all part of the program. One teacher explained that robotics is a tool to help students enjoy lessons, and improve how they understand and remember the lesson material better and faster.

> I think for our Robotics curriculum, we try to integrate the core subjects. So we are not just building robots, but we cultivate the learning of mathematics, English and Science for every level. So the robot is just a tool to make lessons more enjoyable and [children to] want to go for the lesson. It also helps them to understand the core subject matter. So when pupils enjoy the lesson they actually learn faster. So I think we believe that it is through fun learning that they actually grasp the concept better.

At first, the move toward greater curriculum innovation and changes in pedagogy at Rulang made many teachers apprehensive. The principal remembered how everybody was "telling us—'Why bother?'" In a school with a strong academic record, many teachers felt that "the national examination result was the only thing that mattered."

Singapore's Primary School Leaving Examination at the end of Year 6 is not just one more standardized test. It carries astonishingly high stakes. Pupils' scores affect the status of the secondary school they or their parents might be able to choose and the stream (or track) that they will be assigned to. Innovation that is achieved at the cost of maintaining or improving academic success is inconceivable to many Singapore educators.

Principal Cheryl Lim was neither insensitive about these issues, nor naive. She knew all about Michael Fullan's "implementation dip" where proficiency can become worse rather than better for a while, when people have to adjust to new ways of doing things.[4] Even her teacher leaders were realistic in recognizing there would be "hiccups" in implementation. What were Rulang's principal and staff to do? Being cavalier about examination scores as if they did not really matter, in a school with a hard-earned academic reputation, was out of the question. Abandoning the idea of innovation altogether would be opposed to the direction in which Singapore education was officially moving. Mrs. Lim and her staff put this dilemma right on the table.

Everyone understood that "the innovation cycle definitely requires a period of time for it to settle before we can look at the exponential growth."[5] But the principal also asked her staff: "What is the range that you are willing to let your results drop over the next few years?" She recalls: "When I asked them to tell me [what] percent they wanted to drop, nobody agreed that it must drop. All of them said 'No, No.' We will maintain. We will improve. We will not drop." The principal explained:

> [I] needed to let staff know that when we change, it doesn't mean that everything is always successful the first time round. In that first year or second year, you will find that because of difficulties [of varying levels of staff commitment] and implementation problems, results may not be as what you hope it to be. And be realistic that if there is this dip, it is something that will likely happen. And if there is a dip, what else are we going to do in the meantime? So there is a long-term strategy but there must also be short-term strategies. You cannot wait until five years later and hopefully things will just work out well.

There is a widespread belief among Singaporean teachers that teaching in a highly ranked school involves great amounts of extra work. "A lot of people come into Rulang thinking that if you're a high achieving school having excellent results, your staff must be feeling very rotten because they must be working many donkey hours and as a result cannot enjoy life." Cheryl Lim appreciated that if the staff were going to commit to a new direction, there was a need to "achieve results while saving time." How could this be done?

Well, the staff joked, they learned to "pray very hard" that the results would not fall. For just a year or two, school leaders also strategically assigned the best teachers to the years where results were formally tested and therefore most at risk. And they drastically reduced the number of worksheets that pupils had to trudge through—45 revision worksheets a year across three different classes, in one teacher's case. Like all effective innovators, they knew what they had to abandon as well as start.

> "We want the staff to enjoy work, enjoy family, and yet produce results." –Cheryl Lim, Rulang Primary School

But the most important response was to *transform* the relationship between work and life. There was a steadfast belief that increasing the enjoyment and engagement of students' and teachers' work would, by itself, yield positive measurable results, especially if continuous attention was paid to monitoring the effect of the innovation on achievement outcomes.

> I think that was our main purpose. We do not want a staff to work many hours here and yet not produce any results. We want the staff to enjoy work, enjoy family, and yet produce results. Sometimes, it can seem contradictory but we look at the framework and see whether that is possible.

Rulang, like Singapore in general, is a paradox. It is traditionally highly competitive yet also a pioneer of technological and pedagogical innovation. Alongside its innovative orientation, the school is "anchored in Chinese values." Yet again, the pupils and their traditional families are also "very cosmopolitan." They "step out of Singapore" to engage in "correspondence with other schools globally." At Rulang Primary School this occurs through language immersion visits to China and in undertaking community service for two orphanages in Cambodia. Both are supported by a Ministry of Education "twinning" fund that enables and expects all Singaporeans to experience and learn from other cultures.

Rulang Primary School is animated by innovation, but also anchored in tradition. The first thing you notice when you approach the school and its entrance is a large wall display with bold pictures of the school's humble beginnings. Rulang began as part of a small rural shop house in the 1930s.[6] At the time, it was an example of Attenborough's earlier depiction of the entire country in the 1950s and 1960s—just a few small sheds on a muddy track. Photographs of its founding leaders in the school and the community commemorate these origins to this day. Rulang is deeply proud of its past, and some of its earliest leaders still retain close ties to the school and its community. There is a constant effort to keep reiterating the foundational spirit and traditions at Rulang, as people come and go within the community.

> Mrs. Lim brought us through our history of the education system in Singapore. [She set out] in the future, what she wants us to reach. That's the binding—to let us see that in the journey that we are about to begin, there is an end in mind. Then every year we will go through this process again. This time round, we will probably be looking at our vision again and our mission. That's how we slowly convince our staff that we are on the right track.

Rulang Primary School is a captivating conundrum. It is truly "glocal": both local and global. It embraces the future and the past. It is traditionally Confucian in some ways and dynamically cosmopolitan in others. Its teachers know how to innovate and also how to maintain conventional results. They can think outside the box yet keep on performing well inside the box. They work hard and are also happy.

> As teachers, we need to believe that our kids can be stretched and that's the reason why we are willing to come together to plan to write curriculum for the kids. Not for Mrs. Lim. You know, I think that's the culture here. We work very long hours, but we also derive fun and joy in working together.

It is teachers' capacity to capitalize on these paradoxes that makes Rulang Primary School successful. Hard work is driven by teachers' sense of moral purpose, yet a light-hearted spirit accompanies everyone's aspirations for the children to excel. These are the things that make Singapore enlivening and enjoyable—so "surprising," in the words of the country's tourism board.

> "What anchors us is the fundamentals, where a good teacher engages students in class and makes the subject come alive."
> –Adrian Lim, principal, Ngee Ann Secondary School

About half an hour's drive from Rulang Primary School is Ngee Ann Secondary

School. It epitomizes many of the new directions in which Singapore is moving as well as the cultural paradoxes that make this movement possible. Adrian Lim is the school's young and dynamic principal. Adrian has a passion for information and communication technology (ICT) but he and his staff understand that "the pedagogy must lead technology and not the other way round." He explains, "We don't use ICT for every single lesson. There needs to be a balance and we also need to bear in mind the teacher-student relation. At the end of the day, what anchors us is the fundamentals, where a good teacher engages students in class and makes the subject come alive. ICT is not the silver bullet."

ICT is very important as one way to enhance the dynamism and impact of innovative and effective pedagogy at Ngee Ann. In many schools and systems, ICT throws students and teachers off track —but not here. One of the school's teachers had actually been opposed to ICT in her previous school because "there were really no goals in what we were doing." But when she came to Ngee Ann, that changed.

> There was a lot of support given. That really changed my perspective entirely. And my ex-colleague was really quite surprised. He saw that I was presenting [about ICT] at some conferences. He is, like, "ICT, are you kidding?" you know. So I bought into the idea because of Ngee Ann.

Technology and pedagogy are sometimes in tension, of course. But Ngee Ann teachers and their principal don't deny the tensions. They find creative ways to overcome and work with them. Take two examples.

First, the school has won many worldwide awards by using MSN messenger as a teaching tool. It has created icons of Isaac Newton, William Shakespeare, and Dmitri Mendeleev (the inventor of the periodic table). The students ask science and literature questions of these figures and receive answers compiled in hundreds by teachers from frequently asked questions that students typically pose. Of course, as one teacher said:

> We can't expect Newton (in the system) to answer everything in the world. But for any questions that Newton cannot answer, I can actually look at the log file. So basically it opens a window to a student's thinking at that time: "What questions did he ask?" "How come he asked this question and not *that* question?" Forty students can talk to Newton with 40 different questions getting 40 different replies, which (the teacher) cannot do in that kind of time.

The teachers do not believe that technology can replace teachers' and students' more probing or open-ended questions. Nor does the school imagine that interacting with an icon of Shakespeare is a substitute for reading Shakespeare himself. But teachers do find that using "technology to put a different spin on how Shakespeare is taught" gets students "excited about Macbeth," for example. Technological change leads students toward traditional knowledge. Instant messaging opens windows to deeper thinking.

A second example is the use of cell phones. In the United States and many other countries, student cell phones are seen as constant sources of interruption as well as dangerous devices for teasing and cyberbullying. In line with a protectionist philosophy of technology (for the adults as much as for the students, perhaps) almost 70% of U.S. high schools typically try to ban them.[7] At Ngee Ann Secondary, however, cell phones are employed as teaching and learning tools, especially through the use of the 140-character communication tool, Twitter. Twitter is regarded as a "perfect tool for summary." It enables otherwise shy or quiet students who do not normally speak up in class to record their responses to their learning in real time. It provides teachers with data about their students' learning and therefore about their own teaching that they can review after class. Students are also "more engaged because they are using something they are very familiar with and very good at." One teacher commented:

> [Whereas] I [might have] asked a student to keep a vocabulary notebook 10 years ago, today when we go over that word in class, I would tweet that word and we would see how we would use it in a sentence. That's how we keep track of the learning.

This does not mean the school is innocent about the hazards and risks of cell phone use among teenagers in schools.

> There will be issues—for example, if the students use the cellphone in class when the teacher is teaching. Now, I have a policy that is a "No, No." I will confiscate the phone for about a week or two. You know that with privilege comes responsibility. We return phones later. The first phone you confiscate from them is usually their best phone!

Technology may be changing teachers' everyday lives but, in most places, it is proving much harder to get it to change their teaching. Some teachers share the views of challengers to and protectors from technology that too much technology can be harmful—bombarding young people with short-term distractions that undermine deeper concentration, foundational knowledge, engagements with nature, and compassionate relationships.[8] The classroom, they feel, should not add to this digital maelstrom but be a shelter from it. Others fear loss of classroom control and professional authority if children can instantly challenge their teachers' knowledge or use their mobile phones and digital tablets to divert their attention to something else. Then, as Larry Cuban mentions, there are those who harbor the objections of teachers that technology interferes with the interpersonal relations of the classroom.[9]

Wise use of technology can open up traditional knowledge, rather than suppressing it or pushing it to the side.

Paradoxically, though, Ngee Ann Secondary School in particular, and Singapore more generally, illustrate that when technology is harmonized with worthy learning goals in the service of effective pedagogy, it can strengthen rather than weaken teachers' relationships with their students. We do not have to choose between teaching or technology. We can instead become professionals who use technology mindfully to enhance and support good pedagogy. Wise use of technology can open up traditional knowledge, rather than suppressing it or pushing it to the side. In today's tussle for the future of schooling, it often seems as if people are being pitted against machines, as if we have to choose between the teacher and the mouse. At Ngee Ann Secondary School, improvement and innovation go together. Technology and the teacher live side by side.

PARADOXES OF HIGH PERFORMANCE

The relationship between technology and the teacher in Singapore seems like a paradox. Technological innovation enhances access to tradition. Mobile devices improve face-to-face relationships. Singapore is full of paradoxes like these. Rulang Primary School and Ngee Ann Secondary School express paradoxes of high performance that are visible not merely in these schools but in the system and the society as a whole. An essential capability of leadership and change today is the capacity to tolerate, work with, and capitalize on states of paradox.[10] Beyond one Singaporean strategy or another that other countries might think about emulating, it is the existence of these paradoxes and how Singaporeans deal with them that defines the essence of their school system and society.

An essential capability of leadership and change today is the capacity to tolerate, work with, and capitalize on states of paradox.

In Western thinking, oil and water don't mix. But in Chinese cooking, they do. Singapore succeeds because it is able to turn apparent contradictions into creative paradoxes that drive the country forward. There are at least five of these paradoxes of educational and social change that underpin the country's high performance:

1. the paradox of control: more autonomy, more control;
2. the paradox of technology: class conventions, digital inventions;
3. the paradox of pedagogy: teach less, learn more;
4. the paradox of change: structured insurgency; and
5. the paradox of space and time: back to the future, inside out.

1. THE PARADOX OF CONTROL: MORE AUTONOMY, MORE CONTROL

There was a time, not very long ago, when Singapore, like Japan, was a global poster child for centralization, standardization, and bureaucratic alignment in education. If you gave a speech that contained an idea that a senior education official liked, the joke was that within 72 hours, it would be fully implemented with complete fidelity across the entire country.

Over two decades, through the 1980s and 90s, educational reform in Singapore went through what has been called an *efficiency-driven* period.[11] Following the establishment of universal primary education in the 1970s, Singaporean policy makers pursued effectiveness and efficiency in all schools, and started to concentrate their energies on secondary school reform where universal access, increased opportunities, and reduced dropout or "wastage" were their priorities.

In 1979, a defining government report led to the institution of a highly centralized and prescriptive curriculum.[12] This was accompanied by streaming (or tracking) to narrow the ability range in classes, in order to support teachers whose existing capabilities were then often limited. Channelled by a centralized curriculum and driven by a highly competitive regime of examinations and tests, Singapore's standardized educational system became the world's top performer in mathematics and science by the mid-1990s. To some overseas admirers, this system of top-down control and individualistic competition is the one that still prevails and that, in their view, other nations should adopt today.

Singapore's success would not be everlasting, though. The nation's economy had been dependent on electronics manufacturing and was hit hard by the 1990s Asian financial collapse when consumption shifted to the digital domain. Singapore's political leaders wanted to avoid further collapses by reducing the nation's dependence on particular economic specializations. To survive and prosper in the future, they knew that their country would need to be a flexible, innovative, and high-performing knowledge economy that could invent and reinvent its way out of any crisis or trouble that might head in its direction in the future. So in the midst of the Asian financial crisis, Prime Minister Goh Chok Tong launched the country's new economic and educational vision of flexibility and innovation under the banner of *Thinking Schools, Learning Nation.*[13]

How could a country be so dynamic, creative, cosmopolitan, and inventive when it is often seen as being paternalistic, hierarchical, and competitively meritocratic?[14] How could it innovate if it still retained its traditional tests? How could it release classroom decision making and curriculum development to teachers and schools, yet also maintain overall control across the system?

Part of the answer is structural. The Singapore government encourages flexibility and innovation by decentralizing power to the schools. Schools have been granted increasing autonomy from regulation and intervention, and made responsible for their own improvement by developing their own plans. At the same time, the government retains responsibility for providing high value for public money and aligning what schools do with the nation's social and economic strategies. The Ministry of Education spells out broad strategic requirements while tactically empowering schools to fulfil those requirements in their own way. Schools set their own goals and assess progress annually in a school excellence model aligned to desired outcomes.[15] The structure lets people go their own way and keeps a grip on what they do at the same time. But the question still remains—how does everybody pull all this off in practice?

2. THE PARADOX OF PEDAGOGY: TEACH LESS, LEARN MORE

> Communication would not just flow from the top of the Ministry of Education down to the schools, but schools would be organized in networks to interact with and learn from each other.

Following on the heels of *Thinking Schools, Learning Nation* was an even more courageous and counterintuitive policy announcement in 2004, called *Teach Less, Learn More*—or TLLM, for short.[16] Prime Minister Lee Hsien Loong's speech during the 2004 National Day Rally proclaimed that "We have got to teach less to our students so that they will learn more."[17] "White space" was introduced, occupying up to 20% of school time for teacher-designed curriculum. Children would be prepared for the "test of life," not a "life of tests."[18] Communication would not just flow from the top of the Ministry of Education down to the schools, but schools would be organized in networks to interact with and learn from each other.

Just as the Finns understand that students don't learn more by teaching them more things, more often, TLLM is about transforming learning from quantity to quality. It aims, in the words of one former minister, "to touch the hearts and engage the minds of our learners. It reaches into the core of education—why we teach, what we teach and how we teach."[19] TLLM makes room for teachers to introduce their own programs, to undertake pedagogical innovation, and to give students the space to shape their own learning.

> In Singapore, teaching less isn't about lowering standards or doing less. It is about putting *learning* first, including the learning of teachers themselves.

Teaching less isn't an easier option. It's actually harder work, requiring greater planning, more differentiation, and constant adjustment.[20] In Singapore, teaching less isn't about lowering standards or doing less. It is about putting *learning* first, including the learning of teachers themselves. This involves reducing central prescriptions but not relaxing expectations, among politicians or parents. Standards still matter. And just like in Rulang Primary, the results must not "drop." Teaching less, learning more; thinking in and out of the box at the same time—these things are easy to say but hard to turn into action. The answer, we will see, is in the culture—in the nature of leadership and of relationships across the entire system.

3. THE PARADOX OF TECHNOLOGY: DIGITAL INVENTIONS, CLASSROOM CONVENTIONS

Nowhere are the tensions between traditional and innovative pedagogies brought into starker relief than in the paradox of technology. How can you live in and with a digitally transformed world, when your school operates with large classes, traditional lessons, age-based cohorts, standardized tests, and whole-class teaching styles that are relics of 20th century and even 19th century organizations? How do you implement educational technology that epitomizes flexible innovation, within a structure that still supports and excels at traditional and tested achievement? If young people and teachers spend more and more time looking at screens, how can they sustain the face-to-face relationships of caring and personal connection that seem essential to Singapore's educational success?

Ngee Ann Secondary School, we have seen, knew how to combine good teaching with new technology: how to put innovation and improvement together. Government policy in Singapore is moving in the same direction. When Singapore announced its *Thinking Schools, Learning Nation* vision in 1997, it regarded new technology as a central part of its economic and educational future. After supplying hardware access and appropriate infrastructure, the Singapore government subsequently realized that the major challenge now was not whether or not teachers were using digital technologies but *how* they were using them—to reinforce or enhance traditional teaching, or to transform learning for their more self-directed and collaboratively inclined students. Teachers, one minister said, "need to still base effective outcomes on sound pedagogical principles when they use ICT tools to bring out a learning point."[21]

4. THE PARADOX OF CHANGE: STRUCTURED INSURGENCY

There are many ways to change. Not all of them can be managed in the same manner. When creativity is the goal, schools must have their own platforms to network and innovate. Reform models that push or drive narrow tested priorities in literacy down from the top through middle level tiers such as school districts and finally down to schools are unsuited to this highly adaptable environment. Innovative behaviors do not result from micromanaged control.[22]

In the past, Singapore approached educational policy like a precision engineer, step by logical step, tightly managed from a highly capable center of extremely well qualified ministers of education and their staffs.[23] But when innovation is the desired outcome, it cannot be secured by autocracy as a method, however benign. At the same time, when many schools, not just a few, need to be open to and engaged with using new technologies, innovative efforts cannot be entirely voluntary either. So how is it possible to balance autonomy with control?

Adrian Lim's answer at Ngee Ann Secondary School is what he calls "structured insurgency."

> I am talking about putting innovation in different departments and not overly focusing on just one particular department. So, when you plan well and seed the idea of innovation in every department, you are going to get structured insurgency. At one point in time, it will blow up and it will grow. I think when teachers start small and experience success, then success begets success.

To change the metaphor, this is a deliberate strategy of planting change and then cross-pollinating it through networks and interaction. It also occurs in Singapore's systemwide support for clusters of schools that each focus on teaching and learning issues like cooperative learning or multiple intelligences. In addition, educators are also connected to leading edge practices and ideas from around the world through international visits and conference participation, and through periods of paid leaves that enable teachers and leaders to study in the best universities overseas. In these ways, structured insurgency turns into systemwide change.

> We can and should nudge people forward in directions that are beneficial for them and also serve the common good–yet still leave them in control of the choices they ultimately make.

Structured insurgency is not about driving change through people, pushing them against their will, or making them deliver policies that others have determined. Nor is it about leaving people with a completely free and open choice either. In their best-selling and politically influential book *Nudge,* Richard Thaler and Cass Sunstein argue that we can and should nudge people forward in directions that are beneficial for them and also serve the common good—yet still leave them in control of the choices they ultimately make.[24] Making more fruit than candy bars easily available at school lunches, and putting new teachers next to highly experienced and innovative colleagues are examples of how to nudge people's practices in positive directions. Structured insurgency is nudging on a large scale.

In Singapore, the paradox of change is about constantly pulling people toward a certain mode of thought and action, as the key way to create momentum, direction, development, and coherence. In all these interactions, there is persistent encouragement in continuous communication and valued relationships. Teachers are supported when they want to try a new experience, switch to a new career track, undertake study abroad, move up into leadership, or take on a difficult assignment in a challenging class or school as a mark of their professional accomplishment and as part of their service to the nation. Structured insurgency embeds innovative practices across different parts of the environment. It nudges neighbors into knowing about new practices that are right next door. This enables them to discover what Steve Johnson, in his analysis of six hundred years of innovation, calls "the adjacent possible."[25] Networks and clusters connect people to embedded innovations and to each other. In Singapore's educational system, thousands of elbows constantly nudge each other. Nudge after nudge draws increasing numbers of teachers toward one another in a process of intense and endless interaction that defines Singaporean culture.

5. THE PARADOX OF TIME AND SPACE: BACK TO THE FUTURE, INSIDE OUT

The Roman god Janus could see in opposite directions at the same time. This was not a liability or a two-faced act of hypocrisy, but a distinctive asset for the pagan god of beginnings and transitions, of endings and time. Janus guards gateways. Singapore is a global gateway of trade, culture, and learning. It looks forward into the future and back into the past. It looks inward to its own culture, and outward to the world around it.

This Janus-like character is one of Singapore's assets. Outside Singapore, teachers might be working more with each other in professional learning communities, but far too many principals are not. Because more and more schools are now in direct competition in many school systems, outsiders are often viewed as rivals. Insiders collaborate; outsiders compete. Schools compete with their neighbors for the most marketable families and their children, and for the best teachers and leaders. Their survival may depend on it. Charter schools or academies compete with all their surrounding public schools for human as well as financial resources. Why collaborate with your neighbors, when they might use your ideas to surpass you?

Singaporeans understand that it doesn't have to be this way. Their schools and principals engage in an unlikely mix of fierce competition and intense collaboration. This is what the business literature calls *co-opetition*—where collaborating with competitors actually adds to one's own competitive edge and collaborative advantage.[26] Singapore has many arenas for school competition. Yet, among schools, there is also considerable collaboration. This is not only officially encouraged. It is expected.

A much acclaimed cluster system in Singapore isn't just a way for a middle tier of administration to implement policy effectively. It provides a platform for schools to show what they have achieved and for other schools to learn from those achievements. At Ngee Ann Secondary School, for example, the school had opened itself "to over 65 schools to learn about ICT because [the] assumption is that [it has] nothing to hide."[27] Adrian Lim acknowledges that

> there are good schools around the east. So, we are always competing for students in that sense. But we have never failed in competing for students and so we are not afraid of the competition.
>
> I think if you are afraid of the competition, you are going to be at the back end. So, just think about working with the schools as part of the process of really sharpening each other. There are many things we picked up from other schools. As

> Giving away or openly sharing your best ideas with other countries externally keeps you on your toes, and makes you keep on innovating further in order to stay ahead.

long as schools are forthcoming and they are willing to share, I think it helps both schools level up together. So, we are very open about such things.

In Singapore, people like Sing Kong Lee, the director at the National Institute of Education, believe that giving away or openly sharing your best ideas with other countries externally keeps you on your toes, and makes you keep on innovating further in order to stay ahead. Current education minister Heng Swee Keat has called on schools "to form more collaborative partnerships to pursue excellence as a team, so that more schools, if not all schools, can achieve excellence."[28]

The Singapore system is always eager to engage with thought leaders and system leaders from overseas who come to visit the country. It sends its own educators abroad to present at conferences, study at leading universities, and learn from other schools and systems—all the while coming back with ideas that might benefit their own system, and reaffirming their loyalties to the country as they do so. Singaporeans are successful because they are local and global, competitive and collaborative. They are able to look inward and outward all at the same time.

Just like Janus, Singapore schools and the school system can also look forward and back in time. Adrian Lim appreciated that although he had set his school on a technologically innovative path, his three principal predecessors had built the stable and successful foundation that made this possible. At the same time as it embraces cutting-edge innovation, Singapore does not abandon traditional Confucianism that places a premium on virtues of discipline, respect, good education, and hard work. Add this to strong traces of the traditional British colonial educational system, still evident in the persistence of streaming or banding and in the prominence of the Secondary School General Certificate Examinations at age 16 and you have a family culture, work culture, and educational culture in which hard work, perseverance, respect for authority, and individual competitiveness are accorded high priority.

The OECD acknowledges the power of these cultural characteristics:

> Schools play a major role in inculcating Singaporean values and character, and civic and moral education play a major role in schools. Honesty, commitment to excellence, teamwork, discipline, loyalty, humility, national pride and an emphasis on the common good have been instilled throughout government and society.[29]

Educational reform strategies often present themselves *vertically* as being top-down, bottom-up, or increasingly a combination of both, as in Singapore's joint tendencies toward centralization and decentralization. They have also been represented *laterally,* as incorporating networks in side-to-side interaction—and, as we have seen, Singapore has a lot of this.

Singapore adds two further paradoxes to the space-time continuum of change. *Radially,* it takes ideas and people in, and also sends them out overseas in ways that advance the country's collaborative and competitive advantage. *Temporally,* Singapore connects its innovative future to its national past in ways that make these two periods in time apposite and not opposites. Singapore, in other words, is a four dimensional paradox of space and time that is vertical, lateral, radial, and temporal.

CULTURE AND COMMUNICATION

The unifying key that holds these opposites together is culture—the enigma that overseas visitors find so hard to understand, as the education minister informed us. Structure is about roles and responsibilities, papers and plans. Culture, on the other hand, is about habits and beliefs. It goes deep beneath the surface, takes considerable time to understand, and is much more difficult to transpose. Structure is about what to do. Culture is about how to be.

Singapore is first and foremost a highly compact and sometimes, to outsiders, a rather claustrophobic culture. Singapore's schools are packed together in dense urban concentrations. They are often very large by the standards of countries outside Asia, with primary school populations regularly running into four figures. The country has only 360 schools within a maximum range of one hour's driving time. If the minister of education wants to announce a new policy, he can call on every principal to come to one room, so they all hear the same message. This occurs at the annual Ministry of Education Work-Plan Seminar, for example, which communicates the Ministry's overall direction, sets out its policies for the coming year, and facilitates interaction among school leaders about the implications for implementation. While Singapore is well coordinated nationally as a system, the country is so compact that it has many of the features of a local system as well.

Just as Singapore has a numerically manageable core of school principals, it is also able to establish coherent strategies of teacher training, educational leadership development, and educational research by having just one higher education–based program of teacher education. The National Institute of Education, with a staff of around a thousand, is the sole provider of teacher education, leadership preparation, and educational research. There is little chance that training programs will be of inconsistent quality, that leadership preparation will be disconnected from system priorities, or that research will be unrelated to overall policy directions. The director of the National Institute of Education meets with the minister of education or his very senior officials on a weekly basis. Each side knows what the other is doing, all the time, and there is a commitment to moving in a common direction.

When it is decided that high-quality teachers must be recruited from the top 30% of the graduate range by starting salaries that are competitive with engineers, or that by 2022, 20% of the teaching force will possess master's degrees, or that new university-based leadership training programs will be the culminating component for principal selection rather than just a baseline qualification, this can and will be achieved swiftly by the Ministry and the National Institute of Education working together. This achievement results not from specially convened meetings, or elaborate paper plans, but mainly because of the continuous relationships between the two institutions among senior staff.

To be in the Singapore educational system is to be engaged in numerous meetings, constant interaction, and endless gatherings where good food is enjoyed and *guan xi* (or connections) are made. Driven by a sense of purpose and urgency, all this occurs at breathtaking speed.

Within the Ministry of Education, officials are given informal process targets in terms of the number of schools they should visit each year—not to assess or inspect them, but to communicate with and learn from them. To be in the Singapore educational system is to be engaged in numerous meetings, constant interaction, and endless gatherings where good food is enjoyed and *guan xi* (or connections) are made. Driven by a sense of purpose and urgency, all this occurs at breathtaking speed. As we heard more than once: "We eat and we run! We eat and we run!"

The intensity of all this interaction up and down the hierarchy, across school clusters, and between the Ministry and the National Institute of Education, is double edged—like all paradoxes. It is about trusting and also about watching; it is about careful oversight as well as personal support. Education officers engage in regular professional and supervisory interactions with teachers about how well they are performing and about which one of three career tracks they might choose or possibly transfer to. Potential school leaders are identified and groomed long before they are selected for and enter their formal period of six-month preparation at the National Institute of Education. Rising future leaders are invited for tea periodically where in a one-to-one discussion with a superior, they discuss their progress, reciprocally communicate values, and explore aspirations. All of this is done with a view to helping them fulfill their potential, using measures that are calibrated and recalibrated as they progress through their career.

Beyond the schools, another way to keep communication circulating is to move staff regularly across the system—between the Ministry and the National Institute of Education in particular, or between the Ministry and the schools. This staves off professional boredom; it breaks down the cultures that normally separate research communities from administrative ones; it establishes relationships across institutional and sector lines; and it builds understanding of institutional partners and peers among senior leaders in the system. Lateral interaction among schools within their clusters promotes the sharing of ideas, reaffirmation of values, and setting of new directions—all under the supervision of the cluster superintendent.

In Singapore, the five paradoxes of performance are therefore largely resolved by the culture. Control is achieved by knowing, watching, and being with your people, as they make and follow their own choices, but not in isolation. As in a large traditional family, the process may sometimes be a bit paternalistic, but it is also highly participative and intensely engaging. Teachers who regularly interact with other teachers can figure out how to teach less in order that pupils will learn more, and how to embrace technology without abandoning good pedagogy. Keeping a grip on good pedagogy while letting people go with new technologies are simultaneously secured by a lot of "hand-holding." Educators learn how to nudge and to be at each other's elbow, without pushing and shoving. And they know how to look both ways at the same time. It's not typically Western, it's not mechanistic, it's not top-down deliverology, but it is immensely successful. Communication is the catalyst; culture is the key.

CONCLUSION

So much of what we have seen in Singapore at every level—from the National Institute of Education, to the Ministry of Education, to the teachers and students in schools, and the people in the city's shops and streets—coheres and concurs with the explanations for the country's success among the cornerstone international organizations of policy and change. In its comprehensive account of why Singapore is such a strong performer, the OECD emphasizes the country's policy strengths.[30] These are:

- a forward-looking, integrated planning system that connects education to future economic needs;

- a tightly coupled policy system, with swift implementation and minimal variation between schools, in a manageably small system;
- close links between policy implementers, researchers, and educators;
- effective human resource management in the selection, development, and retention of teachers and leaders;
- commitment to continuous improvement and constant comparison with and learning from best practice around the world; and
- commitment to equity and merit that leads to intense competitiveness on the one hand, yet participation of almost everyone in the public school system.

All this, the OECD emphasizes, is achieved in the context of nation building, where the nation comes first, the organization comes second, and the individual is last. The OECD's summary of how all these elements interconnect is largely in tune with our own understandings and interpretations.

Prescription has been replaced over time by a system that treats teachers as respected professionals with good judgment.

None of the criteria for calculating performance-related pay in Singapore refers directly to student test scores or other measurable achievement outcomes.

McKinsey & Company echo some of these elements, placing particular emphasis on how the nation develops its teachers and leaders.[31] To reach its high levels of capacity, McKinsey & Company argue, Singapore has been able to foster teacher collaboration in professional learning communities and to establish a strong system of school clusters that constitute a mediating layer for policy implementation and organization. Prescription has been replaced over time by a system that treats teachers as respected professionals with good judgment. Top-performing teachers in Singapore, McKinsey & Company note, are given a bonus of three months salary.

The NCEE, like McKinsey & Company, concentrates much of its attention on Singapore's scrupulous attention to teacher and leadership development. The NCEE declares its admiration for pay for performance in this high-performing nation. "The Singaporeans," the NCEE says, "provide substantial bonuses to teachers to do outstanding work."[32] However, our corner store analysis acknowledges more explicitly that none of the criteria for calculating performance-related pay in Singapore refers directly to student test scores or other measurable achievement outcomes. This avoids any possible misunderstanding that the United States and its promotion of linking individual teacher pay to student test scores is consistent with practice in high-performing countries such as Singapore.

Our corner store approach has been able to add to the existing cornerstone understandings of Singapore's educational success by digging a little deeper into the culture and life of Singaporeans and Singapore schools. In doing so, it has unearthed two key factors that contribute significantly to Singapore's outstanding educational record and that the country's minister of education alerted us to right up front. These are the distinctive nature of the country's culture, and the pragmatic capacity of its people to work with paradoxes that might divide or defeat many of their counterparts abroad.

In a land where towers are built on swamps, where oil mixes with water, and where innovation and traditional improvement are able to coexist, Singapore holds out important lessons for the rest of the world. These are not so much particular practices that can be picked off and teleported—like career tracks, reward structures, or selection programs. Nor are they the country's systems and structures that others might be misled into believing could be easily implemented elsewhere.

As in Finland, Singapore's lessons are not so much about *what to do,* but about *how to be* as a culture and a country. They are about how to believe in and be loyal to a purpose greater than oneself, how to play with and profit from paradoxes, and how to be personally ambitious and also serve the public good. Singapore shows us how it is possible and even desirable to combine hard work and joyful play, to compete and also collaborate, to reconcile participation and paternalism, and to be grounded in tradition yet open to change. This small city-state is a global leader in how to place technology in the service of good pedagogy, and how to value communication with others within and beyond one's own borders as a school and as a nation.

When Singaporeans compare themselves with other countries, they are not just engaged in the worst kinds of competitive international bench-pressing. They are engaged in genuine international benchmarking and policy learning—in a disciplined cultural quest of constant curiosity that defines a dynamic way of life. The most surprisingly successful thing about Singapore, we can now see, is not its transferable systems or structures, but its transformative paradoxes and cultures, its attention to and even obsession with constant communication and endless nudging, and its capacity to innovate and keep on learning without abandoning the traditions that have been its foundation.

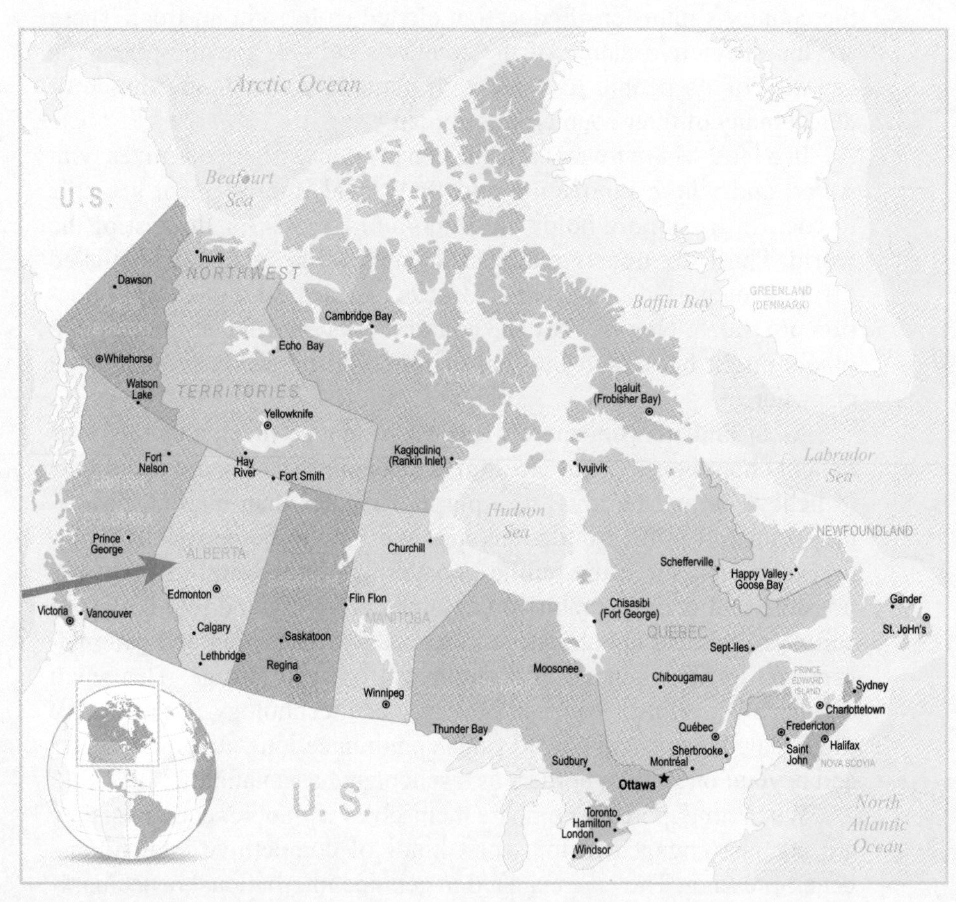
Arctic Ocean
Beafourt Sea
U.S.
Inuvik
NORTHWEST
Dawson
YUKON TERRITORY
Cambridge Bay
Echo Bay
Whitehorse
Baffin Bay
GREENLAND (DENMARK)
Watson Lake
TERRITORIES
NUNAVUT
Iqaluit (Frobisher Bay)
Yellowknife
Fort Nelson
Hay River
Fort Smith
Kagiqcliniq (Rankin Inlet)
Ivujivik
Labrador Sea
BRITISH COLUMBIA
Hudson Sea
NEWFOUNDLAND
Prince George
ALBERTA
Churchill
Schefferville
Happy Valley - Goose Bay
SASKATCHEWAN
Edmonton
Flin Flon
Chisasibi (Fort George)
Gander
Victoria
Vancouver
MANITOBA
QUEBEC
St. JoHn's
Calgary
Saskatoon
Sept-Iles
Lethbridge
Regina
Moosonee
Chibougamau
PRINCE EDWARD ISLAND
Sydney
Winnipeg
ONTARIO
Charlottetown
Fredericton
Québec
Thunder Bay
Saint John
Halifax
Sherbrooke
Sudbury
Montréal
NOVA SCOYIA
Ottawa
U.S.
North Atlantic Ocean
Toronto
Hamilton
London
Windsor

Chapter Five

ALBERTA

Innovation With Improvement

In more than a few British novels and films, when a character has to be disposed of in a bloodless way, the simple line "and then he went to Canada!" is usually quite sufficient. From that point on, this character is heard of no more. No harm comes to him, but he achieves no greatness either. He just disappears into the vast wilderness that makes up most of the world's second largest country.

With the possible exception of ice hockey, Canadians don't usually boast about their considerable achievements—in literature, music, and international advocacy for human rights, for example. Globally, Canada mostly flies under the radar of international news, which is easy to do when the United States is your neighbor. Most Canadians are the epitome of understatement. When we drove through Toronto a while ago, we spied a bumper sticker that said it all. It didn't proclaim "God Bless Canada" or even "Proud to be Canadian." It simply read "Content to be Canadian!"

And that's the country in a nutshell. Canada scores quite well (but not spectacularly) on a range of international indicators: 8th in human development, 25th most equal, 14th least corrupt, and exactly half way on UNICEF's index of child well-being.[1] Notwithstanding its weather, Canada is a country that avoids most extremes and sits quietly in the middle most of the time.

Except in education! In 2010, when the OECD's PISA results were released, the big story was that eight of the top ten performing systems were Asian. What almost everyone overlooked was the strong performance of Canada. Canada ranked sixth overall—the highest English-speaking and French-speaking nation in the world.[2]

The oversight didn't persist for long, though. Canada is now a go-to country for educational inspiration and policy learning. With 90% of the Canadian population living within 100 miles of the U.S. border and the two cultures being similar in many respects, U.S. educators and policy makers are especially and increasingly curious to learn about what is happening just a little to the north.[3] Canada is culturally and geographically closer to them than Finland or Singapore. How has Canada accomplished so much, while avoiding favored and fashionable U.S.-style reform strategies like pay-for-performance, charter schools, and punitive responses to school failure? The answer is not so simple.

First, Canada is a vast country of ten provinces and three territories, with no central Ministry of Education. At a time when the United States and Australia are each aggressively implementing common core standards and curricula that encompass all their states, Canadians are maintaining K–12 education as entirely a provincial responsibility. Each province has its own distinctive demographics, parties of political control, and educational policy strategy. Despite the tendency of international policy organizations to highlight the success of only one province—Ontario—in truth, no province can or should stand for or be equated with the whole of Canada. If you try to imply that, the other nine will be after you like a shot. Imagine the uproar there would be among Americans if California or Texas were equated with the whole of the United States! It's no different in Canada.

Second, looking at PISA results province-by-province, four Canadian provinces perform particularly well, not just one.[4] Interestingly, these four provinces are also the ones where you will find the greatest urban diversity and the highest levels of immigration—in Toronto, Montreal, Vancouver, and Calgary. On the PISA scores for reading literacy, Alberta leads, followed by Ontario and British Columbia. For numeracy or mathematics, Quebec comes first, followed by Alberta and Ontario. For science, Alberta is ahead, followed by British Columbia and Ontario.[5]

Yet the policies and strategies, the parties of political control, and the relationships between governments and teacher unions, for example, are often quite different and sometimes dramatically so. During the past quarter century, for example, Ontario has been under the political control of all three political parties, at different times. Alberta, by contrast, has had four decades of Progressive Conservative government—the nearest thing Canada has to the Republican Party in the United States.

Alberta's single teacher's federation (that also includes principals and central office personnel) collaborates closely with other professional organizations and with the government; Ontario has to orchestrate the views of four different teachers' federations (from which principals have been forcibly excluded by government legislation since the 1990s); and British Columbia's government and its teacher's federation have locked horns in unending conflict over many years.

For all their policy differences, the high-achievement results across the top four provinces on PISA are very similar—often varying by just 2% or so. The same pattern is evident on the Trends in International Math and Science Study (TIMSS). When you score up in the 90s, the only place that one or two extra points truly matters is on a basketball court!

If consistent high performance can be achieved in provinces with very different populations and policies, we need to look, first of all, at what it is about Canada as a culture and country that transcends the specific policy frameworks of particular provinces. The OECD picks out Canada as one of its strong performers internationally and summarizes some of the reasons for overall Canadian success:[6]

- *Supportive Family Culture.* "Parents in Canada are generally supportive of their children's education. . . . Canadian students are more likely than any other children in the world to read daily for pleasure."[7]
- *Strong Welfare State.* "Children and their parents have access to national health insurance, and adults are protected from the vicissitudes of capitalism by a strong social safety net. . . . The idea that health care and other social services are a right and not a privilege carries over into education, where there is a broadly shared norm that society is collectively responsible for the educational welfare of all of its children."
- *High Quality Teachers.* "Canadian applicants to teachers' colleges are in the 'top 30%' of their college cohorts. There are perhaps 50 [teacher training] institutions in all of Canada, as opposed to hundreds across the United States, which allows for greater monitoring of training quality."

If the four most populated provinces perform very similarly on PISA, it is important not only to look at the recent policies and strategies that seem to differentiate them, but also to examine the policies, strategies, and professional histories these provinces share in common over time. It is the longer-term profile of policies and strategies that affects current results as much as the impact of this or that recent reform.

As a society, Canada has some striking commonalities with Finland, the only non-Asian performer above it in the OECD rankings—not just in weather and latitude, but also in cultural climate and attitude. Canada also has some unexpected similarities with Singapore. All three countries value teachers and teaching and insist on a professional program of university-based training for all public school teachers in a contained and controllable number of teacher education institutions: there are 8 in Finland, just 1 in Singapore, and around 50 or so in far more populous Canada. There are no fast-track programs like Teach for America in the United States, or Teach First in the United Kingdom, or other alternative programs to bring people with minimal training into the profession. Working conditions in all three countries are favorable with good facilities, more than acceptable pay, wide availability of professional development, and discretion for teachers to make their own professional judgments. All three countries have a strong commitment to public schools and a very modest private sector in education.

Outside formal education, all three countries have strong social welfare and public health systems with broad safety nets to protect the youngest and most vulnerable members of the population. Parental leave benefits in Finland and Canada enable most parents to stay home with their infant children and nurture their crucial early development. All three nations are characterized by deeper cultures of cooperation and inclusiveness that make them more competitive internationally.

This extends, in two out of the three cases, to their approaches to diversity. Although Finland still has low rates of immigration, Singapore pays solicitous attention to integrating its different ethno-cultural communities. Canada is an officially bilingual, multicultural society that sees itself more as a mosaic of different cultures than a U.S.-style melting pot that blends them more into one. This is reflected in progressive, evidence-based policies that support second language learning, and that enable accommodations for second-language students when they take standardized tests. In Canada, it is fine to be half-Canadian—Irish Canadian, Chinese Canadian, Jamaican Canadian and so on—for

> Much of what makes Canada such a strong educational performer is a professional ethic and social fabric that values education and teachers, supports families and young children, welcomes and integrates all kinds of immigrants, is internationally cosmopolitan in outlook among its people as well as its politicians, and prizes the public good.

to be half-Canadian is regarded as an addition to individual and collective identity, not a subtraction from it.

Much of what makes Canada such a strong educational performer is a professional ethic and social fabric that values education and teachers, supports families and young children, welcomes and integrates all kinds of immigrants, is internationally cosmopolitan in outlook among its people as well as its politicians, and prizes the public good. Canada is no longer a place for lesser literary characters to be exiled to. It is a high-performing country for others to learn about and to emulate.

THE FRONTIER OF CHANGE

For more than a decade, Alberta has been Canada's highest-performing province on PISA and the highest English- and French-speaking jurisdiction in the world. With more than three and half million people, Alberta is Canada's fourth most populous province, straddling the prairies on the east and the Rockies on the west. Despite its superior educational performance within Canada and beyond, cornerstone policy analysts have so far largely overlooked Alberta—an intriguing omission and an open opportunity for an alternative corner store approach.

This chapter compensates for that omission. Drawing on our own extensive research, it provides the first investigation and explanation of the reasons for Alberta's exemplary educational performance. It begins at the top, with the former minister of education, Dave Hancock.

> "If every project is a success, we're either not being honest with ourselves, or we're not experimenting enough." –Dave Hancock, former minister of education

Hancock's father was the last fur trader for the legendary Hudson's Bay Company in the far north of Alberta. His wife is an elementary school principal, and Hancock himself was minister of education for the province until 2011. In 2009, this son of a fur trader addressed a large audience of school teams and their leaders from all over the province. They had been designing their own innovations in their schools with government funding. "I hope you'll celebrate and share your successes within your local learning communities," Hancock said to them, as any minister might. Then his speech took an unexpected twist.

> We also need to acknowledge that not every project we do in our schools must be an unqualified success. If every project is a success, we're either not being honest with ourselves, or we're not experimenting enough. There's nothing wrong with failure, as long as we learn from it. So be brave. Be creative. Be bold.[8]

Hancock's remarks would have been unusual coming from any education minister in a world where failure in teaching or in school change efforts is frequently punished rather than praised. But if the effort to change is professionally sincere and is something that teachers are willing to learn from, then mistakes can be made with the government's blessing. This is how Hancock understands and acknowledges one of the basic principles of organizational innovation and improvement.

Dave Hancock's comments were even more remarkable coming from the lips of a minister of education in a Conservative government—one that had been in power for 40 years. This government had been a Canadian and North American leader in inaugurating standardized achievement tests for accountability purposes, long before they were introduced in Ontario or many U.S. states. It had also been in charge of the first province to experiment with charter schools in the 1990s, although barely a handful took root. In a province that seemed to be Canada's greatest political bastion of Second Way bureaucratic accountability and market competitiveness, Hancock and his government were advocating for a systemwide commitment to educational innovation and risk.

When Alberta's Progressive Conservative government took this counterintuitive direction, it was not just offering vague encouragement to education professionals. It was supporting its own uniquely radical policy and strategy to promote innovative learning and develop teacher and student engagement in almost all of its schools. It was a strategy that could not have had a more improbable beginning.

THE ALBERTA INITIATIVE FOR SCHOOL IMPROVEMENT

In 1999, the Alberta provincial budget allocated $66 million to create a new School Performance Incentive Program that would pay teachers bonuses if they raised their students' results on Alberta's Provincial Achievement Tests or PATs. The Alberta Teachers' Association (ATA), the province's sole teachers' organization, fought this initiative on performance-based pay, arguing that it would not only divide teachers but also be a disincentive to those who had been willing to work with the most difficult students. The ATA won this political battle, and by joining with other associations of school boards and superintendents, it was also able to redirect the funding to a very different purpose: what became known as the Alberta Initiative for School Improvement, or AISI.

The purpose of AISI is to fund teachers, principals, students, and community members to develop their own bottom-up innovations to respond to local needs and to engage teachers in inquiring into and improving their own practice. Generously funded, with $80 million of annual support (about 2% of the overall education budget), AISI spread in its first decade to 95% of Alberta's schools, releasing innovation and empowering educators and students to develop their own classroom pedagogies, curricular units, and diagnostic assessments. Many schools in the AISI network partner with higher education institutions to conduct research together in a way that responds to local needs. Importantly, they cannot receive project funding without a commitment to share their learning with other schools, so networking is integral to the program's design.

In line with Hancock's advice, the point of AISI projects is to support innovation along with improvement. Not every project is focused on basic areas like literacy and mathematics, and they do not have to demonstrate an immediate impact on achievement results. Projects are as diverse as involving First Nations (aboriginal) parents in their children's literacy, building professional learning communities, focusing on diagnostic assessment for learning, developing interest in and knowledge of local history, and employing the Suzuki method of balance and harmony, which is normally used only in music, to enhance learning across the whole curriculum.

In 2009, we were asked by Alberta Education, the province's Ministry of Education, to lead an international team of researchers to undertake a comprehensive quantitative and qualitative review of AISI, its architectural design, and its impact on practice.[9] AISI, our research team found, has a four-dimensional architecture of innovation:

1. *vertical*—top-down and bottom-up;
2. *lateral*—project-to-project, school-to-school;
3. *radial*—outside-in and inside-out research expertise and practitioner inquiry;
4. *temporal*—connecting medium-term and longer-term perspectives.

1. VERTICAL

AISI is steered by the AISI Education Partners Steering Committee and managed by the School Improvement Branch (SIB) of Alberta Education. The SIB works collaboratively with the AISI partners to set priorities and strategic directions for each cycle. The SIB manages three-year project cycles, and the application and approval process coordinates conferences and updates a website clearinghouse to create interconnections across projects. The SIB sees its role not as driving change and having a delivery system to implement it in an aligned way across all districts, but as steering and gently but firmly monitoring and revising this process over time.

From the bottom-up, AISI empowers educators to initiate their own projects based on their own locally created needs assessments. Many of these come from the individual passions or recent professional development experiences of teachers and school administrators that connect to the priorities in the three-year AISI cycle. Others—up to 40% per cycle—are selected by districts in relation to provincewide themes that are also flagged as AISI priorities. These have included differentiated instruction, professional learning communities, and assessment for learning.

The SIB demonstrates *active trust* toward teachers and school leaders as skilled and knowledgeable professionals who produce the hundreds of locally generated initiatives that make up AISI.[10] AISI creates significant opportunities for increased teacher leadership. Teachers become developers, initiators of and inquirers into change instead of just being trained to deliver government strategies. Some are promoted into their local district office for part of their working week. Many are given time in the school day to lead colleagues professionally within and across local schools, without being taken out of the classroom and without having to abandon their commitments and contributions as classroom teachers.

AISI has evolved and adapted its change architecture from one three-year cycle to the next. In the first cycle, AISI supported many different projects but learned that although they created genuine energy, engagement and innovation, they were too reminiscent of First Way–style innovations with individualized projects being disconnected from each other. In Cycle 2, districts overreacted somewhat by defining an "umbrella" focus for their schools' projects. This often meant that initiatives became too centralized and managerial, teacher leaders were overly concentrated in the district offices, and there was an excessive and expensive dependency on transient outside trainers.[11] Too much discipline was stifling innovation.

So in Cycles 3 and 4—partly due to the feedback from our external review—the project re-empowered schools to have their own genuine focus. AISI steered them so they were aware of but not constrained by provincial priorities and expected and enabled schools and their projects to network more with each other. It did this by creating cohesion through regular communication across the system rather than command-and-control alignment within it.

AISI projects today do not just let a thousand flowers bloom. In addition to the very clear strategies of deliberate cross-pollination, projects are developed and conducted in a disciplined way that includes a strong component of accountability. Schools that receive AISI funding are required to complete annual reports of what they are learning, and to use or develop their own indicators of impact at the end of each three-year cycle. These indicators include provincial achievement tests, assessment measures chosen by the schools themselves, and student as well as teacher satisfaction surveys.

2. LATERAL

AISI connects project schools within their districts. Some districts hold celebrations at which teams of teachers share poster presentations of their work, inviting comments and critique from their peers. Others have created districtwide professional learning communities. Provincial and regional conferences create further opportunities for schools to showcase practices and learn from each other. This is especially valuable for small and otherwise isolated rural districts. A website clearinghouse also creates provincewide transparency about AISI projects and enables colleagues to connect with others who are working on similar issues.

One Alberta district was able to connect the learning of students, teachers, and system leaders in an integrated and exemplary way. This is how Brent Davis and Dennis Sumara, who were part of our review team, described the district's work:

> In a rural district of around 300 teachers, each AISI project is selected and defined by its own school, and each has a distinct identity. All schools have used project funding to schedule time for teachers to meet and work in groups. Lead teachers from each school meet at a district level to share ideas. This district has very high cohesion not because of command-and-control alignment but because of a paradoxical combination of high autonomy with intensity of vertical and lateral communication within a shared belief system about the importance of learning as a focus and a process of change.
>
> "Things are always changing in our district," the superintendent explained, so "learning is the work." He was not alone. One teacher explained, "When I first came to this district, I thought I'd be here for only a year or two. What has kept me for many years has been the extraordinary opportunities to learn that have been provided." Learning is collaborative, and this encourages innovation and risk. "We know that if three of us decide to do it," one teacher explained, "it takes the risk

> out of it. We can push ourselves further individually because we have support." A colleague concurred: "Our administrators encourage us to try new approaches. If they don't work, we know we can try something else."
>
> Teachers and administrators in this district tended to use the collective pronouns of "we" and "us" rather than personal pronouns when discussing learners or learning. Because of the frequency of communication, high autonomy and discretion for each school paradoxically increases how well educators know their colleagues and what they are doing. One teacher knew "80% of the 300 teachers in the district." The superintendent could "go to any school and tell you by name who is in each school." There were many opportunities "for people to get to know [him] and one another."
>
> Strong relationships and frequent communication were not just a support system of affirming relationships. They were also a conduit for new ideas. "You can bring your ideas to anyone, anytime," one teacher said. Another added, "Everyone seems to have a voice: parents, community members, teachers—everyone. And our school district accepts all of that. You can talk about anything to anyone."[12]

In creating this network of learning, the district seems to have accommodated considerable diversity of projects, ideas, and opinions. Yet it also maintains a robust internal coherence in terms of a mission and vision of change that is not imposed but that evolves through intense interaction throughout the community.

3. RADIAL

AISI combines inside-out and outside-in change processes that penetrate into its core and out again. Personal intuition and practical wisdom matter as well as scientific evidence. In AISI, university researchers are not intellectual parasites or predators looking to exploit schools for future publications alone, but active partners with districts that often collaborate with faculty members to design surveys, study student achievement data, and modify assessment practices. External stimulation and support are balanced and integrated with internal study and reflection in a radial dynamic of inside-out and outside-in inquiry and assistance. Teachers, it is recognized, create and diffuse new knowledge as well as implement and adapt research-based knowledge from outside. "We are becoming true professionals," one mid-career teacher said. "We are reading and we are talking about what is promising in the field and really trying to implement it. I have to say I have never seen as much of it in my career as I'm seeing now."

4. TEMPORAL

AISI concentrates on middle to long-term time perspectives for educational change. AISI's three-year cycles establish longer time lines for change, action, and results than is common in many other systemwide reform efforts. In political environments that are less stable than Alberta's, reform strategies are usually driven by the demand for measurable, short-term achievement results within one election cycle. AISI's cycles and the projects within them now build more explicitly on each other. The work in one project often provides the foundation for the next. And there is awareness that the significant goal of transforming entire cultures of schools and school districts is longer term still. In the words of one AISI consultant: "It truly took nine years to get to the point where we have a critical mass; meaningful collaboration; honest, open discussion and meaningful connections across districts, within districts. It really did."

To sum up, AISI has a distinct change architecture that consists of

- school-initiated innovation and inquiry, centered on student learning;
- inclusive scope that encompasses more than 95% of the province's schools;
- substantial investment at 2% of the provincial education operating budget;
- long-term operational time frame, persisting over four three-year cycles;
- steering by a group representing all key stakeholders;
- continuous interaction, communication, and networking to establish coherence;
- transparency of participation and outcomes;
- accountability for documenting what has been learned; and
- a culture of risk in an environment of trust.

AISI is not about implementing or delivering centrally determined mandates, on short timescales, in a small number of core and basic learning areas that are linked to a few areas of tested achievement. It is about innovation *with* improvement, about engagement *with* achievement, about professional inquiry *with* integrity.

To say that AISI is specifically responsible for Alberta's high performance on PISA would be misleading. In our review of AISI, extensive statistical analyses could not determine its value-added contribution to student achievement because AISI was closely integrated with other provincial education priorities and because one of its declared purposes was to embed itself into and start to transform the culture of educational change in Alberta.[13] Even so, as a result of AISI, educators said:

> In our school, we've really developed a system where we depend on each other a lot more and we're doing a lot of peer observations. At least once a month, five or six lessons are taught and then everybody gets to go in and see somebody teach a lesson. You get so much out of doing it because the nice thing with Assessment for Learning is that the AISI team has been modeling it, so that gives those people a chance to see how it works. They come to you for feedback. They might set up a similar kind of lesson and then you go and watch them teach it. So we're using each other as the experts. We need to realize that we're good at what we do and we should be depending on each other more. It eventually gets to the point where everybody is watching everybody. It's amazing what you pick up on, just ten minutes in a classroom.
>
> AISI allows us to think big and start big. Usually it's think big, start small. But with the resources, and just the support with AISI, we can start big. We do these fantastic big projects, and take on excellent action research. It's caused us to really dig deeply into research, talk to each other about research, share research with our community.
>
> People are reading common research. They're dialoguing about those things that they read about. You get a common bond based on professional conversation, which is very powerful. I think the regard for professionalism is very important, and when I see it play out in the level of conversation it's not about, "What did you do on the weekend?" It's about, "Did you read this research article?" And, "did you put this practice in place in your classroom?"

AISI has bucked the all-too-common trends of the Second and Third Ways whereby reforms are mandated and professional learning communities are imposed in relation to a fixed agenda of data-driven improvement. As one teacher put it, "I'm more concerned with [the students'] learning as opposed to getting this data that has to be processed." AISI also turned one of the supposed truisms of educational change on its head: that you always have to change people's practice (forcing them to try something new) before they will alter their beliefs.[14] An elementary school teacher leader whose school had used AISI funds to create balanced literacy across the curriculum in relation to differentiated instruction talked about how

> that's such a huge idea, that the philosophy has to come first. And so we were working on developing the beliefs and values and all of that in our teachers and then we saw that as a way to differentiate our literacy.

When teachers are empowered to design and develop their own innovations that they feel have the potential to really improve student learning, then changes in beliefs can and do actually precede changes in practice. Practice changes before beliefs when teachers are being driven to do something that others have decided for them (which may or may not be defensible depending on what it is that has been decided). Beliefs change before practice when teachers work in a culture where the professional responsibility resides in the hands of these dynamos of change themselves.

Practice changes before beliefs when teachers are being driven to do something that others have decided for them. Beliefs change before practice when teachers work in a culture where the professional responsibility resides in the hands of these dynamos of change themselves.

INNOVATION WITH IMPROVEMENT

AISI is not the only educational initiative in Alberta. The province has also, for example, been a pioneer of systemwide achievement testing in Canada. To many outsiders, the government's embracing of both reform directions—teacher-designed innovation and improvement on mandated achievement tests—seems confusing and contradictory. But, as we have seen in the case of Singapore, apparent contradictions can really be positive paradoxes that help explain a system's success. This is very much the case in Alberta.

In particular, a strong teachers' organization that, unlike many international counterparts, still also includes principals within its membership, has been able to develop a largely positive working relationship with a stable, long-term Progressive Conservative government to promote changes that benefit the achievement of students and the professionalism of teachers. While the Alberta government and the Alberta Teachers' Association still battle over traditional collective bargaining issues such as pay and working conditions, the teachers' organization has participated in the design of items on the provincial tests, even at the same time as it has opposed their existence.[15] Indeed, the Alberta Teachers' Association's advocacy for the end of standardized achievement testing, which has been aided by an innovative international partnership it created with educators in Finland, has contributed to the government's increasing recognition of the need to develop an alternative to the existing provincial achievement tests: "first [to] find better ways to understand how students, schools, and the system are doing, and then [to] use that knowledge to improve students' success."[16]

Encouraging and uplifting remarks from government ministers, union leaders, and other professional representatives on the same platform, at the same time, are a commonplace feature of the optimistic branding of the province and its future.

The Alberta Teachers' Association is a prominent promoter of deep learning for students and professional inquiry for teachers and it works tirelessly to build a better future for Alberta's children, Alberta's teachers, and Albertans as a whole. By working with a four-decades-old government that is not always looking for quick gains in time for the next election, both sides have been able to forge a dynamic partnership with each other. There is a high frequency of professional summits, conferences, and other learning events in Alberta, in which the Alberta Teachers' Association consistently takes a leading role. At these conferences and events, encouraging and uplifting remarks from government ministers, union leaders, and other professional representatives on the same platform, at the same time, are a commonplace feature of the optimistic branding of the province and its future.

Albertans know that they need to innovate in order to prosper. They are also keen to maintain their record of more conventional improvement as they do so. Albertans live in a boom-bust economy that is as volatile as the expensive-to-extract energy reserves that are embedded in the province's costly-to-extract oil shale. The province knows its future must rest on a more diversified and flexible economy, and a highly educated population that can work in it. Teachers and schools are regarded as being essential to developing social cohesion in a province where the city of Calgary is now the third most diverse in Canada and has North America's first Muslim mayor.

CONCLUSION

Canada's overall success educationally is rooted in the strength of family cultures, and in the common commitment to a strong welfare system and overall public good. Canadians are noteworthy for their positive attitudes toward immigrants and for the persistent policy supports they have provided for those immigrants, including their second language learning needs. Even in the absence of a national Ministry of Education, Canada evinces a consistency of policies across provinces and over time that respect and promote high levels of teacher professionalism in recruitment and selection, and in the importance that is assigned to professional collaboration and continuing professional development.

This case study of Alberta shows that in the nation's highest-achieving province, Canadians know how to live with paradox. They don't have to be a melting pot. They know how to be a mosaic. Given all these qualities, perhaps U2's Bono put it best when he said, "I believe the world needs more Canada."

Our own inquiry into educational improvement *with* innovation in Alberta, and the window it opens into Alberta education as a whole, provides the first extended account of the change architecture of this key high-performing culture and system. This has shown that Albertans know how to

- develop a Fourth Way approach to innovation and collective professional autonomy within a Second and Third Way system of test-based accountability;
- combine disciplined innovation and continuous improvement without sacrificing one to the other;
- have governments and teacher organizations become educational allies even though they will also be occasional adversaries;
- make teacher inquiry and learning permanent conditions that support improvement, not passing phases of professional practice;
- keep pushing learning forward by networking with other schools and also countries;
- create long term visions by capitalizing on political stability; and
- develop an educational culture that thrives on risk and is supported by trust instead of being held back by constant performance anxiety.

The words of former Edmonton Oilers hockey legend, Wayne Gretsky, epitomize the orientation to change of Albertan educators. "Statistically, 100 percent of the shots you don't take, don't go in." Alberta has scored well in education because it knows where the goal is for the future of the province and is not afraid to shoot for it. Its shots have often been courageous and bold, and its results indicate that it should no longer be overlooked by any of us who are looking for proven examples of educational success. Alberta offers an object lesson in intelligent international benchmarking from which all of us can and should learn a great deal more.

Arctic Ocean
Beafourt Sea
U.S.
Inuvik
NORTHWEST
TERRITORIES
Dawson
Whitehorse
Watson Lake
Cambridge Bay
Echo Bay
Yellowknife
Fort Nelson
Hay River
Fort Smith
Kagiqcliniq (Rankin Inlet)
Baffin Bay
GREENLAND (DENMARK)
Iqaluit (Frobisher Bay)
Ivujivik
Labrador Sea
Hudson Sea
Churchill
NEWFOUNDLAND
Prince George
ALBERTA
Schefferville
Happy Valley - Goose Bay
Edmonton
Flin Flon
MANITOBA
Chisasibi (Fort George)
Gander
Victoria
Vancouver
Calgary
Saskatoon
QUEBEC
St. JoHn's
Lethbridge
Regina
Moosonee
Sept-Iles
Chibougamau
PRINCE EDWARD ISLAND
Sydney
Winnipeg
Charlottetown
Thunder B
Québec
Fredericton
Sherbrooke
Saint John
Halifax
Sudbury
Montréal
NOVA SCOYIA
Ottawa
U.S.
North Atlantic Ocean
Toronto
Hamilton
London
Windsor

Chapter Six

ONTARIO

Inclusion, Interaction, and Local Diversity

With Henry Braun

Among the international leaders of educational achievement, the Canadian province of Ontario is at the very pinnacle of attention. Ontario is one of Canada's highest scorers on PISA and therefore one of the top performers in the world. Yet the reasons it receives so much attention compared to other countries and Canadian provinces extend far beyond its numerical accomplishments. These include:

- *High Immigration.* Ontario's population is 27% immigrant, and there is no difference in results on PISA between children from immigrant families and Canadian-born children. This makes it a much more realistic model for change for those countries that have much higher levels of diversity than Finland, for example.[1]
- *Large Population.* With a population exceeding 13 million and a system containing nearly five thousand schools, Ontario operates on a scale that is more plausible and comparable for many foreign visitors and leaders than smaller jurisdictions such as Finland, Singapore, Alberta, or Hong Kong.
- *Politics and Administration.* Ontario has a structure of school districts and a form of Western political democracy that is more recognizable to leaders of Anglo-American and European educational systems than the systems and politics of most Asian countries.
- *Policy Focus.* The province's recent policy focus on making measurable achievement gains and narrowing achievement gaps

in tested literacy and numeracy and in high school completion rates is close enough to the design of target-driven systems in places like England, the United States, and Australia as well as countries that are also moving in this direction to feel familiar. At the same time, the policy strategy is sufficiently different from many other countries in its methods of accomplishing these targets, especially in terms of their greater investment in the development of professional capital, to attract their curiosity about how to move further forward.

- *Performance Record.* Alongside its high-level performance on PISA, Ontario has increased the credibility of its approach by demonstrating success on its own measures in securing gains over four to five years of around 14% more children reaching proficiency in reading and of 13% more students graduating from high school since 2004.
- *Strategic Clarity.* Ontario's high performance has benefited from the political leadership of the province's premier, Dalton McGuinty, who has made educational reform a key component of his political platform. It has also been advanced by the intellectual leadership of the premier's education advisor, Michael Fullan, and the administrative leadership of former deputy minister Ben Levin. Together, they have eloquently articulated Ontario's reform strategy through many high-profile publications and through maintaining close associations with leaders in cornerstone international policy organizations such as the OECD and McKinsey & Company.[2]

A PROVINCE IN PERSPECTIVE

The planned, stated, received, and recommended theory of change in Ontario has been largely a Third Way reform strategy. As we saw in Chapter 2, Ontario's policies placed a focus on literacy, numeracy, and high school completion. They defined and pursued measurable targets in student achievement. They did this by involving teacher unions, with whom the government established conditions of peace and stability. The Ministry of Education avoided punitive interventions and instead provided extensive support systems to help teachers and schools deliver the goods. The government has also created data systems to track progress and intervene in real time whenever students or schools appear to be falling behind.

As the OECD itself acknowledges, however, in as complex a setting as provincial, state, or national education policy, it is difficult—if not impossible—to attribute achievement gains to one particular policy or another.[3] Many policies and their interaction, not just those that are most prominently emphasized or preferred, explain a system's success. This is partly why high-scoring provinces in Canada with different policies still get very similar results. Indeed, senior Ontario Ministry staff themselves stress that achievement gains cannot be attributed to one specific policy or another. "Trying to figure out what contributed what portion to the success is kind of hard," said one. "You won't be able to isolate variables. You have to put it in context of the school effectiveness planning process, the board effectiveness planning process, aligning all of those with the use of data," another added.

We therefore need to consider how *a wide range* of Ontario's policies and their interactions affect student achievement, including those that have not yet been so prominent in international commentaries or provincial self-advocacy.

This chapter focuses on one of these other policies: an ambitious and inclusive strategy to make whole-school changes to benefit students with special educational needs. The policy is important not just in its own right, but because it overlapped closely and was deliberately integrated with other aspects of the province's strategy, in particular its literacy focus and its attention to test-score results.

ONTARIO'S SPECIAL EDUCATION POLICY

In 2005, the Ministry of Education of Ontario released a visionary new provincial policy document, titled *Education for All* (EfA), which sought to "assist teachers in helping all of Ontario's students learn, including those students whose abilities make it difficult for them to achieve their grade level expectations."[4] The guiding beliefs contained in EfA are:

1. All students can succeed.
2. Universal design and differentiated instruction are effective and interconnected means of meeting the learning or productivity needs of any group of students.
3. Successful instructional practices are founded on evidence-based research, tempered by experience.
4. Classroom teachers are the key educators for a student's literacy and numeracy development.
5. Each child has his or her own unique patterns of learning.

6. Classroom teachers need the support of the larger community to create a learning environment that supports students with special education needs.

7. Fairness is not sameness.

The Ministry of Education allocated the prudent sum of $25 million to the Council of Ontario Directors of Education (CODE)—"directors" in Ontario being the equivalent of U.S. school district superintendents—to develop and implement a plan to support the recommendations in EfA. The CODE Special Education Project for 2005–06 was designed to support school districts across Ontario to generate their own initiatives in special education. These district-generated initiatives had to improve academic achievement for students with special education needs, enhance teachers' professional practice so they would have the capacity to secure such improvement, and be connected to each other across the districts. In time, this project came to be called "Essential for Some, Good for All" (ESGA) and it eventually extended over three years. The adventurous idea was to develop strategies that were essential for students with special educational needs but good for all students as well, and to do this in a manner that was appropriate for each individual school district yet also interconnected and therefore coherent across all of the districts.

The CODE leadership team designed the project. The components of the project's architecture included the development of a consistent, equitable, and transparent application, selection, distribution, monitoring, and reporting process. The architecture also involved the creation of a subsequent ESGA project leadership team to mentor and support the development, implementation, and evaluation of each district's plan once the work of the project was under way. An additional feature was the decision by CODE to allocate an equal amount of funding to all districts regardless of their size. A prime focus was to make a one-time change in the way that school districts structured their interactions between curriculum and special education staff, at the district level and also within the schools, so that these interactions became more frequent, focused, effective, and integrated. The goal was to "break down the silos" between those who had responsibility for special education students and those who had responsibility for the rest, so that everyone would develop a sense of collective responsibility for all students.[5] Over the course of the next two academic years, the Ministry provided additional resources to support the initiative.

From 2009, and with Henry Braun, the co-author of this chapter, at Boston College, in collaboration with 10 of Ontario's 72 school districts, one of us conducted and codirected a large-scale study of this special education reform and its implementation.[6] The districts were spread widely across the province; varied considerably in size; were distributed across urban, rural, and suburban locations; and were representative of its three different sectors. In Ontario, these are the public schools in which English is the language of instruction, Catholic schools, and public schools in which French is the language of instruction. All three of these sectors receive public funding. Three-day site visits were undertaken in each of the 10 districts. Senior policy level interviews were conducted with former deputy and assistant deputy ministers as well as individuals with provincewide responsibilities for special education. Staff surveys were undertaken with participating schools in 9 of the 10 districts to determine their perceptions of the initiative and its impact.

Although ESGA projects in most districts were targeted at particular samples of schools or grade levels and therefore did not directly encompass all students with special educational needs, students having special educational needs showed an overall gain in reading scores between 2004–05 and 2010–11 on EQAO across the province of nearly 13% for public school districts, 11% for Catholic districts, and 21% for Francophone districts.[7] Increases in writing over the same period were around 20% across all three types of districts. These increases far exceeded the gains students made as a whole over the same period. Gaps in the percentage of students reaching Level 3 proficiency in reading between nonidentified and identified students were significantly narrowed during this period. The gap decreased by 8.4% for the public districts, 11% for the Catholic districts, and 8.2% for the Francophone districts. In writing, the mean gap decreased by 18.7% for the public districts, 22.6% for the Catholic districts, and 15% for the Francophone districts. In other words, during the time period of this reform and its aftermath, there was a substantial reduction in achievement gaps in reading and writing between identified and nonidentified students.

THEORIES OF CHANGE SUBSTANCE

Most change theories in action distinguish between change *substance* and change *process*.[8] The *substance* of change concerns what is meant to be changed in the core operations of the organization—for instance, the introduction of healthier diets among school-age children, or initiatives such as improvements in literacy achievement.

The change *process* concerns the assumed drivers, mechanisms, and leverage points by which these changes can be accomplished. These might include inspiring leadership, confrontations with disturbing evidence, exerting pressure to try something new along with support to help people succeed at it, budgetary incentives, or tools to get teachers to collaborate.

Sometimes the distinction between change substance and change process is not straightforward. For instance, developing a stronger professional communities among teachers might lead to improvement in classroom teaching practice, but it also could constitute a fundamental alteration in how teachers work together. This in turn could lead to a shift in how the core processes of schooling are performed. Professional learning communities are, in this sense, an example of both change substance and change process.

The principles of EfA concentrated on enabling all students to succeed through increasingly improved and inclusive curriculum, assessment, and instruction undertaken by professionals working together. EfA had no targets, it was multidimensional, and it was therefore difficult to drive through the system in a top-down way. For former deputy minister Ben Levin and his colleagues, in converting EfA from philosophy into practice, "it became pretty clear that a big part of this issue was teachers' feelings of capacity to actually teach effectively with a diversity of kids."[9] Levin continued, "So the idea then became, 'How do we help teachers feel more confident and more competent in having a wider diversity of learners in their classrooms?'"[10]

In practice, the projects that evolved under the subsequent initiative of ESGA concentrated mostly on three areas: (1) inclusive pedagogy, (2) assistive technology, and (3) professional learning communities. As a parallel factor of change process, professional learning communities will be discussed later. We concentrate on the first two elements here.

INCLUSIVE PEDAGOGY

One of the chapters in the original EfA document is devoted to universal design for learning (UDL). This is based on the principles of universal design in architecture—that it is best to design a building at the outset to support its use by the maximum number of people, including the very young, the very old, and those with disabilities, than it is to build a conventional building and adapt it after the fact for all these different groups. The same is true for a curriculum—it should be designed for the widest range of learners from the start, rather than based on some common or standardized idea of a "normal" learner and having to make all kinds of accommodations afterwards.[11]

Differentiated instruction fits closely with the principles of UDL in its emphasis on differentiating the content, process, and product according to student interest, readiness, and learning profile. Seven out of the ten participating school districts made differentiated instruction one of their prime areas of focus. In the best cases, this focus led teachers to assign "respectful tasks," that did not alienate the student and that were tied to the curriculum.[12] These tasks are pitched at the student's level and are developed to make all students feel included in the lesson, regardless of their ability. This curriculum approach requires teachers, like those in Finland, to know their students well–"knowing each of our students" through classroom relationships and also through intense reviews of achievement data.[13] Survey data indicated that teachers were making increased use of differentiated instruction as a result of ESGA. One respondent expressed it like this:

> Students are more engaged. Fewer behavior issues in the classroom. Differentiated and small group instruction works way better than just whole group instruction does. Huge influx of resources. All have had a positive impact on student achievement.[14]

ASSISTIVE TECHNOLOGY

Differentiated instruction was significantly supported by assistive technology. Educational technology is not simply a device, like a laptop or a piece of software. It is an interconnected system of enhancements and supports. Assistive technology is "any technology that allows one to increase, maintain, or improve the functional capabilities of an individual with special learning needs."[15] For students, assistive technology has the capacity to build on individual strengths, increase engagement and motivation, promote independence, raise achievement, and lessen the need for withdrawal from regular classrooms.

In ESGA, many kinds of assistive technologies were introduced for the first time in many districts. Classroom sound systems benefitted students who had permanent or temporary hearing difficulties after ear infections, which is a common occurrence in poorer communities, yet they also supported all students, giving "everyone a front seat."[16] A range of other devices also supported differentiated instruction such as iPods, laptop computers, mobile devices, and software support such as voice recognition programs and programs that prompt young writers with possible upcoming words to assist with cognitive processing.

One district established two learning centers that grew from supporting one group of Grade 5 boys with learning disabilities at a time to encompass boys and girls with these disabilities from Grades 4 to 7.[17] Here, two groups of about 15 students at a time were trained to use a range of assistive technologies to support them in developing their reading and writing skills, to "express themselves and organize their thoughts."[18] The project built their self-confidence by "developing a greater awareness of their learning disability" through learning about famous figures such as Albert Einstein, Tom Cruise, and Keira Knightley who had the same learning disabilities as they did. The students also "developed self advocacy skills" so they could return to regular classrooms as bearers and implementers of their own changes, instructing their teachers on the ways they learned best and requesting accommodations in their teacher's approach to help them succeed.[19]

> "When the whole class feels comfortable in using laptops and assistive technology on a daily basis, then it is more likely that students who attended the center will feel comfortable in advocating for their use as well."
> –Classroom teacher, open-ended survey response

Classroom teachers were connected to the work of the learning centers through periodic visits and structured, experiential, and embedded professional development. Even so, when the regular classroom teacher used little or no new technology, learning disabled students using special devices felt a "huge stigma" and "stuck out like a sore thumb," quickly abandoning the very tools and strategies that could help them.[20] But "when the whole class feels comfortable in using laptops and assistive technology on a daily basis, then it is more likely that students who attended the center will feel comfortable in advocating for their use as well." They are "able to participate more fully in day to day curriculum with confidence."[21]

In Ontario, as in Singapore, technology is only really effective when it is thoughtfully integrated into everyday teaching. So the district has now infused its technological support throughout all classes. It has made a software package of applications accessible from home or in any of the district's schools available to all students, regardless of whether or not they attend the learning centers. In some cases, learning disabled students even took leadership roles in teaching new technologies to their regular classroom peers: "shining the spotlight on them in a positive way."[22]

The superintendent of the district, a former teacher of the hearing impaired, expressed his inclusive ideals in stating that "if we can create environments where the use of such technology seems almost as natural as drawing breath so that you de-stigmatize it and eliminate all those impediments to it, that's clearly the preferred direction."[23]

The introduction of assistive technologies has contributed to increases in tested achievement on the standardized provincial assessment. In 2007, there was a large spike in provincial writing scores, representing almost a 20% gain among special education students at a time when many more students were no longer being exempted from taking the test. This was the first year in which assistive technologies were allowed for identified students who were taking the test. For many students and their teachers, the initiative was a revelation. One teacher noted that "the technology we used really helped our scores" because it permitted some students to demonstrate what they knew without being hindered by the written text-based format of the test.[24] Other children who had disliked previous tests now "were excited" when they could "edit and push pieces around" on the writing assignments. A leader in Ontario's Ministry of Education argued that access to assistive technologies placed many learning disabled students on a level playing field, getting them "to a point of fairness that they weren't able to get to before in terms of accessing EQAO assessments."[25] It was no different than helping visually impaired students by letting them wear eyeglasses, a colleague explained.

As in Singapore, Ontario strives to integrate technology into the curriculum in ways that enhance learning for all students. Ontario educators participating in EfA use it as a way to introduce genuine innovations into classroom learning while also significantly contributing to conventional improvement in test-score results. A key factor, in every district, was how successfully these technologies were integrated into the culture of the school.

THEORIES OF CHANGE PROCESS

Systemic reform strategies address not only *what* to change, but also *how* to generate and interconnect the changes that the system is trying to implement. They involve theories about the purposes of change and about how to move change forward among the educators who will make them happen. They also address how to create coherence and cohesion among the many change components in relation to each other as well as in relation to other reforms in the system as a whole.

This chapter highlights seven interdependent aspects of Ontario's special education reform strategy, giving emphasis to their Fourth Way features. It then shows how they contrast, complement, or cohere with the Third Way features of Ontario's better-known, wider educational reform strategy with its emphasis on tested literacy and numeracy that were discussed in Chapter 2.[26] The seven themes are

1. inspiring beliefs;
2. moral economy;
3. leading from the middle;
4. local authority and flexibility;
5. integrated strategy;
6. collective responsibility; and
7. intensive interaction.

1. INSPIRING BELIEFS

Many change proponents, as we have seen, operate on the assumption that people have to be pushed into mandated practices and be made to experience them before they will have some basis for changing their beliefs. This is what much Third Way strategy is predicated on: make the change non-negotiable, give people targets to motivate or direct them, and then provide lots of support to get them started. It is assumed that only after seeing successful change in a newly required practice will people start to change their beliefs about it.

ESGA—like Alberta's AISI and Finland's education system and society—was largely based on the opposing view: that common and compelling beliefs are a precondition for moving people into action. Building trust, establishing common purposes, cultivating a sense of shared responsibility, raising expectations, developing relationships, and supporting increased collaboration—these strategies of *reculturing* provide much of the underpinning for ESGA. Change what people believe about who can learn and how they learn, for example, or about who is responsible for supporting children with special educational needs, and you will then be able to change what people do.

The head of the Ontario Ministry's Special Education Policy and Programs Branch, just after the commencement of ESGA, concentrated on establishing or clarifying "common shared beliefs and values." Once this was achieved, he said, the point was then to "let people go." This had been his vision when he was a principal of an innovative high school. He understood that "we have to give control of learning to students and they have to have ownership for this." Just as, in his school, "the nature of instruction was one of open-endedness rather than controlled by the teachers who were providing the information," so too, he believed, adults in schools and school systems have to be "involved in decisions that affect them." More than this, "if you let people go who fundamentally believe what you believe and are dedicated professionals, then they will do it," he said.

According to this system leader, policy makers and system leaders "allocated dollars to boards within this concept of EfA and improving instruction for kids." They said the "project should fit somewhere within the guidelines of *Education for All,*" but "that was it." Despite the fact that educators were always "feeling overwhelmed by all kinds of other demands," one ESGA project leader couldn't "imagine a teacher worth their salt who couldn't buy into that philosophy."[27]

The inspiring beliefs that were articulated in EfA resonated with Ontario educators. In the province's many Catholic districts, for example, spiritual mission statements refer to the uniqueness of all children, where, in the words of one school principal, "Every child is a gift from God."[28] The philosophy was also in tune with core cultural characteristics of inclusiveness and diversity embedded in the nation's officially bilingual, multicultural identity. This increased the likelihood that educators would implement the policy with fidelity.

The province's literacy and numeracy strategy has also been underpinned by a clear moral purpose of increasing achievement and narrowing achievement gaps among all students. This purpose and the testing strategies accompanying it worked alongside Third-Way-style strategies of political and professional definition by government with the assistance of top-level stakeholders. By contrast, the beliefs of EfA operated on more Fourth-Way-like principles of voluntary commitment and inspiration. In Ontario's Third Way literacy and numeracy strategy, changing the practice mainly came first. In Fourth Way ESGA, the inspiring beliefs took precedence.

2. MORAL ECONOMY

If the Second Way is about reducing the costs of public education under every possible circumstance and the Third Way is about providing additional resources to develop people's capacity to meet policy targets, Fourth Way strategies of policy financing are about protecting and even improving the core processes of teaching and learning. This can be done by providing additional resources where needed and by reducing costs attached to other items wherever possible. Fourth Way answers to austerity are not to be found in increasing the costs associated with accountability but in reducing expenditure on things like inspection systems and standardized testing that are often extraneous to teaching and learning.

One additional candidate for economies outside the core moral purpose of teaching and learning is the legal and medical costs of special educational entitlements and interventions. When Ontario's Liberal Party took office in 2003, it inherited a special educational needs strategy from its Progressive Conservative predecessor that was legalistic, labyrinthine, and unsustainably costly. The previous government had introduced Second Way education reforms that involved cuts in, and greater central control over, public education funding. At the same time, there was a new process that allocated additional resources to individual students identified as having special educational needs. In former deputy minister Ben Levin's recollection, this was now "the only place" school districts "could get more money. If you could make a kid look bad enough you could get extra money and there was a ton of paperwork with it." This created "huge financial pressures on special ed because the number of kids identified was going steadily up"—10% a year. "So money was rolling steadily out."

According to some of Levin's colleagues in the Ministry, the system of individual identification had turned into a "funding formula driven activity."[29] They explained how filling out forms to drive funding received more effort than "driving the needs of instructional practice."[30] One colleague explained how the process was being "used to generate more money for the districts," while another echoed, "That had got to change."[31]

Bruce Drewett, the Ministry's director of Special Education Programs at the time, has lived a lifetime with physical disability and had many exclusionary experiences when he was a student in school. Along with Levin, Drewett felt that the special education process, driven as it was by separate identification, was a moral problem as well as a monetary one. The escalating rates of funding-driven identification were based on and also boosting "a deficit based type of documentation as opposed to what the kids can do and could be expected to do." Drewett continued, "There was also an emphasis that the kid needs a full-time educational assistant as opposed to the emphasis on the instructional level based on the kid's needs."

The old system that gave priority to identification over instruction was not the best way to help students. A senior ministry administrator remarked how "sometimes you have five educational assistants in a classroom. None of them are coordinated in terms of the whole classroom. And the perception is the assistant is tied to the student." Levin was keen "to try and keep as many kids as possible in regular classrooms." He and his colleagues wanted to create a more collaborative and inclusive way of doing that by attaching resources to instruction rather than to individuals.

Shifting the way that special education was supported was seen as being more prudent, effective, and fair than the previous system. It represented a kind of "moral economy" that reduced costs without hurting children. British historian E. P. Thompson originally used the idea of a "moral economy" to explain food riots in England in the 18th century as a response to free market political economies that had allowed widespread hunger to become the acceptable price of private gain. The riots were directed at restoring a fair and proper balance between economic development and social need. The initiation of ESGA was a less dramatic effort to establish a similar kind of moral economy in the field of special education.[32]

3. LEADING FROM THE MIDDLE

Large-scale educational reforms make little progress unless they have key political support behind them and widespread professional engagement in developing or delivering them. In the Third Way, this means establishing a "guiding coalition" of key stakeholders at the top, and placing pressure on as well as providing support for professionals down through different layers of the system. The Fourth Way makes much more use of the system's professionals as the dynamos and not just the deliverers of change.

Elements of both Third and Fourth Way approaches to reform were present in Ontario's special educational reform architecture. They became evident in the unusual and influential role played by middle-level leaders—the province's district superintendents and directors and their representatives. Leading from the middle took three forms:

1. high-level stakeholder representation on Third Way lines,
2. collective commitment and advocacy of all or most leaders, and
3. development and steering by a team of middle-level leaders.

First, in line with Third Way principles, key district leaders inserted themselves into the province's top-level stakeholder group in educational reform, from which they had felt previously excluded as "second bananas" compared to other constituent groups like the teachers' unions and principals' organizations.[33] Three superintendents of special education wrote to the deputy minister, arguing that the leadership of the superintendents and their directors could be drawn on more effectively in relation to implementing EfA. In a subsequent meeting with leaders of the Council of Ontario Directors of Education (CODE), the minister stated that he would write a check for $25 million for "CODE to do the professional development associated with EfA."[34] The province's district-level leaders were now officially key stakeholders in the province's reform strategy.

Second, following this agreement, the directors and superintendents, with the ministry's blessing, assumed a more Fourth Way form of leadership of the EfA initiative, that went beyond mere stakeholder involvement to building a critical mass for change. Education for All was a complex change to implement because parts of it were more of a philosophical statement of direction than a strategic plan. "The province knew it had to make changes but it really didn't know" what to do. "It knew what it couldn't do, which was mandate a bunch of stuff" as it had in other parts of its Third Way reform program.[35]

The middle-level leaders who initiated ESGA understood that "if the superintendents didn't see it as important enough to empower the people to bring about this change, it wasn't going to happen."[36] But how could they engage all these superintendents and directors across the system? The answer was in the funding. In the past, funding equity for projects across districts had been calculated on a per-pupil basis, "so if you're in Toronto you get a zillion dollars and if you're in [a small board] you get 50 bucks because of your population."[37] If funding had been allocated proportionately, "there would have been very, very little, if anything to give to the smaller districts."[38] Yet, "three quarters of the school districts in Ontario are considered small or medium size."[39]

The ESGA project steering team therefore determined that "the funding was going to be equal no matter what the size of the district."[40] Although this risked alienating the larger and traditionally more powerful districts, the many directors whose smaller districts now benefitted from significant infusions of dollars, and who were already short on resources for special education programming, were in a position "to do something that they could have never afforded in any other circumstances."[41] This provided the initiative with a critical mass of senior level support. "For them to get a big chunk of money and to be able to do something was so empowering they would have stood on their heads and spit nickels for us," one member of the steering team reflected.

All 72 districts therefore participated. "The goal was to get everybody talking about Education for All and everybody involved."[42] Every superintendent and director became an advocate. It "upped the profile in the province in terms of what the project was all about."[43] District-level leaders became the collective dynamos who gave the whole project its momentum.

The third aspect of leading from the middle took the form of a small steering team of retired directors and superintendents from public, Catholic, and Franco-Ontarian districts that the head of CODE appointed to be responsible for designing and developing the ESGA initiative. This steering team knew that, with the deputy minister's full support, it was engaged in "a new way of thinking about how to implement a service."[44] Ministry staff said that they wanted district-level leaders "to have ownership of the project with us because at the end of the day it was about a culture change and movement that we needed them to actually own."[45]

The steering team of retired established personnel was "not a threat to the superintendents" because they were not elected representatives and they exacted no formal control over anyone.[46] "They knew that we got money from the Ministry of Education but they were responding to who they considered to be their colleagues."[47] Also, the steering team "weren't the Ministry, so weren't viewed in the same way by districts. We were able to operate with more flexibility in a more nimble way because we weren't tied into the Ministry," one of them reflected.

Change was not being driven down through the superintendents and directors in Third Way style. Instead, the steering team was more about "bringing forth and *empowering* the knowledge that already existed with the superintendents."[48] The team did not so much want to *push* change as to "to *pull* it from the people."[49] This pulling process occurred as superintendents and others in the districts interacted with the steering group during the process of applying for project funds.

The Fourth Way is about professionally developed change, rather than administratively driven reform that professionals then have to deliver. Professionally developed change can originate in many places and with many groups. In ESGA, it was the group of respected leaders in the middle of the system who had a decisive influence. They exercised their influence in making representations to central government, in building commitment and dynamic engagement among leaders of all the province's 72 districts, and in steering and guiding the project among their colleagues.

> The Fourth Way is about professionally developed change, rather than administratively driven reform that professionals then have to deliver.

4. LOCAL AUTHORITY AND FLEXIBILITY

Earlier, we described how, in countries like England, the United States, and Sweden, there is currently an undermining of local democracy, district responsibility, and community engagement in public education. In ESGA in particular and the Fourth Way in general, however, local authorities or school districts have been central to effective educational change. In Ontario, considerable freedom and flexibility was accorded to districts in how they implemented and interpreted EfA. Every district proposed its own plan and then, after the steering team accepted it, developed it in its own way. In communities with widely varying populations and cultures, this allowed for a great diversity of projects concentrating on themes like early literacy, UDL, assistive technologies, and raising expectations for aboriginal students. The steering team "had to respect the fact that districts were at different places and that they had different needs and that what might work in one district would not be effective in another."[50]

> Every teacher didn't have to do the same thing. Too often a project is, "OK, you will do this and it will happen this year and you will report it." Ours was much more open than that and it was "bring us your best approach, we're going to look at it"—and most of them were approved.[51]

The Ministry "didn't micromanage in any way. They asked lots of questions, but they never came out and said, 'You will do it this way.'"[52] In the province's prior and parallel Third Way educational reform strategy as a whole, it was felt that "a real weakness" was "so much focus on building a common curriculum and working on common goals." As a consequence, "flexibility and variation to fit the context had really been lost."[53] By comparison, ESGA's steering team was given considerable scope to promote and respond to local variations and diversities in cultures and communities:

- A Franco-Ontarian district actively protected multiliterate areas of art and play through which its imperiled culture expressed and protected its defining identity. Preserving this identity was regarded as being at least as important as narrowing measurable achievement gaps.[54]
- A district with an Old Order Mennonite farming community, where many of its young people were expected to leave school before the legal age limit, realized it could not enforce attendance because families would simply migrate to other parts of

their farming network in the United States or beyond. So the school where this community was mainly concentrated focused on making a generational change in attitudes to education by building trust and relationships with families, serving locally grown food for school snacks and lunches, walking with parents back to their homes, and even carrying their groceries for them, if necessary. This trust-building process of empathy and communication helped keep families in the community and connected to the schools when more standardized strategies would probably have driven them away.

- One district in which aboriginal students comprised 40% of the enrollment addressed the fact that many of them had been deprived of their own heritage language and also excluded from the majority language of English. They thus began by developing basic oral language capabilities as a foundation for future learning.
- A district with high proportions of immigrants, which had seen a sharp drop in the achievements of its English language learners in Grade 4, embarked upon an early literacy initiative that broke through impassioned ideological disputes between advocates of structured literacy and of unstructured play. The initiative produced an enriched and engaging literacy program that connected language and words to playful activities with sand, water, and other manipulative materials like floating ducks that had matching letters for upper- and lowercase.

In Fourth Way fashion, the architecture of ESGA allowed for and encouraged responsiveness to the diversity of communities and cultures. It gave districts a strong degree of local autonomy and authority in devising their own change solutions. It worked with diversity, rather than enforcing standardization.

However, local adaptations of focus and approach could not, by themselves, create coherence of overall direction or quality of results. There was sophisticated differentiation and responsiveness; but how could there then also be coherence across the system? The actions of the group of former superintendents who were leading from the middle were absolutely central in creating cohesion and interconnections among all the activities of these different authorities.

5. INTEGRATED STRATEGY

From the outset, with the appointment of its coordinator and its steering team, ESGA reached out to senior leaders of other provincial reform initiatives and to those who worked in other related ministries. Some of these other leaders were surprised by this willingness to involve them from the very beginning, but it led to a more coordinated concentration of effort across government departments, secretariats, and initiatives. It forged a connection between a Fourth Way initiative with lots of diversity and differentiation, and the high-profile and high-priority provincial Third Way strategy. This move to integrate effort and responsibility at the highest level was designed to increase the status of the project and its purposes, to head off potential conflicts and the threat of departments and programs working at cross-purposes, and to increase collective capacity of personnel and resources.

Taking action on special education also fit with the province's other reform priorities. The former deputy minister, Ben Levin, knew that "kids going into special education tend to do worse" than other students in literacy and numeracy, and that there were "big achievement gaps between kids in special ed and other kids on the EQAO results." So one way to try and close the achievement gap was to improve learning and performance in the special education population. As we saw earlier, the results did indeed demonstrate success between 2004 and 2009 in terms of narrowing the gap on EQAO tests between identified and nonidentified students in reading and writing.

6. COLLECTIVE RESPONSIBILITY

A recurring theme of the Global Fourth Way that characterized the cases of Finland, Singapore, and Alberta is collective responsibility for all students in the school community. The ESGA project, it was initially thought, would be for just one year. It was treated as a one-time chance "to fund opportunities for districts to experiment with new ways of doing business with regard to special education."[55] The plan was to make a short-term change that would have a long-term impact—the creation of a structure and culture of collective responsibility for all students, and for the quality of differentiated instruction that would be provided for these students.

ESGA set about breaking down "silos" within school districts between the curriculum and special education departments and their superintendents.[56] Schools, in turn, were encouraged to make "better use of the roles and responsibilities of the special education resource teachers in relation to classroom teachers as they shared collective responsibility for all students."[57] Superintendents for both curriculum and special education in each district were required to "sign off" on the project budget together as a condition of funding.[58] *Restructuring* was being employed in order to achieve *reculturing* of district relationships. In addition to the cultural pull of people's common beliefs, restructuring exerted a strong nudge toward engaging people in different professional conversations and relationships.

Collective responsibility was a prime reason why one of the elementary schools in the project had been able to turn its achievement results around.[59] Like many of its counterparts in the district and beyond, this school had instituted an eight-week teaching-learning cycle, whereby students were assessed and tracked at the end of each cycle on their progress in literacy and mathematics. They were also reviewed periodically in the cycle, and each student's progress was displayed on a data wall in green, amber, or red colors, so as to pick up any child, in real time, who might register as falling behind.

Within the framework of this very Third Way, data-driven process, the principal added a Fourth Way approach of convincing all the staff to take collective responsibility for every student. In time, *all* the teachers came to care about *all* the students, not just those in their class or grade. Grade 1 teachers shared responsibility for how students were doing in Grade 6, because they used to be in Grade 1. Special education teachers worked alongside other teachers in regular classes to help all students who needed it—not just those who had been formally identified. This stimulated intense conversations that put children's faces on their performance numbers and that encouraged a common focus on student learning and how to improve it.

Collective responsibility was encouraged and supported by the belief system of EfA and by putting an end to the silos within school districts. Educators learned to employ and make thoughtful use of common language and tools such as data walls and anchor charts to stimulate committed professional conversations. Anchor charts, for example, were handmade posters that were widely used to communicate things like common objectives and concepts across a grade level in a way that even students could use to guide their learning and help them advocate for the kind of instruction they needed from their teachers. These charts existed prior to ESGA but were used much more frequently after its start.

Collective responsibility was deliberately created across the whole system, and it started to come alive in Ontario's classrooms. The project "gave us money to be able to get together and work as a team—team building, common planning time."[60] On a 5-point scale, surveyed teachers registered an average of 4.13 in acknowledging that staff felt more collective responsibility for students with special educational needs, and 4.21 in relation to the statement that there was better collaboration among all professionals

The Fourth Way puts "faces" on the data, so that teachers take collective responsibility for knowing and responding to the real children that the data represent.

in relation to these students.[61] Teachers who were interviewed about the impact of ESGA on their practice, said things like, "There's a change from *my* students to *our* students." With the greater integration of special education support teachers into regular classrooms "it's not all on the classroom teacher. They never feel like they're responsible for this one child."[62]

The Second Way isolates and individualizes teachers—separating them from, and sometimes making them compete against, their peers on measures linked to extrinsic incentives like performance-related pay. The Third Way brings teachers together in professional learning communities, but often within a specified focus on analysis of achievement data and related spreadsheets, in order to drive up tested achievement scores. The Fourth Way, by contrast, continues to take data seriously as a focus for a professional community, but now puts "faces" on the data, so that teachers take collective responsibility for knowing and responding to the real children that the data represent.[63] Through ESGA, schools brought classroom teachers and special education teachers and their counterparts in school district administration together to work collectively and intensively on behalf of all the children for whom they shared responsibility. In Ontario, collective responsibility is one of the key areas in which the Third Way meets up with the Fourth.

7. INTENSIVE INTERACTION

How can a provincewide array of locally responsive projects be brought together coherently? In ESGA, district projects were held together by a number of means including the guidance of the respected middle-level steering team, and by their pragmatic and political integration with, and "piggybacking" on, other reform priorities. The projects were also interconnected by an intensive process of constant communication that, we have already seen, is essential to the success of other high performing systems like Singapore and Alberta.

In a short space of just a few weeks, as districts submitted applications for their projects, each member of the ESGA steering team took responsibility for communicating with ten districts, establishing "relationships with the superintendent or staff person in charge of the project."[64] A coaching and mentoring process was established where this intermediary group of superintendents went back and forth with districts during the application process to ensure that everything hung together in line with the project's guiding principles. Again, this was a process of always nudging people forward, as well as a constant pull into the whole project.

In a number of instances, the approval process could become "quite sticky."[65] Some proposals were initially rejected. The steering group "went back sometimes and said 'No, it didn't have the support of the team. Here are the things you need to do to change it.'"[66] This might have been because the proposal did not have enough of a student focus or because it had insufficient emphasis on getting special education resource teachers and classroom teachers to work together, for example.

One month after the projects commenced, in October of 2005, a team of 30 to 35 "monitors" that the steering team appointed went out to visit the districts and their schools in teams for the first of two visits in the first project year. As former senior school district staff who were "very experienced," the monitors "understood the districts," and had received training to prepare them in what to look for on their visits.[67] Their task was to help districts and schools "reflect on where you are in your project at this point, what the gains have been and so on."[68] The head of CODE described the monitors as "non-threatening" and as "confidantes" who did "not go in and say, 'Hey you have to do it this way,'" but asked reflective questions about ESGA programs.

However, when the call reverberated through the districts that "the monitors are coming, the monitors are coming," this served to "kick-start" the projects.[69] "It really got it into gear fast because districts knew that two people were coming to spend a day talking to them about what their plans were and what they had found out to that point." In practice, "everyone tried to impress" the monitors "with their good work" and "the word spread" that the monitors and therefore the overall project were "actually looking at what we're doing."

The ESGA leadership team and the cadre of monitors were more than Second Way compliance officers. They were not there just to ensure technical fidelity with an imposed program and set of strategies. They were able to appreciate and to adapt to local exigencies. They precipitated mutual learning and provided reflective feedback.

> Cross-pollination and constant communication, rather than enforced compliance, was at the heart of ESGA's strategy of coherence.

In the project's change design, coaching and monitoring were integrally connected through a constant exchange of understandings and ideas. Coherence among a diverse portfolio of projects was intensified through networked communication. Some districts, for instance, were initially unclear what kinds of instruments they could use to measure growth in student achievement. Coaches and monitors would advise contacting another district they knew that had "a couple of tools that they have been using."[70] As one of the ESGA team members reflected, "So, what we were doing was cross-pollinating in our coaching roles. That was our job as the coaches." This cross-pollination and constant communication, rather than enforced compliance, was at the heart of ESGA's strategy of coherence.

CONCLUSION

Ontario is an outstanding international performer in education. The reasons for this success include all the factors listed by cornerstone organizations and by Ontario's advocates as well. Our corner store research shows that other factors are also at work that have clear implications for achievement results. Ontario's well-publicized Third Way reforms in tested literacy and numeracy with strong and also supportive central direction have, in some ways, cohered with the Fourth Way special education emphases of ESGA. ESGA initiatives piggybacked on the literacy priorities in the wider reform environment and included key representatives of the literacy and numeracy secretariat in its strategic planning.

The two reforms' emphases on developing greater collective professional responsibility for all students were also highly compatible and interlinked. Both reforms have been able to build on a deep-seated culture of collaboration among teachers that had grown in Ontario since the 1980s, even if it had gone underground during the cutbacks of the Progressive Conservative government before 2003. Ontario's most recent educational reforms restored professional relationships and dispositions and pushed them further ahead through data-driven inquiry. ESGA, meanwhile, extended collaboration to include breaking down the silos between classroom teachers and special education resource specialists in schools, and between their counterparts in school district offices. The inspirational direction set by EfA also gave the move toward greater collective responsibility a moral and philosophical underpinning.

Sometimes, as we saw in Chapter 2, the relationships between Ontario's Third Way literacy and numeracy strategy and the Fourth Way orientations of ESGA have not been entirely complementary and have even come into conflict with each other. Imposed threshold targets within standardized testing priorities drove some educators to game the system to get the required results by concentrating undue attention on students just beneath the threshold. This was discouraging to teachers who felt that the real and measurable growth they had achieved among students with special educational needs was not acknowledged or prioritized if it fell below Level 3.

At a time when Ontario shows signs of explicitly embracing innovation with improvement, there is a lot it can learn from what it has already achieved with ESGA. ESGA did not deliver central strategies through hierarchical layers of implementation. It allocated substantial discretion and autonomy to local school districts and then created coherence among their strategies through an inspiring belief system, constant monitoring, intensive interaction, and integration with existing priorities. By deliberately structuring ways to break down silos, and to develop new cultures of collective responsibility, it connected the professionally dynamic interactions of the Fourth Way with the continuing focus on achievement results of the Third.

Ontario has achieved iconic status on international benchmarks. This will endure and be enhanced even further if the province is able to communicate other effective elements of its change portfolio, such as ESGA, that have received little attention from cornerstone organizations to date.[71] Taking this broader view, in terms of whether it is a Third Way or a Fourth Way system, we would now regard Ontario as being about a 3.5! Yet it would be a mistake to infer that Fourth Way approaches can always coexist with Third Way policies. Sometimes the policies have to be bypassed or opposed rather than accommodated or appeased. To understand how this can happen, we now shift to England and the fate of a promising school that made enormous progress in serving its cultural minority immigrant students, despite the wider policy environment.

England
1 BEDFORDSHIRE
2 BRISTOL
3 BUCKINGHAMSHIRE
4 CAMBRIDGESHIRE
5 DERBYSHIRE
6 EAST RIDING OF YORKSHIRE
7 GLOUCESTERSHIRE
8 GREATER LONDON
9 GREATER MANCHESTER
10 HEREFORDSHIRE
11 HERTFORDSHIRE
12 LEICESTERSHIRE
13 MERSEYSIDE
14 NORTHAMPTONSHIRE
15 NOTTINGHAMSHIRE
16 OXFORDSHIRE
17 RUTLAND
18 STAFFORDSHIRE
19 TYNE AND WEAR
20 WARWICKSHIRE
21 WEST MIDLANDS
22 WORCESTERSHIRE
NORTHUMBERLAND
Newcastle upon Tyne
CUMBRIA
DURHAM
NORTH YORKSHIRE
LANCASHIRE
Leeds
WEST YORKSHIRE
Kingston upon Hull
Manchester
SOUTH YORKSHIRE
Liverpool
Sheffield
LINCOLNSHIRE
CHESHIRE
Stoke-on-Trent
Leicester
Norwich
NORFOLK
Birmingham
SHROPSHIRE
Coventry
SUFFOLK
Luton
ESSEX
Reading
Bristol
London
BERKSHIRE
WILTSHIRE
SURREY
KENT
SOMERSET
HAMPSHIRE
WEST SUSSEX
EAST SUSSEX
DEVON
DORSET
Southampton
ISLE OF WIGHT
CORNWALL
Plymouth

So far, we have examined four high-performing educational systems. Fourth Way change principles, we have seen, have played a significant, if not always exclusive, part in their success. But what if you work in a lower-performing nation or other system that is below or almost below the top twenty systems on PISA? What do you do then?

This chapter and the next one delve into the role of Fourth Way change principles in bringing about high performance despite the lower performance of the surrounding system and sometimes in direct opposition to it. We begin in England—a country that ranks rather poorly on PISA—and in one of the less fashionable parts of it, in the North. Here, we look at a successfully turned-around school, in a high poverty and cultural minority community, within its relatively low-performing national educational system. What has been the way to excellence here, in conditions that seem to militate against educational success?

The designation of England as a middling performer at best, might strike readers as a bit odd. Of all the countries that outsiders might automatically associate with educational excellence, England would probably have pride of place among them. The country that gave the world the language of Shakespeare, that founded the ancient universities of Oxford and Cambridge, and that transmits the plum vowels of the BBC World Service across the globe appears to be the international epitome of high standards, cultured learning, and good manners. Yet England is an unimpressive performer on most international indicators of educational success. On PISA, for example, it ranks a lowly 24th, well below the United

States. It has some of the widest achievement gaps between children from rich and poor homes in the developed world. And it ranks dead last out of 21 countries on UNICEF's indicators of child well-being.[1]

Impressions of England's elite accomplishments tend to emanate from the bits of the country that have been selectively portrayed in classical literature, modern film, and televised costume drama. This is the England of the pastoral South: of Jane Austen, Thomas Hardy, and Downton Abbey in period drama, and of anything involving the posh pronunciations of Hugh Grant or Helena Bonham Carter in contemporary film.

But there are many other "Englands" that overseas eyes rarely see. These include the old mill towns of the North that gave the world the first great industrial revolution and more recently the Asian communities that immigrated only to find the factories close shortly after their arrival. It is one of these other Englands—the northern mill town of Oldham in Greater Manchester—that is the focus of this chapter.

England may be a relatively low-performing system internationally, and in many parts of the North that is even more true because low-performing schools and districts are disproportionately represented there. But even within lower-performing systems, much higher performance in particular schools and school districts or local authorities still occurs. Between 2007 and 2009, with Alma Harris, one of us codirected a large-scale study of seven such schools and also two local authorities in England as part of an examination of high performance beyond expectations in business, sport, and education.[2] Three of the schools were in Oldham. One of these was Grange Secondary School.

DECLINE AND RECOVERY

Oldham was the site of some of Britain's worst ever race riots in 2001. On indicators of deprivation, some areas of the town are among the poorest 1% in England.[3] Grange Secondary School has been right at the center of one of them. It was the town's "flagship" school when it was established in 1968, drawing in young people from across the community. But as Pakistani and Bangladeshi families came to work in the cotton mills and as the textile industry then collapsed, the staff at Grange Secondary began to struggle and the school fell "into the doldrums."[4] Graeme Hollinshead, who had worked almost all his adult life at Grange Secondary, since 1971, vividly recalls how the school's population changed, and how difficult it was to adjust.

> People's knowledge now about the needs of Muslim children in this school is as good as it is anywhere. But in the '80s, we made girls do PE in bare legs because we didn't know any different. And there were bigger issues than that. We'd carry on with the normal syllabus. There would be no conscious effort made to change things because of the needs of those pupils—because of ignorance, if you want a better way of putting it. And similarly, the curriculum didn't develop. It was the traditional curriculum with no semblance of individual pupil needs. There was no move towards being innovative and looking at things differently. The school was backward.

Ill-equipped with the knowledge required to respond effectively to cultural minority populations where English was not the first language, and challenged by the accelerating incidence of poverty as jobs disappeared with the demise of the mills, Grange Secondary "fell into a malaise."[5] Despite efforts at change through technical and vocational education and the implementation of diagnostic and performance-based assessment reforms, by the 1990s, academic standards had fallen dramatically. The senior leadership team had isolated itself on "the top corridor" where one of them "even used to crochet most of the day." The atmosphere "felt lax."[6]

One teacher recalled how senior leaders "never set foot in my classroom." Turnout at parents' evenings was low and only 15% of students were achieving the standard of five grades C and up in their General Certificate of Secondary Education (GCSE) examination at age 16 (the threshold for most students moving on to university-bound programs after that). Parents "didn't speak English. Some couldn't read English. A lot of them couldn't read their own language."[7]

Grange's deputy headteacher, who had been at the school since 1976, pointed out that the staff's response was "blaming the children, the community for being so poor and the fact that they were on free school dinners and that they don't speak English and that mobility is the problem." "The facilities looked grotty," one senior leader reflected. "In the press, we were muck. The kids didn't have very high expectations of succeeding and we had quite a high staff turnover."[8]

Over the next decade, working with the same community and the same population, the school demonstrated a remarkable turnaround that combined innovation with improvement. The trajectory of Grange's performance results leaves little doubt about its achievements with an identical population that, in 2008, was 84% Bangladeshi and 8% Pakistani, with 24 languages spoken in the school. Grange significantly exceeded the performance and the progress of almost all similarly placed schools, in the entire country. This is evident in numerous indicators:

- The proportion of students achieving five or more examination passes at grades C and up, in the GCSE, increased from 15% in 1999 to 71% in 2008.
- Between 2000 and 2008, the proportion of students not going on to further education, training, or employment fell from 12% to 3%—less than half the national average of 7%.
- Over a decade, attendance improved from 84% to 92.5%, close to the national average of 92.7%.
- In terms of the contribution the school made to growth in student progress between ages 11 to 16 (what is known as its contextual value-added score), in 2008, Grange was positioned in the top 2% of schools nationally, and first among all 16 secondary schools in the local authority.
- Honors and awards included designation as a visual arts specialist school in 2002, becoming the highest performer of 30 such schools nationally in 2005 (and remaining in the top two until the time the school was studied), and winning a number of significant visual arts prizes such as being the regional Arts and Minds winner in 2004.

Successive inspection reports by the English inspection body, Ofsted, support these indicators of improvement. Ofsted's 2002 report upgraded the school to the second highest category of "good," which included "areas of excellence" in the school's work. The report noted that, since the 1996 inspection, "there has been significant improvement in attendance and good improvement in the quality of the curriculum for Years 10 and 11. Teaching has significantly improved and standards are rising faster than nationally."

By the time of the 2006 report, Grange was still a "good school" that now also had "some outstanding features," particularly in terms of supporting and caring for pupils and forming partnerships with other schools. Although examination results were still "below average," they were "much better than at the time of the previous inspection." This is an impressive improvement record after years of underperformance in the face of profound local educational and social challenges and compared to schools in similar circumstances.

LEADERSHIP FOR CHANGE

Grange exemplifies many Fourth Way principles, but it is particularly illustrative of how these present themselves in the kind of leadership and combinations of innovation with improvement that can be effective in contexts of turnaround and conditions of adversity.

A new assistant principal (or in UK terminology, a deputy headteacher), named Colin Bell, arrived at Grange Secondary School in 1994 and went on to become the headteacher in 1997. Graeme Hollinshead, who had started his long career at Grange in 1971, became Bell's deputy in 1997 and succeeded Bell as the head in 2004. This was the perceptible start of the long turnaround in the fortunes of the school. When you are working in an environment where the system overall is not performing especially well, then leadership that can establish higher expectations and pull people together becomes absolutely vital.

The leadership approach at Grange Secondary did not conform to any one of the adjectives normally applied to educational or business leadership, but combined many of them, in a complex and coherent way. Grange's leadership was at times courageous, creative, inspirational, distributed, inclusive, and sustainable. It was not one kind of leadership but many—a fusion and evolution of different styles and approaches across a community and also over time.

COURAGEOUS LEADERSHIP

The low point for Grange Secondary came when it almost failed its external inspection in 1996. Graeme Hollinshead honestly felt the school hadn't deserved to pass. For the week of the inspection, three or four highly capable supply (substitute) teachers were brought in, while a group of weaker staff members were suspiciously "sick for the week." After the inspection, Hollinshead took sick leave for the first time in his career.

Like a number of other dedicated colleagues at the school, he had worked at Grange all his professional life. But the inspection process was a wake-up call. He and the school, he felt, were utterly stuck. Frustrated and despondent, he went to discuss his troubling feelings with a hospital consultant. The consultant listened patiently, then delivered his expert medical advice. This was Northern England, not Southern California, so his feedback was bracing and brutally direct. "He just advised me to get back in and sort it out," said Graeme, "which I did."

Graeme moved up to being deputy head. Bell arrived and was soon promoted to being the head. Together, they started to lead by example, knowing that one of the defining characteristics of leadership is being prepared to go first. They set down firm foundations for improvement by calming down student behavior with a positive discipline strategy. "Behavior was poor, morale was poor, and attendance was 84%. Everything needed improving."[9]

At first, Bell and Hollinshead showed courage and fortitude by leading boldly and resolutely from the front. They took some of the worst behaved students in the school into town and out to amusement parks when they behaved well, even though their staff thought they were crazy for doing so. "We used to do things like getting in our cars and rounding up the kids from the park. There was nothing we wouldn't do. We'd go knocking on doors, saying 'Why aren't you in school?'"[10]

After leading by example, their staff was more ready to follow now that they had respect for their leaders and realized that what they were modeling was actually achievable. The result was a new behavior strategy that produced a climate characterized by "calmness on the corridors,"[11] collective staff responsibility to care for children, willingness to listen to them, and a capacity to understand the students and "where they were coming from."[12]

> Grange's leaders were courageous with their superiors as well as with their teachers and students. They knew how to "manage up."

Grange's leaders were courageous with their superiors as well as with their teachers and students. Like many leaders of schools in challenging circumstances, they knew how to "manage up." For example, Gillian McMullen, who was the head who succeeded Hollinshead in 2009, stood up to unfair inspections and against the judgments of district staff when they did not seem to know or understand the school. This was not out of sheer perversity but in order to assert the school's own solutions to the challenges it encountered that its staff knew to be right for the students.

> We had so much documentation and we could challenge [the inspection team]. We will challenge people out of the school like the local authority. We won't take on board certain strategies they might present and ask us to do. We will say, "No, we're going to do it this way. We've thought about it and we don't want your expertise because we've got it in-house." So we were very, very clued up.

INSPIRING LEADERSHIP

It is not enough for outstanding leadership to be bold and courageous. Going first is not enough if no one is willing to follow. Outstanding leadership has to galvanize followers too. It has to inspire them. Most leaders who perform beyond expectations find ways to lift people's spirits and raise their hopes. Until the middle of the 1990s, Grange Secondary School had been managed by "nice" people, but "there was no initiative at all." Then, "all of sudden we got a deputy head in who's got vision, who's got experience of other things."[13] The new deputy was "not tied to the social history of the school and was like a breath of fresh air."[14]

When he became head, Bell met with the governing body responsible for the school and set out his vision:

> He had plans and he brought them to the governing body, and at a time when the percentage of A-C grades [in the GCSE] was minimal, he was able to look to the future and say, "Well in two or three years time, this is what I want and to get that vision across to everybody and working for it."[15]

Staff felt "he was quite a visionary sort of leader. He started to make people believe that this school could be successful."[16] At a time when the school building was run down, the teachers were "taken out and treated."[17] And, "we all got taken off to the local hotel for inspirational presentations and to hear his vision for the future."[18]

Bell "did wonders for this school in about 4 or 5 years."[19] He was "extremely dynamic; very outward going."[20] One teacher felt the turning point was when Bell gave people the sense "we were definitely going places" so they "realized things could be done"; they now "wanted to be part of it" and knew they could do many things for themselves. Graeme Hollinshead generously recalls how his predecessor "brought tremendous charisma. He was inspirational. He certainly got people doing things."

Bell was welcoming. He "understood the children."[21] He took time to know his people, to learn about the staff, to make even the lowest status teachers and support staff feel they were wanted and valued. One teacher vividly remembers her very first contact with the school as a supply (substitute) teacher, when Bell was in charge of supply teacher appointments and coverage.

> He was asking me a lot of questions and explaining about this new senior leadership team and how they were trying to

One of the acid tests of leadership is how well leaders know and treat the people with the lowest pay and status in their organizations.

> create a team of people who would come in on supply. He asked would I be willing to come in and do different subjects, etc, etc. I said that I would. But at the time I was thinking, "Why are you asking me all this because I'm only coming in for one day?" Anyway, I did my day. And there was just something about the place that made you feel welcome. Maybe it was the fact that the guy took the time to sit down and have the conversation. Now people who come here on supply say there is definitely an ethos of being welcome in the school, which I think is about valuing people from a supply teacher coming in for one day, to the cleaning staff, the kitchen staff and the pupils. I think everybody feels that they belong to the school and that their contribution matters.

One of the acid tests of leadership is how well leaders know and treat the people with the lowest pay and status in their organizations. Leadership involves more than raising people's hopes, though. The power of hope is when its promise shows evidence of fulfillment in action. When better times are evident even in small increments of concrete improvement, this can generate upward spirals of further hope and increased confidence that even greater improvements are possible.

> You went from being a teacher at the school that was the worst performing to someone who was working in a reasonable work environment with good facilities, with students who were improving and this was being recognized. I think all that has a very positive impact on you and encourages you to keep on going.[22]

This spiral of confidence and ever increasing achievement worked across leaders, not just during the tenure of one of them. There was a fusion of their contributions over time.

In school after school in our wider study, teachers described how they had felt lost before a key leader arrived. After years of drift, the new leader finally gave them a sense of where they might be going and how to get there. One of the key features of effective leadership is giving people some sense of direction toward a worthwhile destination. This is what the inspirational and dynamic leadership at Grange Secondary School had to offer.

CREATIVE LEADERSHIP

Leadership often entails taking an unexpected, creative, and counterintuitive approach to a longstanding problem. In many underperforming schools, teachers are simply urged to work harder and longer—tracking, monitoring, and managing individual students so they perform better with the existing curriculum. This may produce incremental improvements, but it will not yield the sort of dramatic transformation in results that was needed at Grange Secondary.

Colin Bell took a divergent approach. He put in many hours observing in classrooms. His experiences taught him that the standard secondary school curriculum did not recognize how Grange's predominantly Bangladeshi students learned best.

In *The Element,* Sir Ken Robinson describes how we succeed when we are "in our element"—engaging in something about which we are intensely passionate and for which we have a profound gift.[23] What people's element might be varies. It may be writing, economics, public speaking, performance art, or computer programming. The problem, says Robinson, is that most schools put only a few of these things on the menu and as such, schools don't help children find their element or engage with the ways they learn best—at a significant cost to achievement and creative human development.

Graeme Hollinshead's predecessor could not have known Robinson's exact words, but in his own way, he grasped that Grange's Bangladeshi students were far from being "in their element." The kind of learning they were required to do in a standard secondary school curriculum did not recognize or include the ways they learned best. Colin Bell did. When he first arrived, he went into classrooms and watched how students learned.

> I remember the first term he was here. I felt very strange around him. He never spoke. He never said anything to anyone. He just watched and listened. He really got to know strengths within the school. And he'd wander into classrooms. He actually said one of the ways that we could make rapid progress is to allow the children to do more of what they're good at and more of what they enjoyed.[24]

The school tested students on their learning styles and found they were "very visual, very kinesthetic."[25] Grange therefore made an innovative move to get the curriculum to fit the child by moving it strongly towards visual arts. This meant introducing more vocational courses, and eventually becoming a visual arts college in 2002. This also brought in a boost of 5 million pounds sterling of new resources for buildings and new technology, as well as a number of visiting artists. This was a great act of what has been called culturally responsive leadership—developing empathy for the assets of a community and using these as a basis for increasing engagement with learning and for reaching high levels of subsequent achievement.[26]

Eventually, Grange Secondary School became one of the top two of 30 visual arts colleges in the country and received a range of national awards. With a wider variety of courses in art now on offer, students "were leaving with a higher number of GCSE [examination] passes"[27] and a stronger sense of pride in their accomplishments. Teachers started to feel that the curriculum really was "designed for" and "fits the needs of [the] pupils."[28] Between 2002 and 2004, results just "zoomed" from 15% receiving five A through C grades on the GSCE in the 1990s, to over 70% in 2008.[29]

> Almost every case of high performance we have examined has taken a path that is counterintuitive.

Almost every case of high performance we have examined has taken a path that is, in many people's eyes, counterintuitive. Finland's teachers know their children better partly because they have enough time to be away from them and to think about their needs. Adrian Lim in Singapore was using Twitter as a teaching device when almost everyone else was forbidding the use of cell phones in classrooms. Alberta's Progressive Conservative government promoted teacher-designed innovation in almost every one of its schools, when other governments were imposing greater standardization and high-stakes accountability. And at Grange Secondary School, the same pattern was evident—responsively fitting the curriculum to children and their culture when almost everyone else was squeezing their diverse students into a homogenized curriculum.

This does not mean that Grange Secondary's innovative approach was undisciplined. The curriculum was carefully designed to suit the students. And all the monitoring and tracking of student progress that characterized the emphasis on improvement in the old Third Way system still persisted in the new one. Innovation wasn't an alternative to improvement. Innovation and improvement went together.

DISTRIBUTED LEADERSHIP

Leadership at Grange Secondary School was not just attributable to single individuals. For one thing, the head and deputies worked as a team. When Graeme Hollinshead was Bell's deputy, he was seen as "the practical one who made sure that things happened," while Bell was "the visionary one" who "had the dreams."[30] They "complemented each other tremendously."[31] As a "really good team," these two leaders "started to bring in funding. The facilities started to improve. There was a big program of rebuilding and improving the facilities including things like the staff rooms."[32] This was "the start of Grange School being on its way up."[33]

Over time, it became clear that Graeme Hollinshead was not just the practical sidekick for his big-picture predecessor. Unlike the town's nationally famous comedians, Cannon and Ball, there was no hard and fast distinction between who was the straight man, and who had all the best lines. In time, Hollinshead came to be seen as a "visionary too," with his own "dreams," though in a different style than Bell.[34]

Eventually, although not always instantly, Grange's most senior leaders encouraged and expected others to take collective responsibility for improvement too. Hollinshead tried "all the time to distribute the leadership" and develop teamwork.[35] The team comprised everyone—teachers, learning mentors, teaching assistants, and support staff. Union representatives were always involved early when new directions were being taken. The business manager was complimentary about how everyone would "rally round"[36] when someone had a problem, how Hollinshead knew how to delegate, and how he "lets you get on with it."[37] The leadership of change at Grange Secondary progressed to being a collective responsibility in which more and more people were engaged. Collective responsibility became a form of leadership in itself.

Hollinshead's successor, Gillian McMullen, continued this approach in her involvement of everyone. "It's very much a team effort," she said. "It's not just a team effort by teachers [but] by every member of staff right down to kitchen staff, cleaners. Everybody is helping one another to do even better."

A senior member of the governors of the school who had spent his political life in this working class town believed that "you shouldn't put leadership on the pedestal." At Grange, he said,

> Leadership is part of the team. They're all teachers. They all work together. There's none of this "I can't go straight to the head or I can't do this"; because everybody's got a right to say what they want, when they want, and how they want it.

Through building a culture of trust, warmth, and loyalty—by pulling people in—distributed leadership at Grange turned into the kind of collective responsibility that was evident in Finland, Singapore, Alberta, and Ontario. Hollinshead observed that "the head can't do everything. He's got to have key people in key positions who are accountable no matter what they do." With this collective, distributed, and inclusive responsibility, the head did not always have to be in school, but could be outside advocating for it, and gathering other ideas and insights that could support it. This "constant networking" or benchmarking, even "internationally" was essential.[38] "We're constantly looking for new things. Better things. We might go to different schools up and down the country if we're looking for specific things to improve."[39] So Hollinshead "goes off all over the place." McMullen, his successor, pointed out that "it's just business as normal. When he's not here, you would not notice."

INCLUSIVE LEADERSHIP

Distributing leadership in schools is not only an internal matter. It also involves the community. Effective school leadership is also effective community leadership. For educators at Grange Secondary, the school is about impacting the culturally diverse and financially impoverished community that influences it. The community is regarded as an asset rather than a liability.

A landmark change resulting from a Labour government initiative on "Excellence in Cities" was the introduction of half a dozen paid "learning mentors" into the school around 2001. In North American terms, "learning mentors" are people from local communities who can help with cross-cultural understanding and awareness. The learning mentors had "no timetable; no teaching qualifications."[40] Yet instead of feeling threatened, staff at Grange welcomed people who had "time to support the children."[41] One member of the governing body had previously been a learning mentor at the school himself. The learning mentor, he said,

> was more of a friend of the pupil, helping them to overcome barriers of learning, truancy and problems at home. We would try and help homes, use outside agencies, if it'd help, place information and see if we can get the best out of the child and make sure they do have a good education by the time they leave.

One of the current learning mentors described how she and her colleagues spent their time in the behavioral support unit, intervened in and mediated school fights, and simply "listened to pupils"[42] before putting new strategies in place for them. She described how she would often meet former pupils in the town that was also her own community, when they would show appreciation for what she and other mentors had done for them.

Several teaching staff at Grange Secondary had formerly been students at the school and now provided role models for current students. Learning mentors and teaching assistants were drawn from the local community.

> When I first came 16 years ago there were very few staff who came from the same cultural background as the pupils that we have now. But yet now we've got ex-pupils as teachers. We have classroom assistants. We have learning mentors. We have technicians, all sorts of people who come from the same community as the pupils. I think that is very, very important because they will bring understanding and knowledge to the school as a whole which will help all staff who maybe come from very different backgrounds culturally, religiously and in language terms. The institution is more reflective of the actual pupils in the school, which is a valuable thing.[43]

This kind of inclusive community leadership widens the circle of trust out to parents and community members, increasing their support for children and their learning, and improving achievement and attendance as a result. It's the kind of community leadership we also saw in many other diverse communities and districts in our study—as in the London Borough of Tower Hamlets which, using similar strategies, rose from ranking 149th out of 149 school districts in 1996, to being above the national average on all key indicators today.[44]

> Inclusive community leadership widens the circle of trust out to parents and community members, increasing their support for children and their learning, and improving achievement and attendance.

LEADERSHIP STABILITY AND SUSTAINABILITY

Although the entire senior leadership team at Grange turned over after the barely acceptable inspection report of 1996, many members of the new team actually came from within the school itself. In 2010, the team included people who had been there for more than 20 or 30 years. The school had "a very stable workforce. Many of the staff is still here. There are lots of people who have been here and nowhere else," one 30-year veteran said. "We've all been here a long time and we've seen absolutely massive changes."[45]

> I've been a teacher here for 25 years. I think in some schools, you do get an attitude that "I'm not going to change, I'm going to stick with what I know." Often, here, the older staff and the ones in the management positions are the most open to change. Obviously, that will drive through what happens with the younger staff.[46]

Research on schools in challenging circumstances repeatedly indicates that communities with adults who have had little success at school themselves when they were children, who experience great instability in many other areas of their lives, and who have seen too much instability and turnover of teachers and leaders in their local school in the past, welcome and desperately need their school and its people to be the anchor of stability they find it so hard to get elsewhere.[47] This is the opposite of what happens under the panic-driven turnarounds of Second Way strategies with their constant comings and goings of staff and openings and closures of schools.

Graeme Hollinshead worked at Grange Secondary School for 37 years. He knew the staff, the students, and the community inside out. "The character and context in the school has changed. Staying in the same place has given me breadth of experience I never could have got by moving around the country." Because he had "seen several generations come through the school," it mattered a great deal that "what we provide for the community, for the students is excellent." Hollinshead was not alone in feeling that

> our kids like stability in staff. They want people who they can trust, they know. I was known in the community. In an all-Asian community that's sometimes difficult and we didn't want somebody new coming in with new ideas—because I had already started loads of new ideas.

Hollinshead was not the only one to "come up through the ranks." Leader after leader, he said, had "come up from being a probationary (first-year) teacher here," "came as an assistant head of department" ten years back;[48] "started a career at this school and has never been anywhere else"; "came as a second in department about 15 years ago"[49] then went on to become a department head. More and more teachers and middle-level leaders were former pupils of the school who returned in order to give back to it. Orderly leadership succession and high leadership stability were vital to achieving persistent growth at feasible rates. In business and in education, turnaround tricksters often try to induce quick-fix miracles by changing all the teachers, or moving the leaders in and out. Second Way systems are still stuck on this failed strategy. Sustainable high performance, however, results from high stability among leaders, but with lots of outside communication and periodic refreshment of some staff. This is also evident in the internal promotion patterns of leaders from within their schools in Finland, and in the unwillingness of Canadian and Singaporean systems to adopt U.S.-style turnaround strategies.

> Turnaround tricksters often try to induce quick-fix miracles by changing all the teachers, or moving the leaders in and out. Sustainable high performance, however, results from high stability among leaders, but with lots of outside communication and periodic refreshment of some staff.

CONCLUSION

Grange Secondary School experienced a remarkable turnaround, and this was due to remarkable leadership. The courageous leadership of two headteachers with an ever-widening constituency of senior leaders provided a practical example of what was achievable, and a platform for further improvement. The headteachers modeled what was needed to their staff, and defended what was necessary against unwarranted bureaucratic intrusion. Their dynamism and inspiration was matched in equal measure by perspiration as subject departments improved, results turned around, and students and teachers developed strengthening loyalties to their school. The headteachers did not try to push their school further and further along the customary grain of conventional, tested achievement. They did not confine the school to incremental improvements alone. Instead, they undertook creative and counterintuitive steps to be responsive to students' cultures and to match the curriculum to their culture and learning styles, so they could all be in their element.

Trust grew, collective responsibility developed, and the leadership became increasingly inclusive and so effectively distributed across the school and the community that headteachers could be absent for a day or more without anyone feeling that they had been abandoned or even noticing that the most senior leaders had left. All this occurred in an environment that welcomed elements of change in personnel but also capitalized on and recombined the expertise of highly experienced educators within the school. This avoided the volatile shifts of direction that have sabotaged Second Way turnaround efforts elsewhere. It supported leadership stability and sustainability instead.

Grange Secondary School exemplifies a number of core principles of a Fourth Way approach to educational change under adverse circumstances. Its early leaders had an inspiring dream or vision of where the school needed to go that meant more than just raising the school in the rankings. It increasingly engaged the whole community as knowledgeable and committed partners in serving the students they shared in common. There was a widespread sense of collective responsibility for students' welfare and achievement that extended to responsibility for exercising leadership in the school as well. The school developed a lot of its own leaders from within and created trust and stability in a community where poverty and uncertainty had been pervasive. And it knew how to innovate boldly and also improve relentlessly at the same time, instead of opting for one over the other.

EPILOGUE

Perhaps you've been inspired by this narrative, and would like to visit Grange Secondary School? We are sorry to say that you can't. The school no longer exists in the form that it did at the time of our study. An externally mandated reorganization of all the schools in the town led to its redesignation and reorganization, along with the town's other secondary schools as an "academy"—the English equivalent of a U.S. charter school—despite its strong performance record. The Fourth Way success of Grange Secondary School was quashed by a Second and Third Way ideology of academies that superseded it. This is bringing in its wake many repeated turnovers of leaders and staff.

> The lesson of Grange Secondary School is to take on a challenge that many others would regard as impossible, to embrace disciplined improvement and innovation, and to take collective responsibility among the school's staff and with the wider community for the eventual results. This is the True North of educational change.

Over 15 years, though, Grange Secondary School has shown what a determined quest for educational excellence can accomplish. It left a Fourth Way legacy that must not be forgotten. Grange Secondary School has shown what an architecture of educational excellence can accomplish in an inhospitable policy environment and why educators must sometimes not just cooperate with or capitulate to government policy but swim against the tide of unhelpful political strategies that are directed toward other ends. The lesson of Grange Secondary School is to take on a challenge that many others would regard as impossible, to embrace disciplined improvement and innovation, and to take collective responsibility among the school's staff and with the wider community for the eventual results. This is, in a metaphorical sense as well as a geographical one, the True North of educational change.

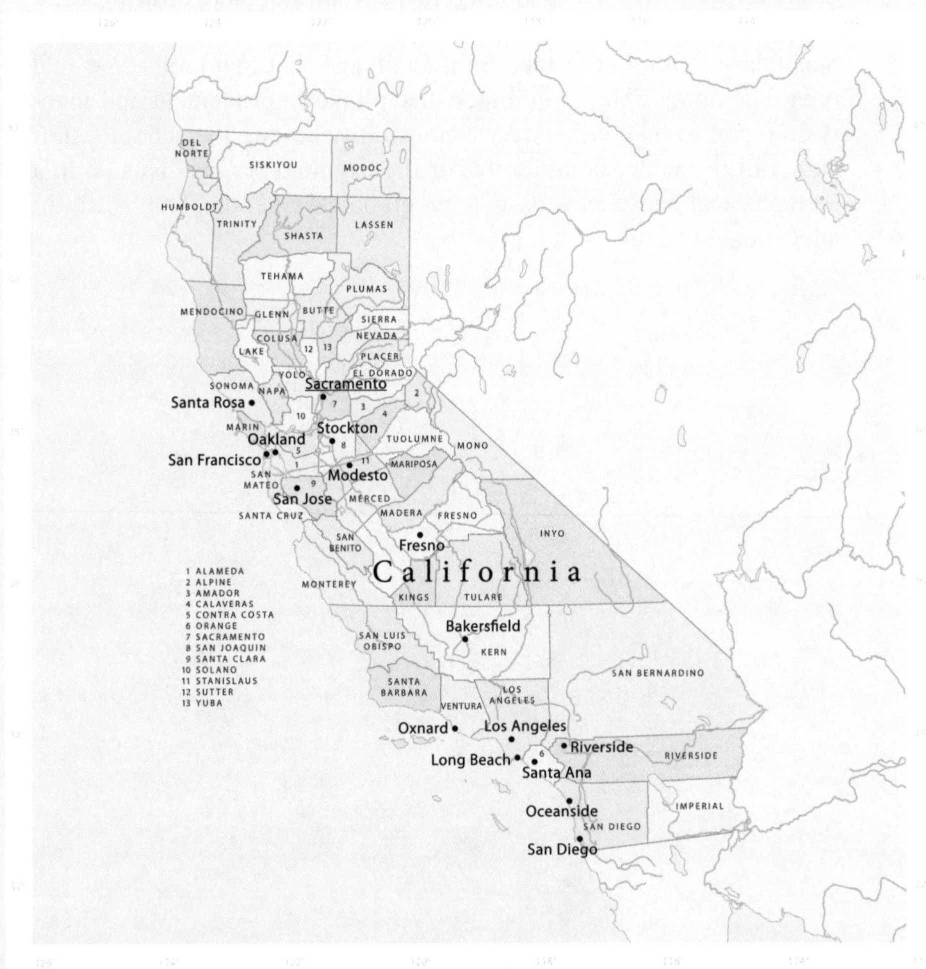
California
DEL NORTE
SISKIYOU
MODOC
HUMBOLDT
TRINITY
SHASTA
LASSEN
TEHAMA
PLUMAS
MENDOCINO
GLENN
BUTTE
SIERRA
COLUSA
NEVADA
LAKE
PLACER
YOLO
EL DORADO
SONOMA
NAPA
Sacramento
Santa Rosa
MARIN
Oakland
Stockton
TUOLUMNE
MONO
San Francisco
SAN MATEO
Modesto
MARIPOSA
San Jose
MERCED
SANTA CRUZ
MADERA
FRESNO
SAN BENITO
Fresno
INYO
MONTEREY
KINGS
TULARE
Bakersfield
SAN LUIS OBISPO
KERN
SAN BERNARDINO
SANTA BARBARA
VENTURA
LOS ANGELES
Oxnard
Los Angeles
Riverside
RIVERSIDE
Long Beach
Santa Ana
Oceanside
IMPERIAL
SAN DIEGO
San Diego
1 ALAMEDA
2 ALPINE
3 AMADOR
4 CALAVERAS
5 CONTRA COSTA
6 ORANGE
7 SACRAMENTO
8 SAN JOAQUIN
9 SANTA CLARA
10 SOLANO
11 STANISLAUS
12 SUTTER
13 YUBA

Chapter Eight

CALIFORNIA

Professional Organizing for Public Good

We have examined systems that perform superbly either as pure or as hybrid models of educational change. We have also looked into a school that turned around against the odds of its challenging and poverty-stricken community and against the lower performance levels and unsuccessful improvement strategies of the wider educational system. Now we turn to an example of systemic educational change that is not only an outlier within an unsympathetic system, but that has raised results by confronting and opposing the system—professionally and legally—to produce better provision, strategies, and outcomes for the most disadvantaged students. This drama takes place in the state of California, and it features two titanic protagonists—the most iconic U.S. living actor-politician, former governor Arnold Schwarzenegger, and one of the world's largest teachers' unions: the California Teachers' Association (CTA).

Schwarzenegger is not averse to self-parody. In the summer of 2004, he was speaking at a place called "Ontario Mills." This was not a small town outside of Toronto, but a large shopping mall in San Bernadino, California. In a stump speech running up to the state elections, in which he alluded to his past career as a bodybuilder and actor, Governor Schwarzenegger, according to the *Los Angeles Times,* "mocked his opponents in the California legislature as 'girlie-men' and called upon voters to 'terminate' them at the polls in November." His legislative opponents, he said, were "part of a bureaucracy that is out of shape, that is out of date, that is out of touch and that is definitely out of control."[1]

This moment of self-parody recalled Schwarzenegger's role as the cyborg Terminator who had returned to the past in order to reshape the future. It was witty, bombastic, and flamboyant. The crowd at Ontario Mills responded by roaring its approval. For observers around the world, it was another piece of evidence that in California, everything was possible—a magic kingdom where truth blends with fiction, all dreams come true, and a bullied child from a small town in Austria could reach the pinnacle of political power. Why put up with the usual bland politicians in grey flannel suits when you can have your very own Terminator eliminating the legislative bad guys and providing endless entertainment along the way?

Californians loved it, and they returned Schwarzenegger as governor in a landslide election in 2006. He was so popular that a grassroots movement began an initiative to repeal Article II, Section 5 of the U.S. Constitution, which requires that all U.S. presidents be born in the country. Schwarzenegger had married into the Kennedy family—his wife, Maria Shriver, was the niece of the late president John F. Kennedy—and with this imprimatur of America's most beloved political dynasty, his pathway to the top seemed assured. But after a series of personal scandals in 2011, the governor's political career was now itself terminated—for the short term, at least.

This was a classic Hollywood narrative—the rapid rise of the improbable outsider to glory as well as his subsequent fall in which the media reveled: a story of rags to riches and back again. This mythic narrative is not just confined to the state's Hollywood-style politics. It is also in the state's schools. In the course of just two generations, California's public schools have moved from being top performers in the United States and the envy of the world, to reaching rock bottom in achievement on almost every indicator.

How has this happened? It can't be because the whole of California is a write-off. California has the world's eighth largest economy, and with 38 million inhabitants, it has the largest population of any U.S. state. There are more Californians than Canadians and more than three times the number of Finns and Singaporeans combined. Silicon Valley remains the undisputed capitol of the global Internet economy. Six out of every ten new patents approved in the United States are issued to firms or universities based in California—more than four times the runner-up state of New York. California is home to more Nobel laureates than any other state and attracts 40% of clean technology venture capital investments—far in excess of any other jurisdiction in the United States or abroad.

But what has happened to California's schools? Back when the Mamas and the Papas were singing "California Dreamin'" and the teen-idol Beach

Boys were wishing that all girls could be Californian ones, the Golden State had a market brand that couldn't be beat. Schools were integral to the allure. Per pupil spending was above the national average, graduation rates climbed year after year, and public universities were tuition-free.

Then in the 1970s, everything started to unravel. First came the oil crisis that drove prices up and supply down. Then came the stock market crash and the unexpected grind of stagflation. In 1978, panicked Californians responded when Proposition 13, the first of many middle-class tax revolts, established a ceiling on local taxes. Packaged as a life-saver for older retirees on fixed incomes, Proposition 13 concealed tax loopholes for the wealthiest Californians and required a two-thirds majority in the state assembly to raise taxes again in the future. The state's schools have never fully recovered. Per-pupil funding fell below the national average in 2000. And by 2003, on the National Assessment of Educational Progress, California's students performed worse than all other states except Louisiana and Mississippi.[2]

This depressing path of increasing disadvantage and accelerating educational decline was not allowed to develop and persist without a battle. As with Grange Secondary School in the North of England and many of its turnaround counterparts, California's educators have had to struggle against fiercely opposing theories of change in action. This struggle is part of our corner store portfolio of successful system-wide change: change that isn't only or always initiated by governments but that is prepared to disagree with and challenge governments and their strategies when children's interests, public life, and the foundational principles of democracy are at stake. In California, the state's architectures of educational change have included Second Way strategies of ever-increasing standardized testing and RTTT guidelines and sanctions that encourage the closure of struggling schools and the forcible reassignment, if not outright dismissal, of the teachers and principals who have worked there. As we will see, these architectures also included legislative provisions that denied poor and minority students the opportunities to learn that were their entitlement.

> In a business-driven world where the word *union* has become as deliberately discredited as "socialist," "public" or even "intellectual," and where millions of dollars have been invested in orchestrated assaults on teacher unions and their members, the CTA provides a remarkable example of positive union involvement in educational change.

Against these reform pressures and legislative barriers, a whole coalition of organizations and forces has battled to defend the rights and opportunities of the state's poorest children and of the professionals who teach them. Not least among them all is the CTA. In a business-driven world where the word *union* has become as deliberately discredited as "socialist," "public" or even "intellectual," and where millions of dollars have been invested in orchestrated assaults on teacher unions and their members, the CTA provides a remarkable example of positive union involvement in educational change. Here, union engagement with change is not a Third Way cooptation by government on terms not of the union's own choosing. It is, contrary to anti-union stereotypes, a Fourth Way dynamo of professionally driven and equity-oriented change that has had to operate within and against the policies and priorities of a tenacious Second Way system.

Over the past six years, we have served as critical friends for the CTA Executive Committee. We have participated in facilitated retreats for on-the-ground leaders of the CTA's reform work, conducted extensive interviews with the CTA and school leaders, and visited schools linked with union-driven reforms. We have witnessed, watched, and sometimes played walk-on parts in a drama of union-driven improvement and innovation that has been motivated by real moral purpose and that has been occurring on a considerable scale. In this respect, our work in this chapter bears some of the hallmarks of an OECD-style case review and some of the characteristics of educational change literature written by change theorists and advisers such as Michael Barber, Michael Fullan, and Ben Levin. Like them, we analyze and write about the reforms and systems which we have sometimes been directly involved in developing.

THE ORIGINS AND THEORIES OF EDUCATIONAL CHANGE IN ACTION

The changes that have been established and driven by the CTA, along with its many partners, have a distinctive theory of change in action that was not perfectly preplanned, but that emerged out of a legislative external battle, an internal institutional struggle, and an emerging professional effort to champion a change that would make a significant difference to the learning and lives of many of California's most vulnerable students. This unfolding drama and what we have been learning from it expresses six distinctive features of the Fourth Way of leadership and change:

1. professional and political capital,
2. courageous leadership,
3. innovation with improvement,

4. intensive interaction,
5. culture of inquiry, and
6. professionals as intellectuals.

1. PROFESSIONAL AND POLITICAL CAPITAL

In 1988, the legislature passed Proposition 98, a measure the CTA supported. It provided a formula for school funding to assure that during lean times, a given percentage of the state's revenues would go to the public schools. This established a foundation for educational funding but professional and political advocacy groups still viewed it as insufficient, especially as legislators found ways to circumvent loopholes in the legislation. Further action was therefore urgently needed.

From 2000 to 2004, a group of plaintiffs from community organizations who were advised by university experts, such as Jeannie Oakes and John Rogers at the University of California Los Angeles, sued the state in *Williams v. California* to remedy funding inequities that discriminated against poor students and students of color.[3] This was a major victory for the families of students from poor and working-class communities in California. Shortly afterward, however, the state again removed billions from the education budget, not only decimating funding gains acquired through the *Williams v. California* lawsuit, but also violating Proposition 98. Governor Schwarzenegger wasn't heroically slaying make-believe opponents on a Hollywood set this time. According to former executive director of the California State Board of Education, John Mockler, the Governor was "consciously and viciously violating the constitution of California."

Incidents such as these have taught educators, students, and the public hard lessons in recent years. Even in the most developed democracies, government is not always the answer in educational change. At times, governments can turn against the very publics they have been elected to serve. At other times, they can seek to circumvent the constitutions they have sworn to uphold. At these moments, teachers' unions, community organizations, philanthropic associations, and faith-based groups have to take the lead instead. This is especially imperative when sectors of the public such as children and young people do not have a voice in the legislative process themselves.

Californians mobilized their collective political capital to battle back against Proposition 13 with Proposition 98. When this remedy faltered, they pushed ahead with *Williams v. California,* which was settled in August 2004. Yet once again they faced another obstacle as more than $5 billion dollars was subtracted from the education budget for other purposes. Now it was the educators themselves, led by the CTA, who mobilized their combined political and professional capital to sue the state (*CTA v. Schwarzenegger*) in August 2005 for failing to meet the minimal funding provision of Proposition 98.

> The Fourth Way shows us what to do when governments fall short.

The Third Way calls on enlightened governments to bring together coalitions of stakeholders who can guide change from the top. Among its other attributes, the Fourth Way also shows us what to do when governments fall short. In California, after direct confrontation and outright conflict, Governor Schwarzenegger was forced to settle the lawsuit in May 2006. Political capital united with professional capital to establish a new platform for equitable educational change.

2. COURAGEOUS LEADERSHIP

The CTA was now in the land of the Chinese proverb—the one where all its wishes had come true. But every victory opens up new territory for additional conflict. Every solution gives rise to a new problem. What would the CTA do with the revenues that had been restored?

A traditional approach would simply spread the funds out across the state on a per-pupil basis. Whether a school was in a middle-class suburb of Sacramento, the opulence of Beverly Hills, or the heart of inner-city Oakland, each student would receive the same amount of money. It all would be spread evenly across the state to implement an idea of equity understood as identical treatment, in which everyone received the same.

But, as in Ontario's special education reform, not everyone agreed that this interpretation of equity would be the fairest distribution of the money, or would produce the best outcomes. Fairness wasn't equated with sameness. For years, Americans have seen how the gap between rich and poor has been widening with every passing decade.[4] One of the consequences of this growing disparity is that the United States has a higher percentage of children living in poverty than almost all other advanced industrial nations, with the only other developed nation behind it in a recent UNICEF study being the United Kingdom.[5] As for the black-white achievement gap that has been the focus of so much policy attention in recent years, the magnitude of the gap remains, in the words of one detailed analysis, "pervasive, profound, and persistent."[6]

In Ontario, when special educators sought to address the needs of their students through the ESGA project, the government was on their side, but in California, the CTA had to force the government to do what was right. The moral stakes were clear. The CTA had been trying for years to help the schools that were struggling the most in the state: those that were serving high numbers of students of color, often in conditions of great poverty. "We had been doing a number of low-performing schools initiatives," Joe Nuñez, the associate executive director of Governmental Relations for the CTA, told us. "They would get funded and there would be these small projects and then a crisis would hit and they would defund the program." Exasperated by the lack of sustainable change, CTA leaders saw a chance with the settlement of the lawsuit to help those students who most needed additional assistance, and to do so with measurable and lasting improvements. CTA had the potential to revolutionize its approach to educational change in the state, but this would also mean a disruptive innovation or change in the role of the union itself.

Many different people and groups—from classroom teachers to activist educators to CTA leaders—had to come together to support a new and better approach to educational change in California. John Mockler was "on the side of investing the money in problems that have been more intractable than others—the most needy, most difficult schools in California." According to Justo Robles, the manager of the Department for Instruction and Professional Development at the CTA, these schools were trapped in a "world of hurt" that existed in a parallel universe to California's abundance. For a former teacher like Mary Rose Ortega, who had worked in such schools and is now on the CTA Board of Directors, the issue was one of simple "equality for Latino kids, especially the Spanish-speaking kids," who most often found themselves in the schools with the least qualified teachers and the least enriched curricula." Ortega believed that behind the financial troubles lay problems that could only be fixed by "empowering the teachers and getting the community into the schools."

Not everyone agreed with this empowerment agenda. Mockler recalled "that argument was fierce. It was strongly opposed by almost every education group. The CTA alone took the bows and arrows." For the CTA, once the dust had settled following the legal settlement, courageous leadership now meant accepting shared moral responsibility for student learning outcomes. It meant taking on public leadership and accepting a measure of accountability, with all the accompanying risks if projects failed. The CTA was transitioning from being an oppositional movement that resisted government reform to becoming a leader of a newly defined statewide alliance for change.

Outwardly, the CTA was leading a disruptive innovation in the California school system. Deep inside, an even more dramatic change was occurring within the union itself. Older sentiments favoring "industrial" or "job protection" unionism over the newly evolving professional model still prevailed among many members of the CTA, as among U.S. teacher union members more broadly.[7] Older educators had no quarrels with an industrial union model that had given them job security and a decent salary they never enjoyed before their unions joined up with the American Federation of Labor and the Congress of Industrial Organizations (AFL-CIO) in the 1960s.

But in many ways this deal with the labor unions turned out to be a Faustian bargain for the teaching profession. Along with traditional industrial unionism came collective bargaining arrangements based on the premise of equivalence of labor in factories organized for mass production. But excellence in teaching bears no resemblances to assembly-line work. Excellence in teaching requires careful planning with an engaging curriculum, knowledge of one's students, and skills in managing large numbers of sometimes challenging and unruly youngsters. Such a skill set calls for judgment, discretion, and adaptability, not an interchangeable circuit of workers repeating manual tasks one day after another. Yet this blue-collar model of labor unionism came to inform and shape the profession in the United States during subsequent decades, with real costs to the unions in terms of members' loyalty to and identification with them.

In California and elsewhere, this older generation of teachers—who looked to their unions primarily for benefits and job security—is ceding place to younger successors for whom job security is no longer enough. Research on teacher unions reveals that inactive union members typically appreciate the *pragmatic* dimensions of their union membership in terms of salary and security and they also acknowledge the *cognitive* benefits they acquire through having an organization that advocates for their professional dignity. They disagree, however, with what they observe to be teachers' unions' readiness to protect teachers who shirk their responsibilities and neglect their students, for example. Younger teachers want their unions to demonstrate not only *pragmatic* sensibility and *cognitive* advancement, but they also want their unions to project the *moral* purpose of their profession. They want their unions to be engaged not peripherally and intermittently but centrally and continuously in improving learning for their students.[8]

CTA leaders had to disrupt their organization and culture to become a professional rather than blue-collar union with an unquestionable moral purpose.

It isn't easy for any organization to change, but CTA leaders saw the trend lines and knew the union would have to adapt. They had to disrupt their organization and culture to become a professional rather than blue-collar union with an unquestionable moral purpose. With the courageous advocacy of activists like Ortega and policy leaders like Mockler, Nuñez, and Robles, the CTA defined a new role for itself as a real partner in an inspiring new government policy. As CTA leaders were delighted to discover, the union's new role in the forefront of a change that went right to the heart of teachers' classrooms suddenly began to increase the levels of active involvement among the union's younger members. Fortune favored the brave.

3. INNOVATION AND IMPROVEMENT

Educators have become accustomed to what Seymour Sarason called "the modal process of change" in which outsiders plan and provoke desired changes while giving teachers little authority in how they implement them.[9] The CTA sought to find an alternative approach to this modal process. "We wanted to build a case that we could show to policy makers," said Dean Vogel, president of the CTA. "We have to give teachers an authentic role in determining the pedagogical needs of students. Don't rest that in Washington DC or the state capitol. Rest it at the school site. Give the teachers an authentic role. That's the real issue."

Over the summer, in collaboration with California state senator Tom Torlakson and John Mockler, the CTA worked out the details of a bold new act to supplement Proposition 98—the Quality Education Investment Act (QEIA). The idea was to create a network of QEIA schools to attack the most persistent problems of educational underachievement in California. All of the designated QEIA schools would be in the bottom two deciles of California public schools as measured on the state's Academic Performance Index (API), which is a composite of different assessments. The schools that now comprise a statewide change network would receive $2.7 billion by the time the program was completed. Those funds would be used to

- reduce class sizes,
- increase the recruitment and retention of qualified teachers,
- enhance the quality of teaching, and
- improve student learning.

Some of these priorities were controversial. For example, for critics waiting to challenge union-driven reforms, the plan to reduce class sizes flew in the face of classic, blind-control studies of class-size effects that show little or no impact of smaller classes on student achievement.[10] Spending resources on reducing class sizes might therefore be viewed as one example of how unions make life easier for their members without providing any benefits to students.

Of course, in some circumstances, reducing class sizes will indeed have little effect. If teachers mainly teach their students from the front of the class, it doesn't matter whether they are teaching a big class or a small one—the level of students' engagement with the curriculum is still pretty much the same. But once the pedagogy gets more sophisticated and differentiated, once it starts to take into account varying student needs, and once teachers start to become capable of teaching in this way, then smaller class sizes do make a difference.[11]

CTA leaders and educators in QEIA schools understood this situation. They also grasped that the nature of teachers' work and the strategies to promote individual student achievement had progressed significantly since the classic findings of class size study. A principal from an elementary school that had climbed out of "Program Improvement" status with the help of QEIA remarked, "If you're using data to target instruction for students and to do one-on-one conferences—if you're providing students with extra time and support—if you're going to provide timely, specific feedback for students—you need smaller class sizes." In today's world of data-driven improvement, of relentless attention to reducing achievement gaps, and of intervening the moment any individual child falls behind, smaller classes are indispensable. Smaller class sizes enable teachers to know their students as individuals, to have the time to assess their work thoroughly and to tailor their responses to every child's needs—especially those with special needs who are on individual educational programs. "What QEIA allowed us to do is incredibly significant," the principal commented. "Without it, our achievement wouldn't have been so steep."

One of the ways to enhance teacher quality has involved taking a different and distinctive approach to school leadership. The CTA's own data from surveying their members have shown that there are two leading factors that persuade expert teachers to move from suburban to urban schools. The first is reduced class sizes to enable them to better meet their students' learning objectives, and the second is the opportunity to work for an outstanding principal who would respect, inspire, and support their efforts.

Unusually, as a teacher's union, the CTA therefore supports identifying and developing high-quality leadership. In this respect, the QEIA provided funding to locate and develop exemplary principals with participatory leadership styles who could harness and empower the professional capital of their staffs and engage parents and community members in improving learning outcomes.

Overcoming earlier funding cuts, the QEIA would provide all high school students with access to guidance counselors, with no school assigning more than 300 students to any single counselor. Each school would have a QEIA site leader who was a classroom teacher. The site leader's role was to ensure changes would be made in the schools to lift student achievement. QEIA site leaders would be responsible for monitoring their schools so that schools would comply with not only the letter, but also the spirit of the law. Funding would go directly to QEIA schools rather than to the central office of school districts. This would ensure that educators within the schools could innovate to determine the best ways to improve the learning of the students at their sites.

To select the QEIA schools, the California Department of Education undertook a purposive sample of the roughly 1,500 schools in the state that were most desperately in need of an infusion of new resources based on their academic progress indicators. The sample reflected the racial and ethnic diversity of California, including socioeconomic factors, English language learners, and rural, suburban, and urban schools. Of the students in QEIA, 80% are of Hispanic ethnicity, 9% are African American, and the rest are Asian-American, of European descent, or Native American. Fully half of the students in elementary schools are English language learners, as are 34% in middle schools and 27% in the high schools. Over one-fifth of the schools are in the Los Angeles Unified School District, the second largest school system in the United States.

The innovative aspect of QEIA was not that it restored funding to struggling schools and students. This has been a feature of federal policy ever since the first passage of the Elementary and Secondary Education Act in 1965. The real creative components of QEIA were threefold. First, the union challenged the state. Second, it took charge of allocating resources to underfunded schools. Third, it made sure that the funds went directly to the schools, and the teachers in those schools. For educators used to operating with little authority beyond the boundaries of their own classrooms, this was a significant step up in real responsibility. This is not outside-in innovation in how to restructure schools by moving teachers in and out of them, or by manipulating teachers' pay to reward or punish a few of them. It is inside-out innovation that builds a platform of professional capital where classroom teachers become the dynamos of change themselves, not in this school or that school, but across hundreds of schools in one of the world's largest systems.

For the first time in their careers, teachers from the QEIA schools we studied said they had the resources and decision-making power to inquire into their own teaching practices and to learn about the pedagogical and curricular issues that they most needed to address. In this respect, they were stepping up alongside their peers in Alberta as leaders of innovation, improvement, and inquiry.

This empowerment of teachers entailed circumventing the central offices of school districts, and channeling resources directly to schools. In some cases this undoubtedly threatened some district administrators who were accustomed to controlling how schools distributed resources. Indeed, some districts had to leave the project because they insisted on bringing in high-priced expert trainers and on concentrating resources on central office positions rather than on directing these resources to embedded initiatives, driven by teachers within the schools.

4. INTENSIVE INTERACTION

In our five other examples of high performance, intensive interaction stimulated and also held together effective improvement and innovation. These included the Singaporean educators who excelled in a fast-paced culture of "we eat and we run" productivity, the educators participating in AISI in Alberta, and the Ontario teachers and principals in the Essential for Some, Good for All initiative. Similar Fourth Way peer networks of teachers learning from teachers were evident with the QEIA in California. Teachers enjoyed working in many different kinds of teams in their schools. These included grade-level cohorts, teams that focused on students with learning disabilities, and project groups that worked on parent outreach programs. "There are so many pieces that we're trying to put together for our students," said one teacher whose school had a Coordinated Services Team to integrate before-school care, afterschool care, and health services for its children. Educators in this same school turned themselves into *de facto* community organizers who worked tirelessly with parents and children in the neighborhood to ensure they had access to athletic clubs, service activities, immigration services, and housing and health care providers. QEIA gave this school additional staff positions so teachers could get release time for home visits to parents of students with the greatest needs.

Teachers knew this freedom would only be successful if they had genuinely strong principals who were open to their ideas, eager to support collaboration, and focused on their students and their learning. One elementary school had an inspirational principal who her staff described as a "total workaholic." She kept her teachers fully informed of QEIA and related reforms by sending them e-mails at all hours of the day and night. The staff at this school felt that beyond the usual procedures for students with learning disabilities, a "student support team" needed to be created "which is more individualized with a deeper level of interventions and strategies that we discuss." Teachers convened and followed an agreed-upon protocol to help them to understand the students' experiences from multiple perspectives and to explore better strategies to keep them fully engaged and consistently learning.

Regardless of the origins of the QEIA program as the result of a lawsuit against the state of California, principals did not need to be rebels or revolutionaries to make the QEIA program work in their schools. Schools we visited were tidy, classrooms were well organized, and students were well behaved. In the words of Jim Collins and Morten Hansen, innovation was disciplined.[12] The quest for flawless execution was obsessive.

In one building, where 99% of the students were on free or reduced-price lunches, QEIA meant the teaching staff was able to build its own professional culture. Some of the teachers' observations of each other were through formal "learning walks" with protocols that they developed themselves to improve their teaching. In another school, teachers said that QEIA funds enabled them "to hire somebody to come in and take over their classrooms so they can go and observe for an hour. We have three days a week now when people are actually in other people's classrooms and we also have time to debrief, which was missing before." Teachers visited each other's classes in a model where nothing was set in stone: "It was all very fluid and it was based on assessment." Along with other established staff support programs, such as peer assistance and review, teachers found they had many opportunities to receive precise feedback to strengthen their instruction.

In the Third Way, data come to matter more than people. In Fourth Way systems, numerical data (along with other kinds of evidence and judgment) become teachers' companions, not their commanders.

How different all this intensive professional interaction is from the "contrived collegiality" of administratively imposed and hierarchically controlled professional learning communities that characterize many Third Way systems.[13] In the Third Way, data often come to matter more than people. Teachers find themselves sitting beside spreadsheets studying numbers instead of being in each other's classes where they could be investigating each other's teaching and identifying new and effective strategies they could use with their own classes. Learning walks or instructional rounds become tools of administrative evaluation and compliance rather than prompts for professional conversation and inquiry. This is not to claim that data don't matter. The point, rather, is that in QEIA, and in Fourth Way systems generally, numerical data (along with other kinds of evidence and judgment) become teachers' companions, not their commanders. Data-driven action is replaced by evidence-informed interaction and intervention focused on children and young people first, and data second.

This does not mean that QEIA was able to cast out the worst demons of data-driven obsessions from its large number of participating schools. Even in the best QEIA schools, educators struggled to learn how to reconcile professional judgment and inquiry that use data thoughtfully and intelligently, with a continuing Third Way state system that still uses test-score data to drive the actions and interventions of teachers' professional learning communities.

5. A CULTURE OF INQUIRY

Eric Heins, a former fourth-grade teacher in the Bay Area who is now vice president of the CTA, chairs the CTA's QEIA Work Group. He recalled that the entire initiative from its very origins in the lawsuit against Governor Schwarzenegger "was completely new" for him. For the CTA to assume this new responsibility, "we had to be able to reach into the schools in a different way."

At the heart of this transformation was a recovery and regeneration of excellent teaching. "I saw QEIA as a program for getting back to good pedagogy," Heins remarked. As a music teacher, he had seen the arts decimated even as his students thrived under his own instruction. A philosophy of teaching and learning grounded in sound principles of cognitive science, such as Lev Vygotsky's "situated learning," was being sacrificed to the imposed models of factory-like standardization.[14] "I saw this as one way of fighting back what was going on," Heins said. Once the lawsuit was settled, QEIA turned teachers back from followers into leaders. It enabled them to bring out their best practices and to develop their practices with others.

Recovering, renewing, and reinventing teaching and teachers builds the basic resources of professional capital that yields repeated returns in continuous improvement and student achievement.

In every case we have examined so far, and in every instance of Fourth Way reforms and even their best Third Way counterparts we have seen, educators who learn from each other and put their learning into direct action, reap benefits for their students. According to one OECD report, "Teachers who exchange ideas and information and coordinate their practices with other teachers also report more positive teacher-student relations at their school. Positive teacher-student relations are not only a significant predictor of student achievement, they are also closely related to individual teachers' job satisfaction."[15] Recovering, renewing, and reinventing teaching and teachers builds the basic resources of professional capital that yields repeated returns in continuous improvement and student achievement. The QEIA strategy has set about building and rebuilding this professional capital among its teachers.

Teachers and principals in the QEIA schools we visited kept detailed notes on their students' achievement data, in striving to identify those areas of weakness that merited increased attention. At one of the schools, the older teachers had previously blamed transient students for low test scores. But when their new principal demanded that they take a closer look at the data, they found that the students who were in their school for a longer period of time than the transients actually did *worse* on state tests. The principal believed that teachers had been holding low expectations for their students. The teachers would say things like "we don't want to stress the kids out with academics because they have to socialize." Educators had not been preserving core instructional time in literacy, for example, and even though the school was not making adequate yearly progress, they were taking students out of class during key instructional units for a variety of pullout programs and movies.

In previous top-down turnaround strategies, the response might have been to impose a prescribed program or to fire some of the worst teachers, perhaps. But the deeper problem was that the school had no culture of professional collaboration or inquiry. The previous principal had separated the teachers from each other in a strategy of "divide and conquer." Older teachers learned to keep their heads down in a culture where critics of the principal were punished in small-scale wars of attrition. Critics would be assigned new grade levels every year, overlooked for funding opportunities when they arose, and denied field trip requests. New teachers confessed that the school was "scary, to be honest. The lack of motivation among the kids was shocking," one teacher remembered, but the previous principal had made no effort to bring the adults together to develop a collective response.

The new principal responded by "asking a million questions," in the words of one teacher. "It was so exciting. He was a person willing to learn. We started exchanging articles and books." Older teachers who had participated in the nationally renowned Bay Area School Reform Collaborative for many years, but had learned to go underground during the previous principal's leadership of the school, were able to replicate ideas they had gathered there using "critical friends" protocols to address issues like race and language differences that often go unaddressed in orthodox professional learning communities. This principal's openness to and acceptance of the great and sometimes superior instructional skills and knowledge of his staff created a spirit of collective exploration and risk taking. "He had never been a principal before, and that put us all at the same level," one of the older teachers building recalled. The principal modeled curiosity and expected the classroom teachers to do the same. "What he did was empower the teachers," the district superintendent said.

Working together, the educators in this school created a new professional culture of risk and inquiry. Experienced teachers were revitalized as their questions were honored and their aspirations for their students were affirmed and also challenged. They became intensely interested in the learning of each and every child. "Personally, the human relationship is far more important and the data come after that," one fifth-grade teacher said. Daily classroom observations of children were brought together with student achievement data in a process of mindful data analysis.[16] Evidence of learning on multiple measures provided points of departure for reflecting on what was actually transpiring with the students.

Engaged inquiry, not imposed intervention, proved to be the secret of turnaround success. API indicators "went off the charts." Teachers stopped requesting transfers out of the school and dug down deep to exploit new pedagogies that they learned about through QEIA-supported professional development opportunities and site visits to other schools. Years of the loss of middle-class parents to a charter school and another public school with a more affluent population base stopped. Surveys no longer indicated that students' favorite parts of school life were recess and their friends, but showed how students loved learning and being able to read and to write. Intensive interaction among professionals and their partners led to definable improvements in students' engagement and achievement.

6. PROFESSIONALS AS INTELLECTUALS

> It is not just the job of system leaders to be thinkers in action. It is a fundamental right and responsibility of all true professionals–including teachers and principals in their schools.

However important the CTA as an organization might be, in the end it is only the educators who are in a system's schools day in, day out, who can provide the necessary stability and sustainability for improving learning over the long haul. Principals and teachers have to recognize their central leadership role as dynamic thinkers and actors who drive learning forward in their schools. It is not just the job of system leaders to be thinkers in action. It is a fundamental right and responsibility of all true professionals—including teachers and principals in their schools. The intellectual caliber of the principals and teachers we met in QEIA schools and their school districts, and the ethical integrity they brought to their work, are impressive in this respect.

- One principal had studied John Rawls's *A Theory of Justice* and brought Rawls's eloquent advocacy for the dispossessed to his everyday life as a school leader.[17]
- A superintendent had read the research of Anthony Bryk and Barbara Schneider on trust in schools,[18] shared his dissertation on the subject with other leaders in his system, and grasped that innovations will be unsustainable if the culture of the adults is permeated

with mistrust. This leader spread social trust to others so they would take risks to identify their areas of weakness and ask for assistance.

- A third educational leader applied the research on professional learning communities to help her teachers pursue their own areas of inquiry with their colleagues, in ways that connected classroom and standardized test data to their day-to-day interactions with and observations of children.[19]
- Veteran teachers, whose professional knowledge had been recognized by the participatory leadership style of their principal, had accumulated abundant professional capital over many years of their careers by being involved in powerful national networks of teacher learning such as the National Writing Project and the Critical Friends network.

In professions such as teaching, everyone needs to be an intellectual who constantly inquires into their practice and pushes the boundaries of that work through how they understand and reflect on it. Being an intellectual can't be an elite prerogative, and it can't be carried out in privacy without colleagues to challenge and expand one's ideas. It has to be a shared professional imperative.

RESULTS

What has been the impact of these union-driven strategies of innovation and improvement? Have they just made the lives of their teachers a bit better, or have they had a positive impact on student learning and achievement? Overall, there was a significant increase in growth in student achievement in the QEIA schools from the planning years of 2006–07 to subsequent years until 2010. The schools that were selected to participate in QEIA are outperforming comparison schools by a substantial margin at a number of levels. Especially encouraging are the results for traditionally underachieving students.[20] In its *First Progress Report* to the legislature and the governor, the California Department of Education stated that "an analysis of the Academic Performance Index (API) of participating [QEIA] schools indicates that their average performance exceeded the average performance of schools statewide, as well as an appropriate comparison group of schools (i.e., those eligible but not selected to participate), in the early years of the program."[21]

A separate analysis by Vital Research, an independent research agency in Los Angeles, found that "on average, QEIA schools are making greater gains in API with African-American and Hispanic students, English Language Learners, and socioeconomically disadvantaged students than similar, non-QEIA schools."[22] These gains are especially large at the elementary level. QEIA elementary schools have done well when contrasted with those in a control group, and there have been significant gains for QEIA schools compared to non-QEIA schools when it comes to vulnerable populations in certain areas at the secondary school level.[23] Significantly greater gains for QEIA schools compared to schools with similar demographics have been posted for African Americans in mathematics, Hispanic students in English/language arts and mathematics, and socioeconomically disadvantaged students in English/language arts and mathematics.

Although the outcomes data are still at an early stage of the change process, as an aggregate they validate QEIA as a union-led strategy. They show that an outside-in *challenge* to the government, succeeded by the outside-in legislation and nature of QEIA that then supports inside-out processes of professionally driven innovation and improvement, has reaped benefits for students who otherwise would have suffered unfairly. Tables 8.1 and 8.2 show outcomes data for QEIA as an aggregate and at the elementary school level.

Table 8.1 Academic Performance Indicator Growth in QEIA and Non-QEIA Schools Overall

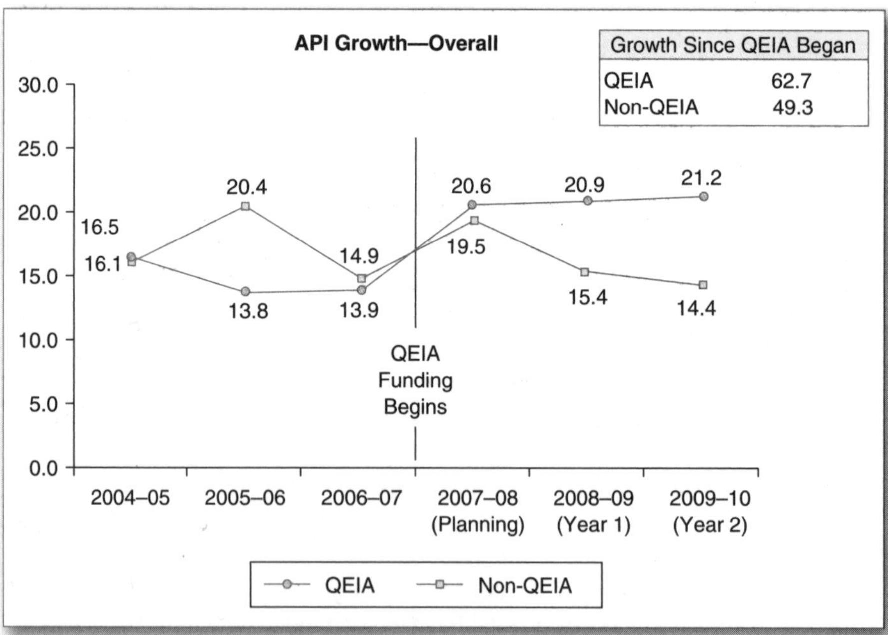

From Malloy, C. L., & Nee, A. K. (2010). *Quality Education Investment Act lessons from the classroom: Initial success for at-risk students.* Los Angeles: California Teachers Association.

For information on the nature of the scoring and growth measures on California's Academic Performance Index, see http://www.cde.ca.gov/ta/ac/ap/

Table 8.2 Academic Performance Indicator Growth in QEIA and Non-QEIA Elementary Schools

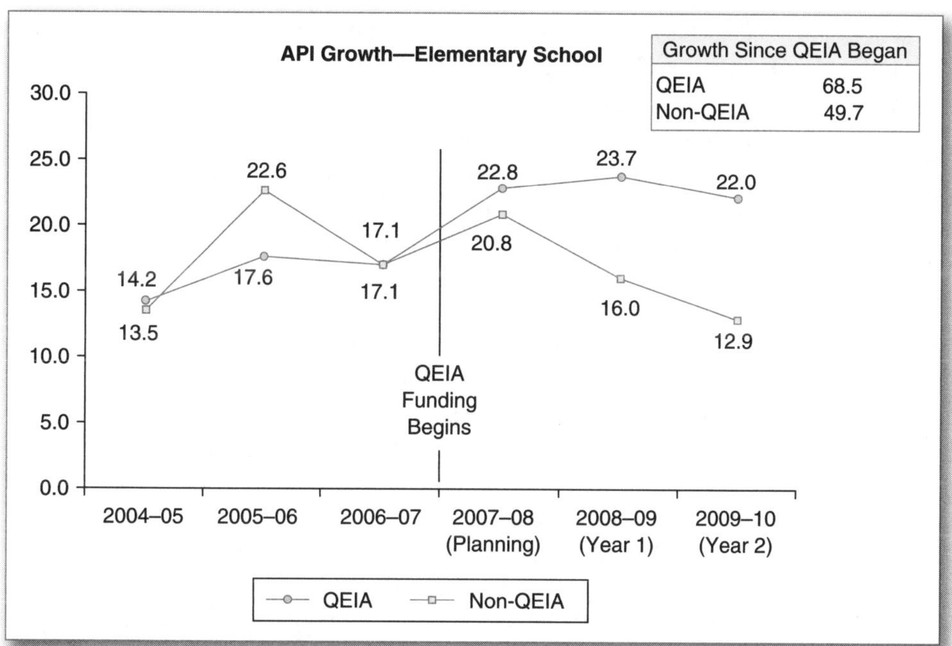

From Malloy, C. L., & Nee, A. K. (2010). *Quality Education Investment Act lessons from the classroom: Initial success for at-risk students*. Los Angeles: California Teachers Association.

For information on the nature of the scoring and growth measures on California's Academic Performance Index, see http://www.cde.ca.gov/ta/ac/ap/

EXPLAINING THE IMPACT

To understand how schools achieved these gains, we interviewed teachers and principals working in QEIA schools. The findings from Vital Research corroborate other studies of large-scale reform. Schools that exhibited high degrees of growth had visionary and inspirational leaders who distributed responsibilities equitably, were inclusive in considering faculty requests for targeted professional development, and studied a range of data and evidence (not just standardized test scores) to guide and monitor their progress. Teachers in these schools were effusive about the high levels of collaboration and professional responsibility they were experiencing and, with their principals, were driven by a mission of raising achievement for all students. These teachers were leading from within, between the world of the system and the student.

There were, however, some limitations to the impact of the QEIA reforms. These were evident in two areas: the absence of consistent impact on high schools, and resistance by principals and district administrators to some QEIA provisions.

First, like many large-scale reform initiatives elsewhere, high schools proved to be harder to change than other parts of the system. High schools in general are much more difficult to improve than elementary schools, in part because of their size, and also as a consequence of their "balkanized" departmental structures.[24]

These internal problems of high school cultures can be magnified by external conditions. One recent survey of 277 high school principals in California indicated that policy turbulence has created numerous problems for high school reform in particular.[25] As a result of the global financial crisis that began in 2008, the state of California has been battling off bankruptcy and the impact on high schools has been devastating. Of the principals surveyed, 49% indicated that their students have experienced fewer instructional days since 2008, 32% reported reduced afterschool programming, and 65% stated that they had either eliminated or reduced summer school programs. Furthermore, 86% reported that their teachers' access to professional development has been reduced and 78% stated that they had experienced cuts in school improvement programs. These cuts occurred in a system that was already spending $2,371 less per child annually than the national average before the credit crunch occurred in 2008.[26] In the words of John Mockler, California is "a very asset-depleted school system. The state, in the last few years, has decimated school systems."

A second limitation in QEIA implementation was one of leadership. California is a large, underfunded system, and even with QEIA school site leaders in place, problems still arose. Some principals circumvented the spirit of the law and did not include staff in decisions about professional development funding. Instead, they conspired with central office administrators at the district level to control QEIA funds and to use them for their own favored programs. "It's just been an incredible struggle for us for the money to flow to the right places," one CTA leader stated. "But if I was one of those guys and I was trying to keep my school alive or trying to keep my district alive and I had that big chunk of [QEIA] money sitting there, what some of them do is they allocate it in chunks. They hold onto it. It's kind of like their savings account."

A common complaint among administrators in education is about "resistant" teachers who fail to demonstrate fidelity to the system's programs and thereby undermine promising reform initiatives. QEIA sometimes had the opposite problem: principals and central office personnel who resist union-led and professionally driven change strategies to improve student achievement when they threaten the system's monopoly over budgets and its mechanisms for maintaining control. This has led the CTA and the California Department of Education to discontinue membership of those schools in the QEIA network. Professional unionism requires careful guardianship of scarce public resources.

A FOURTH WAY NETWORK IN A SECOND WAY SYSTEM

Some of the struggles of QEIA's Fourth Way reform are directly attributable to having to operate in the state's continuing Second Way (and slightly Third Way) environment. In California, resources are scarce, tested performance data are dominant, and threats of closure or intervention—due to failing to meet threshold test targets on adequate yearly progress—have been ubiquitous and imminent. The potential for disruptive innovation within QEIA, in this respect, always has to face the push for improvement on state test scores. While some administrators, along with their counterparts in other systems, endorse new assessment cultures with enthusiasm, teachers are often more dubious about their benefits because the annual test score is "the only data point that they use to talk about whether a school is doing a good job or not." Staff in one elementary school stated that over 80% of their instructional time and all of their data entry and analysis were dedicated to just three subjects: reading, writing, and mathematics. They longed for a broader curriculum with more potential for creative teaching and learning but found this was constantly pushed to the margins in the single-minded push to raise achievement. Despite all the achievements of QEIA within the existing state context, it was able to make little impression on the constraining system of data and testing that drove the wider policy system.

However, the state itself, like many systems elsewhere, is now registering signs of taking a new direction. Twice former governor Jerry Brown, who replaced Governor Schwarzenegger in January 2011, refused to sign new legislation in the form of State Bill 547 that proposed to add yet more tests to the schools. Governor Brown dismounted from the dead horse of standardized reform, and commented:

> Over the last 50 years, academic "experts" have subjected California to unceasing pedagogical change and experimentation. The current fashion is to collect endless quantitative data to populate ever-changing indicators of performance to distinguish the educational "good" from the educational "bad." Instead of recognizing that perhaps we have reached testing nirvana, editorialists and academics alike call for ever more measurement "visions and revisions." There are other ways to improve our

> schools—to indeed focus on quality. What about a system that relies on locally convened panels to visit schools, observe teachers, interview students, and examine student work?[27]

Elsewhere, state after state has challenged the prevailing U.S. federal reform strategy by securing waivers from Washington concerning NCLB's adequate yearly progress provisions. If every state has a waiver, it's like every child having a hall pass. When everyone is an exception, the credibility of the rule has collapsed. Given this breakdown of the Second Way, it may be that QEIA is less of a change exception, and more a harbinger of better reform designs for the future.

CONCLUSION

> The QEIA is a Fourth Way demonstration of what can happen when educators stand up for students in underresourced schools, shift from an industrial to a professional model of unionism, and undertake the necessary advocacy to provide the needed revenues to those schools.

The QEIA is a Fourth Way demonstration of what can happen when educators stand up for students in underresourced schools, shift from an industrial to a professional model of unionism, and undertake the necessary advocacy to provide the needed revenues to those schools. The early achievement results in the QEIA schools indicate that additional resources matter and are being used to improve student learning. They are QEIA's idea of a moral economy. From teachers' perspectives, the changes capitalize on their foundational professional commitments to help children learn. "It's the norm," one teacher said. "That's what we do. It's intrinsic within us." For this reason, as union advocacy goes deep into the heart of classroom practice, young teachers become inspired and feel that this more professionally oriented and morally centered union is the right place for them and their activism.

The CTA has mobilized professional and political capital to address unfair policies. It has breathed Fourth Way spirit into schools struggling within and against Second Way policies. But arguably the most disruptive aspect of its innovation is that in doing all this, it has started to transform itself from a First Way boomer generation union—one of basic collective bargaining and contract agreements—into a broader Fourth Way professional association—one that puts its teachers in the vanguard of improving teaching and learning.

Chapter Nine

POINTERS FOR PRACTICE

The Global Fourth Way in Action

The four cases of Finland, Singapore, Alberta, and Ontario, along with the two from within England and California, point to six distinct yet interlinked examples of educational excellence. Finland is the most pure of the Fourth Way systems. Its stringent qualification criteria secure the highest professional standards for educators. The public has high investment in and trust of its schools. Within a framework of general steering by the central government, the collective responsibility of educational professionals and democratically elected local authority guide all decision making.

Singapore, Alberta, and Ontario have each been moving from the Third Way to the Fourth through their own distinctive approaches. Along with Finland, they also have high levels of teacher qualification, strong trust in public education, and an ingrained ethic of professional collaboration. Unlike Finland, they do place some emphasis on centralized and standardized test results, yet, paradoxically, they also show countervailing tendencies toward innovation in their schools through the Alberta Initiative for School Improvement; the Teach Less, Learn More policy in Singapore; and the inclusive strategy of Essential for Some, Good for All in Ontario.

The cases of school-generated change against the odds in England and of union-driven reform in California reveal the challenges that face educators when they battle to assert Fourth Way philosophies and practices but are constantly pushed back by data-driven pressures and standardized testing procedures in the wider system. These pressures limit

The Fourth Way is also *not* a Way whereby official policy statements scapegoat educators or teachers who then react defensively by falling back on the contract or by refusing to pursue any kind of collective commitment to improvement whatsoever.

how far educators can go in promoting innovation along with improvement. Yet despite surrounding systems that are unsympathetic to their goals, the success of these educators is still considerable.

The six cases reveal how hard, yet how necessary it is to distill common change principles from these varying examples of educational excellence. Let's start with what we *don't* find in Finland, Singapore, and Canada. We *don't* find governments pushing charter schools, fast-track alternative certification programs, and salary bonuses for teachers who get the test scores up. We *don't* see systems testing all students in Grades 3 through 8 on reading, writing, and mathematics with a national Ministry or Department of Education setting the goals from afar, year after year. We *don't* come across governments setting up escalating systems of sanctions and interventions for struggling schools and endless rotations of principals and teachers in and out of schools that erode trust and destroy continuity. And we *don't* find a centralized and standardized curriculum that is prescribed and simplified to the point where it might be teachable by people with little preparation or with only temporary commitments to teaching as a career. The Fourth Way is also *not* a Way whereby official policy statements scapegoat educators or teachers who then react defensively by falling back on the contract or by refusing to pursue any kind of collective commitment to improvement whatsoever.

What *do* we find instead? We *do* find a lot of leadership stability and sustainable improvement at the system level, that establishes a platform for innovation to take off in districts and schools. We *do* find educators who have gone through excellent university-based preparation programs that are also backed up by extensive practice in schools, and who study research and bring a stance of inquiry to the work they do with their students every day. We *do* find a highly respected profession along with an engaged public that lets these trusted professionals bring their individual and social capital to bear in their work.

In high-performing countries and provinces, there is a strong teaching profession backed by powerful and positive professional associations that are in the forefront of educational change. There is also a strong public system, a means to forge a common good and a shared future in a better life for all.

In high-performing countries and provinces, there is a strong teaching profession backed by powerful and positive professional associations that are in the forefront of educational change.

There is also a strong public system and a widespread belief throughout the society that public education is not just a way to provide opportunities and advantages for individual children, but also a means to forge a common good and a shared future in a better life for all.

The evidence of our corner store case studies that is largely consistent with the repeated findings of international cornerstone organizations like the OECD is clear: marketplace models, and carousels of principal rotation or endless openings and closings of schools, are not part of high-achieving systems. These policies create panic in the short term and fail to lift up the profession or develop its collective capital in the long run.

There is a better way ahead for everyone—a Global Fourth Way of educational change. Not all the elements of this Fourth Way are present in every example of high performance in this book. But the ones we pick out are evident in enough of them to comprise something that stands above and beyond any one case—something that provides a direction for educational success that takes us on a different route and toward another destination than that of market competition, bureaucratic control, and stalled attempts to achieve success. To summarize and synthesize, these key principles come down to 15 Fourth Way factors. The first six principles comprise the basic pillars of purpose that establish a system's purposes and direction, support it in doing its work and enable it to innovate and improve in ways that benefit all students and the society. The next group comprise five principles of professionalism that give the system its dynamic energy, underpin its ethics, and build its shared professional capital. The final four factors act as catalysts of coherence that hold the system together and it give it the stability and sustainability to complete its work well. Together, these 15 principles revisit, revise, and recast the defining features of the Fourth Way that are outlined in our earlier book and that are summarized in Figure 1.1 within this text.

THE SIX PILLARS OF PURPOSE

1. *an inspiring dream* that moves a nation or a system forward and places teachers in the forefront of shaping that nation's or system's future;
2. *education as a common public good* that secures widespread support and participation from the vast majority of the people;
3. *a moral economy of education* that provides sufficient resources to boost the system's capabilities wherever it can, and makes

prudent economies in areas that do not undermine educational quality or equity, whenever it must;

4. *local authority* within broad central parameters, as a process of public engagement, a way to respond to diverse communities, and a means to forge collective professional responsibility for curriculum development and school-to-school assistance;
5. *innovation with improvement* as a disciplined and integrated process, not as a set of mutually exclusive options, or necessary sequential stages;
6. *platforms for change* that enable people to have the capacities to help and develop themselves, rather than pipelines for delivering reform from the center to the schools.

THE FIVE PRINCIPLES OF PROFESSIONALISM

7. *professional capital* that is created by selecting teachers from the top end of the achievement range, by engaging them together in curriculum development and shared inquiry, and by increasing retention of teachers until they reach the years of experience where they will be at their best;
8. *strong professional associations* that agitate for positive changes to benefit students, rather than just opposing reforms that are seen to do the opposite;
9. *collective responsibility* for all students and the improvement of teaching, rather than individual autonomy from any interference, or imposed accountability that eliminates professional discretion;
10. *teaching less to learn more* to support learning in depth rather than superficial coverage of imposed curriculum content;
11. *mindful uses of technology* that concentrate on how to improve teaching and learning rather than becoming fascinated by new programs and devices for their own sake.

THE FOUR CATALYSTS OF COHERENCE

12. *intelligent benchmarking* where many educators learn from the successes of their counterparts in other nations and systems, rather than policymakers engaging in competitive bench-pressing to outperform each other in the international rankings;

13. *prudent and professional approaches to testing* that do not distort the quality of teaching and learning as a result of testing almost every grade, or as a consequence of linking test results to high-stakes targets for system improvement or to competitive incentives for performance-based pay;
14. *incessant communication* as way to create system coherence through the strength of that system's culture rather than through the rigidity of its aligned bureaucratic structures; and
15. *working with paradox* rather than striving for sameness and standardization.

These are the fundamental principles of the Global Fourth Way. But wherever you are, whatever you do—whether you are a teacher, a school leader, or a system leader—the most significant issue now is what these principles mean for your own work. How can you turn these principles into action? What pointers do they provide for your practice?

"Pointers" are like the signs and signposts that are encountered on a hike. Sometimes they can be wooden posts with arrows that literally point you in the right direction. In other cases, they may be a splash of paint on a tree or a rock—reassuring you that you are on the right track, indicating that you have to take a sharp turn, or letting you know how far you still have to go. They indicate ways to go, paths to follow, and steps to take that will help you reach your destination.

This chapter sets out what we believe are the most helpful pointers for bringing the Global Fourth Way to life in your professional practice. They are directed to three different constituencies within the profession. The first pointers are for the leaders who are responsible for developing, changing, and steering whole systems. The second set of pointers is for principals or headteachers in charge of individual schools. Last, but by no means least, the final set of pointers is for the teachers who make up the thousands, and in some places, millions of change agents who affect all the young people in a nation in ways that can last for the rest of those people's lives. Every level of influence is important, but these pointers for practice will have their greatest impact if they are addressed by all parts of the profession together.

SYSTEM LEADERS

It doesn't matter how much bottom-up ferment there is in a system or how much lateral learning is occurring among teachers, principals, and schools—there will always be an imperative for excellent leadership at the top. System leaders don't only have to take care of indispensable administrative requirements. By design or default, they also set the direction for and shape the overall professional culture of their schools. Without their careful stewardship and constant vigilance, even the best educators and the most eager students will falter.

Based on the detailed evidence of our six cases of high performance, Global Fourth Way system leaders, we believe, must pay attention to six pointers for their practice:

1. Create an inspiring and inclusive dream.
2. Communicate incessantly.
3. Benchmark intelligently.
4. Test prudently and professionally.
5. Develop professional capital.
6. Preserve local authority.

1. CREATE AN INSPIRING AND INCLUSIVE DREAM

When Nelson Mandela was imprisoned on Robben Island, and all reading matter was forbidden, the dream that he and his fellow prisoners would one day be the leaders of a racially just South Africa gave them the determination and the ingenuity to steal discarded newspaper fragments from the sandwich wrappings of their jailers. They knew that without literacy, there would be no leadership for them in the future.[1] After Finland's economy collapsed and one in five adults was unemployed, the dream of the nation's leaders and then its people was to become a world-leading knowledge economy. Following years of cynicism about public education, Ontario's incoming premier decided to make the improvement of education his top priority. With a long-standing reputation for resisting other people's changes, and after considerable inner debate and struggle about its mission as a union, the CTA courageously and counterintuitively decided to lead a mammoth effort to turn around hundreds of the lowest performing schools in California.

In 1996, the London Borough of Tower Hamlets, which had a student population similar to that of Grange Secondary School, was the worst performing local education authority (school district) in England, but when Christine Gilbert took over as its director of education, she insisted that poverty would be no excuse for failure.[2] Neighboring Hackney was England's newly lowest performing local authority and one of its six poorest boroughs in 2002. But when the head of the independent organization that took over control of the authority started his new job, he announced that "I believe that at the end of this journey you are going to be proud to work in Hackney. People are going to recognize you because you work in Hackney."[3]

These were impossible dreams. But look at the results. The African National Congress, once branded as a terrorist organization and spurned by many nations, led its country beyond apartheid. Finland became the world's highest-performing national educational system and a global leader in economic competitiveness. Ontario now has a world-class reputation and provides practical lessons for others in advancing systemwide reform. Within a decade, Hackney and Tower Hamlets were performing well above the national average. And California's QEIA schools are showing clear signs of improvement on the very measures that the CTA once derided.

The Global Fourth Way begins with an inspiring and inclusive dream. The more impossible the dream, the more inspiring it will be. The greatest dreams take an organization's biggest problems and turn them into its greatest triumphs. What is your inspiring and inclusive dream for your organization? Don't just think about it and keep it to yourself. Share it with others. Talk it into existence, day after day, one conversation after another. Follow it with action. Persist despite all obstacles and incomprehension. Tell people they will be proud, and then show them something or lead them through something they can be proud of. Unless we have dreams, we have nothing. Be inspired. Dare to dream.

2. COMMUNICATE INCESSANTLY

Finnish educators approach everything with a problem-solving mentality and a sense of collective responsibility. Singapore's society and its schools are held together and animated by endless intensive interaction. AISI leaders create lively learning communities in which educators share new ideas they are piloting in their classrooms with one another. The new leaders of Grange Secondary School took the time to communicate their vision to everyone—even the lowliest substitute teachers, and the learning mentors from the community. The CTA has a teacher leader in every one of its QEIA schools.

The style of interacting may look very different in Finland than it does in Singapore or Northern England. But constant communication is an indispensable feature of all six examples of educational excellence. Be with the people you lead to show interest in their work and constantly check for "weak signals" in everyday relationships rather than through episodic evaluations. This is the essence of Global Fourth Way thinking and acting.

3. BENCHMARK INTELLIGENTLY

Successful organizations never rest on their laurels. They are always searching for ways to keep moving ahead. *Bench-warming* organizations just sit on the sidelines and don't get involved in the game. They ignore international research and when they want to improve they only look at themselves and never explore elsewhere. They are too busy watching their own game to learn from anyone else's.

Bench-pressers are interested only in outmatching competitors. Their aspiration is to find a fast way to outdo them at any cost, in an obsession with victory and performance numbers for their own sake. It might be becoming number one, belonging in the top five, or something similar. Driven by their competitive quest, they become blind to the value of everything else.

Bench-markers, on the other hand, want to *learn* from other high performers, so they interact and exchange ideas with them constantly. Adrian Lim in Singapore sends his teachers to conferences all over the world, so they can share their successes and learn from the successes of others. His country's leaders say they give away their best ideas because this makes them keep inventing their own. Two of PISA's highest performers—Alberta and Finland—have formed school-to-school exchanges and partnerships with each other, learning more about vocational education in one case, and afterschool activities in the other. The leaders of Grange Secondary School networked nationally and internationally with other schools and also partnered with lower-performing schools that needed their assistance. These are examples of intelligent benchmarking in which educators compare themselves against others to learn things for themselves.

So how can you benchmark intelligently? First, challenge the mentality that international benchmarking is just "edu-tourism" and an expensive waste of time. Often your critics are the ones who want to keep all the external trips and internal control to themselves, while they keep you in the dark to struggle on your own. In an age of relentless globalization and demographic change there is no substitute for directly engaging with educators in other systems to see what is change mythology and what is real and practical success. Join one of the growing number of international networks of schools and school systems. Travel abroad with your colleagues and select some ideas and strategies that hold promise for your own situation. If your school has started to achieve success and has accomplished real improvements with innovation help a lower-performing school or system in your area to get better. In helping others, you will also find that you learn a lot yourself.

Take a vacation out of the country and while you are abroad, visit another school or system for two or three days that is still open for business. There's nothing like wandering about in the classrooms and corridors of another country to see with fresh eyes the things you had come to take for granted in your own. Reach out. Be inquisitive. Learn from the best. And try to ensure that you give your people chances to do this as well, instead of hogging all the travel opportunities for yourself.

> Never believe that your system or country is so infallible that you have nothing to learn from anyone else.

Above all, never believe that your system or country is so infallible that you have nothing to learn from anyone else. After Deng Xiapoing visited Singapore in 1978, he went home to Beijing to introduce the power of markets to his country. Sometimes the tiniest nations have a lot to teach the mightiest behemoths.

4. TEST PRUDENTLY AND PROFESSIONALLY

Tests are a part of life. Without driving tests, there would be carnage on our roads. Without health checks, we might miss the early warning signs of potentially fatal illnesses. And without clear performance data about passes that have been made or shots that have been blocked, players and their coaches would be less able to pinpoint the weaker points of their game.

Education is no different. In a busy classroom with many insistent demands, tests can give teachers feedback about how well each of their students is or is not progressing. Tests enable educators to make early identifications of and interventions for children who have learning disabilities. The challenge of the Global Fourth Way is not about whether to test; it is about what kinds of tests should be used and how often testing should take place.

A prominent part of the Second and Third Ways is high-stakes standardized testing of student achievement and, to a greater or lesser degree, teacher and school performance. This practice is defended in terms of ensuring public accountability, setting transparent targets for improvement, and providing objective data that pinpoint the interventions that are needed to ensure excellence and equity. Even in the best Third Way systems, though, we have seen that the attachment of testing to high-stakes outcomes leads to perverse incentives that distort the teaching and learning process and drive many teachers to focus mainly on those students who will provide the biggest and quickest yield in achievement results. These limitations in the testing system detract from the other real strengths of Third Way reforms, and make it much harder for educators in reform networks like QEIA and at schools like Grange Secondary to maintain their extraordinary success against the odds.

What are the alternatives? Finland's high-achieving educational system does not subject students to annual batteries of high-stakes standardized tests. Finnish students *are* tested frequently by their classroom teachers for diagnostic purposes on a curriculum that teachers have largely developed themselves. But while the system confidentially tests samples of students, there are no public annual assessments of everyone's performance.

Finland is not the only answer to the excesses of high-stakes testing, though. Other countries such as Scotland have also operated without high-stakes tests, but with comparatively weaker results. At the same time, nations that perform on a par with Finland, such as South Korea, have done so while retaining standardized tests in some form or other.

Finland shows us only that it is *possible* to achieve exceptionally strong results without high-stakes testing; not that it is *necessary.* So, taking all the international high performers together, what are the crucial testing criteria that separate the Fourth Way from its Second and Third Way counterparts?

Like Finland, Singapore and Alberta do not establish annual governmental targets for student attainment that then drive and distort the behavior of teachers and leaders throughout the system. Along with Ontario, systemwide tests are also administered in only one or two grades, so any distortions that might occur tend to be restricted to just one grade level or another. Testing in these systems is *prudent,* not pervasive. It is part of the system but does not dominate or distort it.

Testing is *prudent,* not pervasive. It is part of the system but does not dominate or distort it.

Moreover, all of these high performers are now looking to moderate their existing testing systems, or mitigate their most negative effects. Singapore's former education minister has insisted that the nation's students must be prepared for "the test of life," not a "life of tests." Alberta is committed to finding a better alternative to its existing testing system. Calls to review Ontario's EQAO are also gathering momentum, especially given conditions of economic uncertainty and austerity when reductions in testing can yield savings for the budget.

Pulling back from high-stakes testing does not mean an end to educational assessment, though. Albertans have made assessment for *learning* a favored part of AISI cycles and a systemic component of improvement along with innovation across the province. Ontario educators use assistive technologies to help special education students improve their achievement on provincial tests because the goal is to improve *learning* and the ways in which all students can demonstrate it. *Learning* is the true purpose of schools and the point of testing and all assessment should be to support that learning, not diminish and distort it. Assessment and testing, in this sense, should be professional more than political—to improve practice and enhance genuine outcomes rather than gaming the system to get the best-looking results.

So if you are system leader, avoid testing almost everyone, every year. Develop the skills of all your teachers to select, design, and deploy their own assessments. Invest in research and development to create high-quality diagnostic tests. Circulate them around professional learning networks. Make them available to everyone by putting them on the web.

At a system level, sample student achievement on a variety of different subjects that change and cycle through from year to year to maintain effective monitoring without encouraging people to game the system.

Make sure that *all* subjects—including science, foreign languages, the arts, and social studies—are assessed with purpose and prudence so that students experience an education that is deep and balanced rather than shallow or narrow. Concentrate on developing the quality and capability of all your teachers, because the more the public trusts its teachers, the less it will feel the need to keep checking up on them.

5. DEVELOP PROFESSIONAL CAPITAL

Anglo-Irish playwright George Bernard Shaw, famously or perhaps infamously coined the expression "Those who can, do; those who can't, teach."[4] In high-achieving systems, though, the public doesn't disparage teachers but honors and supports them. In Singapore, civil servants from the Ministry of Education and faculty from the National Institute of Education are regularly "seconded" to schools to connect their work to the realities of teaching and learning. Finns would rather marry a teacher than someone from almost any other profession because their qualifications are impressive, their work is fulfilling, and their prestige is high. A huge system-level turnaround began in Ontario when voters threw out politicians who had stigmatized teachers as being lazy and ineffective in favor of ones who would prize and promote the assets of the profession.

Valuing the profession starts with signals sent by system leaders and policy makers at the top. The signals are evident in how leaders speak about teachers, of course—whether they praise teachers as influential professionals who shape the future of the nation, or disparage them and their unions for perpetrating failure and obstructing political change. The signals of symbolic capital that leaders send out are also apparent in what leaders do. System leaders can't become so bogged down in the details of their jobs that they have no time to visit schools and to talk with students and their teachers. Fourth Way leadership begins with leaders showing up, so they feel the pulse of learning that is beating in their system's classrooms and schools.

Fourth Way leadership begins with leaders showing up, so they feel the pulse of learning that is beating in their system's classrooms and schools.

There is a lot that others can do to develop teachers' professional capital. The leaders in Grange School and the QEIA schools distributed their leadership to develop professional capital among the teachers around them. Alberta develops teachers' professional capital by engaging teachers in designing innovations that improve teaching and learning. Singapore offers different career tracks for teachers to maximize their opportunities for professional growth. Finland involves teachers in curriculum development that unavoidably also turns into excellent professional development.

Developing professional capital is an opportunity you should rightfully be offered, and a personal responsibility that should never be spurned.

But whatever the system provides in the way of support, developing professional capital ultimately has to begin with professionals themselves. Educational professionals have to do what *all* professionals do: study research, observe one another, accept critical comments along with positive ones, and constantly upgrade their skills to promote their clients' good. Developing professional capital is an opportunity you should rightfully be offered, and a personal responsibility that should never be spurned.

6. PRESERVE LOCAL AUTHORITY

It's easy to understand why critics of public education have had a field day attacking local control of schools. Competitive elections are necessarily adversarial, and who wants to listen to adults hurling insults at each other when children's futures are on the line? Except when there is virtual one-party rule, as with the People's Action Party in Singapore or the Progressive Conservatives in Alberta, the leadership transitions that are part of local self-governance can sometimes undermine the stability that is needed to carry through long-term plans.

Districts and local authorities can sometimes be slow, ineffective, and lack urgency. They can be subject to patronage and corruption. As we have seen in California, they can stifle the energy and initiative of professionally driven changes. Takeovers of districts by the state, private organizations, or nonprofits have sometimes produced superior results to the ineffective districts they replaced. In England, the Cooperative movement has not only now become the sixth largest part of the banking sector as the public seeks to invest in more responsible forms of capitalism, but the movement has also started to form large chains of schools, based on cooperative principles, and working together for the common good. These developments point to the inexorable urges to reestablish community even when free markets threaten to destroy it. At the same time, just as the existence of ineffective corporations or the onset of financial collapse should not incline us to put an end to markets, the damage caused by some poorly performing school districts and local authorities should not be an excuse to eliminate these forms of local authority and control altogether.

Now is not the time to put local democracies up for auction. It is time to galvanize them into action.

Ontario's school district leaders have been the dynamos of the province's special education strategy. Finland's educational excellence rests upon a foundation of common good and commitment to community that is the strength of local municipal democracy. It is therefore important to preserve local control of public schools where it is already effective, and to reinvent it where it is not. Now is not the time to put local democracies up for auction. It is time to galvanize them into action.

As a system leader, develop your personal sense of local authority by having visibility and legitimacy among your schools and your staff. Be present; be available; be known. Distribute as many new resources as possible to the schools where they will make a difference, rather than concentrating them in the district office. Support the capacity of schools to help themselves and each other by funding their capacity for mutual assistance. Resist creating more and more district positions that produce legions of temporary consultants and armies of intervention specialists in burgeoning bureaucracies of top-down control. Control less; lead more.

SCHOOL LEADERS

In *The Talent Masters: Why Smart Leaders Put People Before Numbers,* Bill Conaty and Ram Charan found that the best corporations recruit top people and give them progressively more difficult tasks with increasing levels of support so that they will find their careers engaging and their talents fully utilized.[5] In too many educational systems around the world, we are missing a "talent masters" approach, and it is not helping students.

The Global Fourth Way of educational leadership recruits school leaders who have long tenures as teachers in schools so that they have the necessary professional capital to inspire and guide classroom teachers. They have abundant support from inside and outside of their schools as they step into new and unfamiliar roles as principals. They prosper from relative stability in their roles so that they have time to know and build trust among their teachers, capacity to develop and distribute leadership among others, and credibility within the communities they serve. They benefit from opportunities to network, interact with, and find support and stimulation among other leaders. Stability, support, stretching, and challenge—these are some of the things that systems can provide for their school leaders. But what should school leaders do for others and themselves? Four pointers for practice can help school leaders advance the Global Fourth Way in their schools:

1. Embrace paradox.
2. Be courageous, not fearless.
3. Personalize; don't just customize.
4. Improve and also innovate.

1. EMBRACE PARADOX

> "A foolish consistency is the hobgoblin of little minds, adored by little statesmen and philosophers and divines." –Ralph Waldo Emerson

"A foolish consistency is the hobgoblin of little minds, adored by little statesmen and philosophers and divines." These are the words of American philosopher Ralph Waldo Emerson.[6] There is too much foolish consistency in education today. High-achieving systems thrive not on consistency but on paradox. Grange Secondary School showed that a successful route to school improvement is through curriculum innovation *combined* with the persistence of tracking progress and test-score monitoring. Finns spend more time out of the classroom than teachers in other nations, in order to understand their children better within it. The California Teachers' Association sued their state before moving on to long-term collaboration with it. Singapore has been able to reconcile competition with cooperation, central coordination with school-based innovation, and teaching less with learning more. It embraces the future and the past. The teachers' organization in Alberta opposes the very tests that its members have participated in developing.

A paradox is a seemingly contradictory statement that on closer examination turns out to be true. Fourth Way leadership is all about working with paradoxes, not striving for linear alignment. If you give away your leadership, it will strengthen your authority. Embrace the oxymoron of disciplined innovation. Show that increased creativity need not threaten performance on standardized tests. Be an instructional leader who recognizes that you are not the school's greatest expert on instruction. Give away your best ideas so that you will be under pressure to keep inventing new ones. Understand that helping others will also help yourself. These are some of the positive paradoxes of the Global Fourth Way.

2. BE COURAGEOUS, NOT FEARLESS

Leadership needs courage: the courage to head into unknown territory, to overcome resistance, to make a judgment call when the evidence isn't clear, and to take the first step forward when fear holds everyone else back. One of the world's greatest experts on the psychiatry of leadership, Manuel Kets De Vries, reminds us that courageous leaders are *not* fearless.[7] Only emotionless psychopaths have no fear. It is what we do with our fears, how we face them, and whether we do the right thing anyway, despite the wounds that may be inflicted upon us, that defines whether we are courageous leaders or not.

Alberta's education minister Dave Hancock didn't only urge his school leaders to be bold. He was bold enough himself to state in public that true innovation necessitates occasional failure. Three Ontario special education superintendents took the brave step of "managing up" by writing to their deputy minister and urging him to engage and recognize the province's middle-level leaders by giving them the resources and responsibility for serious special education reform. Do you have the courage to "manage up" when circumstances demand it?

The CTA led the lawsuit against their governor because the Constitution and the life chances of the state's most disadvantaged students demanded it. A male principal in a California school was courageous enough to acknowledge that his largely female staff knew a lot more about instruction than he did. He followed their instructional leadership so he could provide school leadership more effectively. Can you find the courage to admit that you don't know everything and that you need to follow your teachers' leadership sometimes?

A dream is only a fantasy unless you have the courage to follow it through. What pain are you prepared to suffer, what ridicule are you willing to endure, what opposition are you ready to face down in order to fulfill the dreams that will transform the lives of others? Lack of courage is rarely displayed by a giant leap in the wrong direction. It is usually to be seen in a gradual shuffle to the side, away from the spotlight, beneath the parapet—a result of many tiny steps that slowly take you to a lesser place where you never dreamed you might end up.

Lack of courage is rarely displayed by a giant leap in the wrong direction. It is usually to be seen in a gradual shuffle to the side, away from the spotlight, beneath the parapet.

Being courageous means taking on a challenge. Challenge your teachers to raise their expectations for all their students with the help of every resource you can muster. Support and challenge your superiors to meet their responsibilities, provide the necessary assistance, avoid the easier options that are available to them, and be the best leaders they can be. But most of all, when the Olympian heights of political and corporate power entice you, when testing agendas distract you, and when the policy fashions of the day start to diminish you, challenge yourself to be the courageous leader that your own parents and children would be proud for you to be.

3. PERSONALIZE; DON'T JUST CUSTOMIZE

It's hard not to notice that online companies recommend books and films based on your past consumer choices. Your musical playlists can now be selected for you, based on the artists or genres you enter into a music choice program. In business or advertising, these kinds of adaptations are often referred to interchangeably as *personalization* or *customization.* Whichever term is used, the idea is to draw on the memory tools of digital technology to support and attract customers by directing them quickly and easily to the sorts of products they have frequently purchased in the past.

In education, advocates of personalization and customization argue that students should be able to choose courses that are available online and in school and to organize schedules and curricula that accommodate their preferences. They want to replace factory schools with digital tools. If students don't like history in general but enjoy military, women's or black history, why not let them choose curricula that appeal to those interests? If they find that they are wide awake at midnight but sound asleep at 8 a.m., why not let them take an online course in the evening instead of marching them off to school to the sound of the bell before it is barely light? If the life of your aboriginal family is dictated by the hunting seasons and the movement of game, or if your traditional rural community makes demands on its adolescents as it has always done during the times of planting and harvest, then shouldn't schools be open all hours and all year, and couldn't educational staff be available anytime, anywhere to provide education for diverse communities with different schedules and lifestyles? In schools as in farming, there is a time to reap and a time to sow, and a need to recognize that this time is not the same for everyone. By adapting the goals of schools to students' diverse personalities and interests, advocates of personalization and customization claim, we can capture students' motivation to learn more effectively.

But personalization can be taken too far. Just because something is fun or effortless doesn't mean that it is educationally sound. Being able to click and drag a computer image or YouTube clip onto a digitized class presentation isn't the same as, or an adequate substitution for, analyzing a difficult text or defending a point of view. Should students not learn about climate change or the Holocaust because they might find these topics upsetting? Should they not be required to exercise the discipline of going to school at a regular time even if that means that can't sleep in when they like, as training for work, a lesson for life, and a way to ensure they will not jeopardize their long-term future by giving in to short-term gratification?

> *Customization* is the proper term to describe flexibility, adaptability, individual preference, and personal choice in student learning and consumer behavior alike. *Personalization* should be reserved for deeper forms of personal exploration and discovery.

We can reconcile these opposing arguments for choice and constraint respectively by distinguishing more carefully between what is personalization and what is customization. *Customization,* we believe, is the proper term to describe flexibility, adaptability, individual preference, and personal choice in student learning and consumer behavior alike. *Personalization* should be reserved for deeper forms of personal exploration and discovery. These terms and what they signify are not mutually exclusive—you can have an education that is both personalized and customized—but they do address different issues.

Here we draw inspiration from the Latin expression *cura personalis*—the "care of the entire person"—that is part of the philosophy of education at Boston College, the Jesuit and Catholic university where we teach. Although neither one of us is Catholic, the important tradition of Jesuit pedagogy asks educators to work with students as whole people, who should not just be indulged with entertaining platforms in their classes but should also be deeply engaged and involved in personal quests for meaning. As a landmark UNESCO report pointed out some years ago, education is not only about learning to know and learning to do—though these things are, of course, important. It is also about learning to be, personally and spiritually, and learning to live together in community and society.[8]

> Education should not just be reduced to point and click activities–it should also be about developing personal meaning and engaging with the purposes of life.

Grange Secondary School connected its curriculum to the life interests and purposes of its predominantly Bangladeshi student population. Singapore students have to put the needs of the nation and the community before the interests of themselves. Finland requires that all students engage with the visual arts until the end of secondary school, with musical instruments paid for by the state. Education should not just be reduced to point and click activities—it should also be about developing personal meaning and engaging with the purposes of life.

So *do* integrate technology as a teaching and learning resource in all your classrooms so that everyone, especially but not only those with the greatest disabilities, can access and respond to their learning in ways that maximize achievement and engagement for them. And *do* make school schedules and online options as flexible as possible to increase opportunities for all students—particularly those from impoverished backgrounds where parents may be working all hours, or from violent neighborhoods where conflicts and gunshots turn sleep into an elusive luxury.

At the same time, also ensure that the curriculum engages students with the life purposes of their diverse communities—that it engages with the struggle for understanding and meaning in their own lives and cultures. And, through excellent and inspiring pedagogy, with and without technology, *do* introduce all students to the great plot forms of classic literature, to the powerful generic ideas and not just the easily memorized formulae of mathematics and science, and to the heroic quests and struggles that are embedded in world history and ancient mythology.

Don't persist with a curriculum that is standardized, factory-like, depersonalized, and alienating. But don't reduce deep personalization to mere customization either. Above all, true personalized learning requires educators to treat students as flesh-and-blood human beings, not as customers who can be pacified with gateways and gimmicks.

4. IMPROVE AND ALSO INNOVATE

Innovators and improvers usually divide into two camps. Indeed, there are many who believe you have to do one instead of the other, or even before the other, in a necessary sequence of staged development. Just like pain comes before gain, grueling scales precede glorious melodies and art can only be indulged after the basics, so too, it is believed, must risky innovation be attempted only once a firm foundation of incremental improvement has already been established.

Based on their observations of improving school systems around the world, this is exactly what the cornerstone consultancy group McKinsey & Company recommends. They have proposed a set of developmental stages that begins with tight structures, strong prescription, and central control.[9] It then progresses through successive and carefully calibrated stages of slowly relaxing control, to culminate, only at the very end, with the innovative and democratically inclusive pinnacle of Finland.

This sounds persuasive and makes intuitive sense to people who believe you have to be strict before you can be kind, that you must eat your broccoli before your steak, and that you have to hold tight before you let go. At a basic level, the developmental strategy carries an essential truth. It is true enough that you can make little positive change of any kind until you have laid down some ground rules, made the environment safe, and established some basic trust: just like the leaders at Grange Secondary School in the early stages of its transformation. And over many years, it is also true that Singapore and even Finland had a lot of centralized control before they began to embrace innovation. But the principle isn't universal, and in its extremes, it may not even be desirable.

Consider the examples of educational excellence we've observed. Ontario has had more than eight years of a centrally driven and somewhat prescriptive literacy and numeracy strategy, following a chaotic period of conflict and disinvestment in public education. But before that, in the memories and within the capacities of most of the province's teachers, change strategies were highly innovative and professionally inclusive. They had a systemic and sustained focus on professional collaboration, for example, that one of us, along with other change leaders like Michael Fullan, had contributed to since the early 1990s.

The CTA has started to drive up results by abandoning the repetitive failures of external control and intervention in favor of returning to the first principles of good teaching, developed and led by teachers themselves. As soon as it had calmed down the school's behavior problems, Grange Secondary School moved toward culturally responsive teaching and learning that connected the curriculum to the students' lives and learning styles. This was the alternative to shackling them and their teachers down with imposed standardization, or to insisting that the school had to go through numerous intermediary stages of change before it could finally do what was truly needed.

So if your school or system is in chaos, you may have to go down to the basement command and control center for a while to put things straight. But don't stay in the war room too long. It's easy to get accustomed to power and control and hard to let go of it. If you keep saving innovation until last then you may just never get around to the best parts at all. Your addiction to your own power and to the lure of repeated quick wins can make you too tempted to hang on, when you really need to let go.

Most people need to innovate and improve simultaneously–not put one before the other.

Confidence in your existing success, in the improvements that you have already driven, can also make you reluctant to innovate, to let people have more of their own freedom to take risks, and to do something new. This, as Clayton Christensen and his colleagues warned, can be the start of your undoing because the payoffs of past incremental improvement are probably already coming to an end. Most people need to innovate and improve simultaneously—not put one before the other.

For more than a decade, Alberta has known how to innovate in almost all of its schools, without sacrificing its record in conventional tested achievement across the system. Under the official radar of centralized reform, Ontario's success also incorporates an inclusive special education strategy and teacher-designed innovations in the present, as well as a history of professional collaboration and curriculum integration that spreads back over more than quarter century into the past. Grange Secondary School's disciplined approach to innovation brought into being an arts-centered curriculum but persisted with relentless tracking and monitoring of every student's performance as well. And the CTA's model of teacher-led reforms with measurable outcomes that principals rather than teachers had to buy into is perhaps one of the most innovative changes any system has seen at all.

Don't always leave the best until last. Take a pointer for practice from Grange Secondary School and find out how your students learn best. Then create a system, as Ontario's special education strategy has, that is flexible enough to enable schools to respond to its students' unique learning needs. As you innovate, use the new benefits of real-time data to check your progress and pick up weak signals quickly, in order to avoid false trails that lead to lost gains and improvements from before. Innovation can and should be harmonized with improvement. Indeed, the step-changes that many of our schools now need demand it.

GLOBAL FOURTH WAY TEACHERS

Some teachers who work in Second and Third Way systems find our descriptions of the Fourth Way disheartening. While it's interesting to know that there are strong public school systems in other places, this message of intended hope can offer cold comfort if you are in a micromanaged environment that drains your spirit and your energy every day.

If you are a teacher, please don't read our book this way! We included Grange Secondary School and the QEIA schools in our examples not because their struggles to go against the grain are *perfect* but because they are *instructive.* They show that teachers need to be placed at the zenith, not at the nadir of school systems.

Teaching is the largest profession. It is the one that almost everyone has experienced the most, as students, parents, and sometimes teachers ourselves. Teachers shape the minds of the future. Paraphrasing Shakespeare, we often say to children that the world is their oyster. For teachers, the world is a vast bed of oysters. It is no real surprise to learn, that statistically, teaching is the strongest influence within schools on student achievement. In our hearts and in our own memories of teachers who made a difference to us and for us, we have known this for decades. There are examples of educational excellence without accountability, or common standards, or digital technology. But there are no instances of educational excellence without high-quality teachers and teaching.

All this points to the importance of what other people in schools and school systems can do to support and challenge teachers. But there are also important pointers as to what teachers can do for others and what they should do for themselves. This section sets out five pointers for teachers' practice that can enact the Global Fourth Way of educational change:

1. Teach less, learn more.
2. Transform your professional association.
3. Promote collective autonomy.
4. Become a mindful teacher with technology.
5. Be a dynamo.

1. TEACH LESS, LEARN MORE

Finnish secondary school teachers exude an air of quiet professionalism when compared to their U.S. colleagues. And why shouldn't they? They teach 40% less than their American counterparts, so there is a lot of time every day for lesson planning, one-on-one meetings with students, collaboration with colleagues and correcting student work.[10]

How can students learn more if teachers are teaching less? Consider recent U.S. evidence. One of the latest flavor-of-the-month reforms with which American policy makers and foundations have become enamored is *expanded learning time* (ELT). As a result, programs increasing the amount of time children and young people spend in schools each day have proliferated in a number of cities and schools, often in spite of vehement opposition from teachers and students. What are the results of these programs?

The most detailed study to date has been conducted by Abt Associates, an independent research group based in Cambridge, Massachusetts. The group studied a multimillion dollar, five-year ELT initiative in urban schools in Massachusetts. Shattering the hopes of reformers, the research team found that "improved academic achievement outcomes for students have not materialized as expected across ELT schools as a whole." In addition, compared to schools without ELT, "significantly fewer students in ELT schools reported that: they look forward to going to school; like being in school; that all of their classes are important to them; and that they like the length of their school day." Schools also had "statistically higher suspension rates than would be expected in the absence of ELT."[11]

Reform programs like ELT opt for simple-minded *quantity* solutions over the more laborious and fundamental issues related to *quality*. They ignore the problems of uneven teacher quality that exist in almost all of the urban schools where the ELT programs are based, so that children often are simply receiving more instruction from beginning teachers or weak educators who have not mastered the basic skill set essential for the profession. Teaching more will not lead to learning more if the teaching, the teachers, or what has to be taught are no better than when the students were learning less.

Singapore's Teach Less, Learn More (TLLM) policy points in a more promising direction. Here, teaching less means taking on different roles in addition to traditional instruction and polishing skills as observers and questioners to make lessons more interesting and engaging. Teaching less doesn't mean less work—far from it! It means that lessons have to be prepared assiduously and artistically to engage students productively, differentiate instruction effectively, and follow the different paths that students might pursue.

Chinese-American scholar Yong Zhao views "teaching less" as being central to creating the "world-class learners" who will create the knowledge economies of the future.[12] Zhao has spent many years studying education in China and the United States and has observed the frustrations of Chinese leaders who complain that their schools produce excellent test takers but no inventive entrepreneurs. What some have viewed as traditional weaknesses of U.S. education—abundant electives at the high school level, lots of local control and diversity, and haphazard alignment across the system—Zhao views as strengths that allow for all kinds of bottom-up and side-to-side creativity.

From this perspective "teach less, learn more" isn't so much a catchy phrase as an economic and social imperative. Too many great inventors detested their time in school because they had no role to play beyond submission and deference. Schools did not help them to find their "element," in Ken Robinson's sense.[13]

So, as a teacher, let up on the relentless push to cover all the standards wherever you can. Instead of constantly searching for more entertaining and dramatic ways of teaching, step back from time to time to look at how your students are learning. Get your students to think about what they are learning and how they are learning it. Encourage them to be like the Ontario students with special educational needs who learn to advocate for themselves with all their teachers, so teachers can adjust their teaching to the ways that students learn best. Learn more, teach less.

2. TRANSFORM YOUR PROFESSIONAL ASSOCIATION

In *Teachers in Trouble,* Stuart Piddocke, Romulo Magsino, and Michael Manley-Casimir undertook a fascinating study of the kinds of disciplinary cases that get referred to teachers' professional associations and regulatory bodies in Canada, and of the judgments that are reached about those cases.[14] The examples cover illegal acts such as cattle rustling, egregious acts of sexual impropriety, and embarrassing acts such as the shoplifting of chicken parts that are more a problem of how students respond to media coverage by taunting their teachers than of the illegality of these sorts of acts themselves. Fascinating as this book is as a study of teacher misconduct and how professional associations deal with it, the reader will search in vain through the text for examples of misconduct in the area of classroom incompetence, or of failures in professional dedication.

Critics of teacher unions and teacher unionism often make exaggerated complaints against their opponents. But there is nonetheless a clear need for many teacher unions to become much more connected to the core work of their profession—teaching and learning. Ontario's educational reformers understood this when they gave more than $20 million to the province's teacher unions on condition that they spent it on professional development—thereby enhancing a transformation of the culture inside the union. Over 50% of the revenues of the Alberta Teachers' Association are allocated to professional development. This contrasts with a figure of under 5% in most U.S. teachers' associations.

When the California Teachers' Association controversially took on the responsibility to try and turn around hundreds of the lowest performing schools in California and to get more directly engaged with the core work of their profession, this led to an unexpected surge in activism among its younger members. This is another paradox of educational change—taking on more responsibility for professional development and standards doesn't weaken teacher unions. It strengthens them.

These issues are crystallized in the issue of teachers' contracts. A contract is a formal agreement of mutual responsibilities that is usually committed to paper. Contracts are necessary because they clarify our obligations. They protect the weak against exploitation. Like prenuptial contracts, they establish agreements about rights in relationships that are not yet blessed with unconditional trust.

Without contracts, one leader can easily undo the informal understandings reached with a predecessor. Older teachers can be summarily dismissed in favor of younger and cheaper replacements. Employees can fail to show up for work without giving any reason. Teachers can spread malicious gossip with impunity. Employers can bully their staff. They can set them up for failure and dismissal by constantly giving them unfavorable job assignments without them having recourse to due process.

But if contracts are necessary, they are not sufficient. Being a professional means going far beyond what is in any written contract. If you are fixated on your contract then you just have a job, not a profession. Most teachers already go far beyond their contracts, in the preparation they do at home, in the materials they purchase for their students with their own money, in the courses they take during their vacations, and in the calls they take and the e-mails they answer on their own time. They do this whether they have the protections provided by teachers' unions or not. This is because teaching, more than any other profession, attracts altruists.[15]

But this is not true of all teachers. You are not a professional or are not being treated as a professional if you sit in the parking lot until the last second when your contract requires you to enter the building. You are not a professional if you only ever go to meetings within the hours for which you are contracted, or if you refuse to participate in afterschool activities because there isn't a clause that requires it. Furthermore, when you tolerate such lack of professionalism among your colleagues, you undermine your own credibility and that of your guild. You provide evidence that the critics of teachers are right and that teachers don't have the spine to discipline one another when necessary.

You *are* a professional if you go the extra mile for your students and your colleagues whenever the circumstances demand it. You *are* a professional when you undertake professional learning in your own time as well as the time that is allocated to you officially. So go beyond the contract by doing more than the minimum. Endorse the fundamental principle that professionalism in education requires that teachers go above and beyond what is stated in writing, and that no formal contract should prohibit them from being the extended professional that the moral vocation of teaching truly requires. And if this is not what your teachers' organization stands for at the moment, get involved and change it. A new generation of teachers' professional associations is on the rise, and there is a huge opportunity to contribute to the standards and standing of your profession by getting engaged in it.

3. PROMOTE COLLECTIVE AUTONOMY

The essence of professionalism is workplace autonomy. In the old days, this was individual autonomy—the right, once you had gained your hard-earned qualifications, to be trusted and left alone to exercise your own judgment, without interference, in the best way you saw fit. But the unlimited individual autonomy of the First Way is no longer defensible.

The fidelity and compliance of the Second Way was a denial of professionalism, not a realization of it. But having failed to develop their professional capital in the First Way, educators had no arguments to advance on their own behalf when outsiders intervened in and regulated their work in the Second Way.

The Third and Fourth Ways reinvent *individual* autonomy as *collective* autonomy. While there is more exclusive emphasis on data and more focus on delivering external programs and targets in the Third Way than in the Fourth, they both have a strong commitment to shared responsibility for all students, and rigorous inquiry into improvement or innovation. To all this, the Fourth Way adds common engagement in local curriculum development and collective responsibility for professional standards and development as well as individual student achievement.

Collective autonomy is about getting out of the shadows of the profession in order to lead it. You needn't await your principal's or department head's initiative to get started. Collective autonomy begins with you, and some of the ways to start it are very simple indeed.

Be the first to welcome new staff members to your school. Be the first to knock on their door. Sit next to a new colleague or perhaps a more experienced one you have not previously known very well, in the next meeting, and strike up conversation with this person. Ask for a change in grade level or class assignment next year to have the chance to grapple with a new curriculum and meet some new colleagues. Start an inquiry project with a partner, or develop a new curriculum unit together. Organize a staff book club on an educational text, or just one that engages you all intellectually in general. Let your own curiosity guide you. Your books might be about change perhaps, or courage, or something inspiring and challenging in fiction. Find a way to make shared professional development more interesting by combining a professional development DVD with food in a dinner-and-a-movie session in your home, for example. The specific answers are many. The point is to take the lead and to know that collective autonomy begins with you and your colleagues.

4. BECOME A MINDFUL TEACHER WITH TECHNOLOGY

Robotics students in Singapore use digital technologies to design machines of the future. AISI educators receive government funding to pilot innovative new curricula with technology. Special education students in Ontario access universal design for learning and assistive technologies to produce measurable gains on provincial assessments. These examples have shown how combining innovation with improvement as part of the Global Fourth Way can harmonize the very best of the new technologies with excellent classroom pedagogy. This is the essence of a mindful use of technology.

On the one hand, mindful teaching in the current age means being comfortable and at ease with digital technologies, knowledgeable about how students use and also misuse them, and capable of integrating them into everyday classroom practice. It means being open to the ways that technology can genuinely enhance learning by sharing art or writing online, engaging in collective editing work together, assisting students with learning disabilities, and so on.

At the same time, mindful teaching with technology doesn't mean that you have to abandon the best teaching practices you've acquired over many years in the classroom. Interestingly, Silicon Valley executives are very clear what they want where their own children are concerned here.[16] Children of top executives in companies like Yahoo, Apple, Hewlett-Packard, and Google attend the private Waldorf School of the Peninsula in California where they learn how to knit their own socks while studying the origins of wool and the history of clothing; where they learn language skills by tossing around a beanbag while memorizing verses of poetry to get a better sense of syncopation and rhyme; and where they master fractions by cutting up quesadillas into quarters, halves, and sixteenths. You can *feel* wool, *catch* a beanbag, and *taste* a quesadilla. These are *tactile* technologies. We should not cast them to one side because of the fashionable digital alternatives.

Educators at this school keep technology limited in the earlier grades and only add it to their instruction as students advance, so that they are properly prepared when they move on to college and university. This model won't be right for everyone, but it does show a thoughtful approach toward how to harmonize old technological skills like knitting with new ones like tweeting in education today.

If you encourage balance and harmony with your use of technology, what do you teach students by your example? Are you spending too much time online and not enough at the gym? Do you set up technology-free "Walden zones" in your life as William Powers recommended in *Hamlet's Blackberry,* so that the other dimensions of your life are in balance? Do they see you scanning for your own messages in the middle of the school day? And when you go to professional development meetings and conferences, do you use the break periods to exchange ideas with colleagues and process what you have been learning together, or are you a blur of hyperactive thumbs amid a flurry of text messages? Switch on; switch off; stay balanced.

5. BE A DYNAMO

Change theory, like business language, is full of mechanical metaphors. But the metaphors are not always appropriate for education. Leaders speak of finding the *levers* for change, without realizing that, in mechanics, a lever is "a rigid bar used to exert a pressure . . . at one point of its length by the application of a force at a second and turning at a third on a fulcrum."[17] Do we really want change that impacts children as young as five years old to be all about pressure and force?

Others use the language of business to talk about finding the *drivers* of change. In business, a driver is a "condition or decision that causes subsequent conditions or decisions to occur as a consequence of its own occurrence."[18] Whether you are the driver or the driven, this is still a mechanistic and rather uninspiring view of how change happens. Think of students who find school disconnected from their lives and especially from the languages and cultures that they experience at home. How would language about "drivers" that we import from the business literature inspire them so that they would want to redouble their efforts to stay in school and to succeed in mastering the curriculum? So what other terms might we turn to as an alternative? Some educators prefer growth and gardening metaphors. Others opt for ecological ones. But even if we stay with metaphors of the physical world, we can still find more inspiring ones than levers and drivers instead.

On precisely the same day in January in 1867, Sir Charles Wheatstone in England, and Dr. Hermann Werner Siemens in Germany, separately announced the invention of a new machine that used electromagnets, as a kind of generator, to convert energy from one form to another. Werner Siemens named his invention the *Dynamoelektrischemaschine.* In English the literal translation of a "dynamic electrical machine" was unwieldy, so this became known as the dynamo for short.

In physics, a *dynamo* is "a machine for converting mechanical energy into electrical energy."[19] It is a generator of electrical energy. By analogy, we say that a human dynamo is "someone with a lot of energy and determination."[20] Those who possess these qualities are people

> Teachers are, or should always be, the real dynamos of educational change. In high-achieving environments they supply learning and change with their energy.

we think of as being dynamic. They don't just "leverage" change or "drive" it in the way that workers might operate a pulley or jack up a car. Instead, dynamos create and transform energy.

Teachers are, or should always be, the real dynamos of educational change. In high-achieving environments they supply learning and change with their energy. The leaders in the Alberta Initiative for School Improvement understand that by being the designers of their own innovations, teachers also become its dynamos. In Finland, Singapore, and Canada, teachers do not merely implement change. They generate it. In California, CTA teachers are the dynamic leaders of QEIA reforms in their schools, not the mere implementers of reforms that are being driven by others from elsewhere.

So don't be driven by data or anything else. Don't just deliver other people's ideas that have been invented somewhere else. Be a human dynamo: a bundle of energy that lights up everything and everyone around you.

TOWARD THE GLOBAL FOURTH WAY

This last chapter has set out pointers for practice to help you along your own Way. These are not Fourth Way mandates, programs, or even guidelines. No Fourth Way school or system can or should be replicated from one place to another or rented out by one system from another. These have been the mistakes of the Second and Third Ways that took models and strategies that were developed in one place then exported them all around the world to others.

The Fourth Way is a set of evidence-informed philosophies and practical strategies that are different from and, in terms of the results of high performance, superior to the preceding three Ways of change. The pointers for practice are indicators about how to get there, so you can find your own Way forward. The pointers might show you may already be on the right track, or they may indicate a better way to follow.

Do not feel disillusioned if your school is not like Grange Secondary School at its best; if your country seems very different from Canada, Singapore, or Finland; or if your union is unlike the ones in Alberta and California. All the examples of excellence we have described in this book began as something else. But their design and their realization were as deliberate and persistent as they were bold and imaginative. You might be inspired by Singapore or Canada, or by the rebellious spirits of educational change leaders in Northern England and California. But the secret of turning ideas into action is to grasp the common ways through which these examples of educational excellence were achieved, and to pursue them through disciplined habits of dogged persistence. It is this that will truly move you forward, individually and together.

Singapore knows how to collaborate quickly. Grange Secondary School built trust among its Bangladeshi community by employing its people as learning mentors. Alberta treated the strength of its teachers' union as an asset for innovation and improvement. Finland turned the traditional artistic creativity of its people that seemed at odds with modern economic growth into technological creativity that made the country a world leader of entrepreneurial innovation.

So what are the existing assets of your community with which you can already work? Perhaps they are the high aspirations of immigrant parents for their children. Perhaps they are colleagues who are already using technology in inspiring yet also mindful ways that connect new media to deep learning and highly effective teaching. You may know a school leader who makes it her job to circulate from room to room throughout the school day, not with a clipboard in hand to evaluate her people but with a spirit of genuine curiosity and a set of probing questions that can genuinely help. Or there may be system leaders who have become a bit too fixated on spreadsheets or who have pushed their idea of challenging conversations a bit too far, yet who have the decency and openness to respond to the constructively critical feedback you are prepared to offer them.

In the end, although the Fourth Way is something that can only be undertaken together, this does not absolve or exclude you from the individual responsibility that you must exercise as well. Will you welcome the inquisitive school leaders into your room, and respond openly to their questions when they come? Do you have the courage to "manage up" and give leaders, whom you believe have fundamental integrity, the critical feedback they need to become the best leaders they can be?

The California Teachers' Association became part of an improbable project to sue the state's governor in order to address the system's educational inequities. Graham Hollinshead at Grange Secondary School turned his depression and despair into a preparedness to "get back in and sort it out." The Alberta Teachers' Association converted external pressure to implement performance-based pay into an opportunity to create systemwide innovation. In all cases and at all times, these high performers displayed creativity, courage, and persistence to bring into being a new way that would uplift the teaching profession and improve learning for all of the school's or the system's students.

The call of the Fourth Way is to produce new examples of educational excellence—alongside those in Canada, Singapore, or Finland—that have equally bold visions and purposes. These new theories of change in action and their realization can help educators to work *with* rather than *against* the cultural grain of their improbable starting places. They can enable educators to pursue their inspiring and inclusive visions through habits of disciplined persistence and courageous leadership.

Excellence is the asymptotic state that never quite reaches perfection. "Gold cannot be pure, and people cannot be perfect," a Chinese proverb tells us. It is more productive to strive for excellence than it is to pursue perfection. In this sense, to build a new example of excellence is to construct something that will never be completely finished. To follow the Fourth Way is to journey down a path that has no final destination and one where you will never completely arrive. To stride forth and strive further is to keep searching for and struggling to achieve something that can always be even better.

Excellence is the asymptotic state that never quite reaches perfection.

Doing all this should not condemn us to endless disappointment and dissatisfaction because we have somehow fallen short of perfection. It should invite us into a hopeful existence where the world is something that can always be improved, and where we can keep on making a difference. To follow the Global Fourth Way and constantly strive for greater excellence is to believe that children's minds can always be stretched further and that what we now offer privileged students can be made available to all students. It is to believe that each of us, throughout our entire careers, can keep on improving our own professional practice to make the lives of our young people and the world they will inherit a better place.

Every year, our students will come and then they will go. We will meet new students, year after year, as the passage of time brings our own careers to their culmination and eventually to a close. But the Global Fourth Way is never-ending. It is a path that will and should continue forever. As you proceed along this path, you will leave your own unique footprint in pursuit of deeper learning, stronger professionalism, and a greater common good. You will blaze a trail of justice and excellence that will enable others to follow in your footsteps and then open up new trails of their own. You will make your mark, leave a legacy, and bequeath a world to the generations of children and teachers who will succeed you that will be all the better for your efforts. Step forth. Go Fourth. There is no time to waste.

ENDNOTES

PREFACE

1. Metropolitan Life Insurance Company. (2012). *The MetLife survey of the American teacher: Teachers, parents and the economy.* New York: MetLife.

2. Center for Research on Education Outcomes. (2009). *Multiple choice: Charter school performance in 16 states.* Stanford, CA: Center for Research on Education Outcomes.

3. Gunter, H. (2011). *The state and education policy: The academies programme.* London: Continuum International Publishing Group; Gorard, S. (2009). What are academies the answer to? *Journal of Education Policy, 24*(1), 101–113; Gorard, S. (2005). Academies as the "future of schooling": Is this an evidence-based policy? *Journal of Education Policy, 20*(3), 369–377. For a more favorable assessment, see: Department for Education. (2011). *Academies annual report 2010/2011*. London: The Stationary Office.

4. For a poignant illustration of the problems that are created when schools endeavor to replace teachers with technology, see: Herrera, L. (2012, January 17). In Florida, virtual classrooms with no teachers. *The New York Times*. Retrieved from www.nytimes.com/2011/01/18/education/18classrooms.html?_r=2&pagewanted=all.

5. Studies of merit pay have shown for many years that teaching is not a profession that satisfies the conditions under which performance-based pay is valid or efficient. Recent studies have confirmed that the outcomes of merit pay do not meet the intentions of its supporters, while negative consequences often result. Such scholarship includes: Baker, E., Barton, P., Darling-Hammond, L., Haertel, E., Ladd, H., Linn, R., Ravitch, D., Rothstein, R., Shavelson, R., & Shepard, L. (2010). *Problems with the use of student test scores to evaluate teachers.* Washington, DC: Economic Policy Institute; Ballou, D., Hamilton, L., Le, V., Lockwood, J., McCaffrey, D., Pepper, M., Springer, M., & Stecher, B. (2010). *Teacher pay for performance: Experimental evidence from the Project on Incentives in Teaching.* Nashville, TN: Vanderbilt University, National Center on Performance Incentives. For a more positive assessment of merit pay, see: Odden, A. (2008). *New teacher pay structures: The compensation side of the strategic management of human capital.* Madison: Wisconsin Center for Education Research.

6. For a description and analysis of how the educational assumptions, strategies, assessment systems and overall policies of economically powerful nations are exported to other nations see: Ball, S. J., & Youdell, D. (2008). *Hidden privatization in public education.* Brussels: Education International.

In their chapter titled "Privatising Education in the Developing World" (pp. 46–67), Ball and Youdell show how even the most noble endeavors to raise the learning of children in poorer nations—such as the Education for All and Millennium Development Goals of the United Nations—come to carry the imprimatur of policies and interests of global economic elites.

7. Day, C., Stobart, G., Sammons, P., Kington, A., & Gu, Q. (2007). *Teachers matter: Connecting lives, work and effectiveness.* Berkshire, UK: Open University Press; Day, C., & Gu, Q. (2010). *The new lives of teachers: Teacher quality and school development.* Abingdon, UK: Routledge; Huberman, M. (1989). The professional life cycle of teachers. *Teachers College Record, 91*(1), 31–57; Hargreaves, A. (2005). Educational change takes ages: Life, career, and generational factors in teachers' emotional responses to educational change. *Teaching and Teacher Education, 21*(8), 967–983.

8. Hargreaves, A., & Shirley, D. (2009). *The fourth way: The inspiring future for educational change.* Thousand Oaks, CA: Corwin.

CHAPTER 1

1. Rupert Murdoch, the CEO of *News Corporation*, has stated that he sees education as "a $500 billion sector in the US alone.": Resmovits, J. (2011). Murdoch education affiliate's $2.7 million consulting contract approved by New York City. *The Huffington Post.* July 15, 2011. Retrieved from http://www.huffingtonpost.com/2011/07/15/murdoch-education-affiliate-contract-approved_n_900379.html on July 29, 2012.

2. Ravitch, *The death and life of the great American school system: How testing and choice are undermining education.* New York: Basic Books.

3. Anderson, C. A., Floud, J., & Halsey, A. H. (1961). *Education, economy, and society*. New York: Free Press of Glencoe; OECD. (1974). *Towards Mass Higher Education: Issues and Dilemmas.* Paris: OECD.

4. Rowan, B. (2002). The ecology of school improvement: Notes on the school improvement industry in the United States. *Journal of Educational Change, 3,* 3–4; Rowan, B. (2008). Does the school improvement "industry" help or prevent deep and sound change? *Journal of Educational Change, 9*, 197–202.

5. Ravitch, *The death and life of the great American school system,* p. 200.

6. Chappell, S., Nunnery, J., Pribesh, S., & Hager, J. (2011). A meta-analysis of supplemental educational services (SES) provider effects on student achievement. *Journal of Education for Students Placed At Risk, 16*(1), 1–23; Chappell, S., Nunnery, J., Pribesh, S., & Hager, J. (2010). Supplemental Educational Services (SES) provision of No Child Left Behind: A synthesis of provider effects. Research brief. Retrieved from http://eric.ed.gov/ERICWebPortal/search/detailmini.jsp?_nfpb=true&_&ERICExtSearch_SearchValue_0=ED530860&ERICExtSearch_SearchType_0=no&accno=ED530860.

7. Murray, J. (2012, January 16). Education in brief: From academies to apprenticeships. *The Guardian.* Retrieved from www.guardian.co.uk/education/2012/jan/16/academies-special-measures-apprenticeships?INTCMP=SRCH.

8. Fabricant, M., & Fine, M. (2012). *Charter schools and the corporate makeover of public education: What's at stake?* New York: Teachers College Press.

9. Evergreen Education Group. (2011). *Keeping pace with K–12 online learning.* Retrieved from http://kpk12.com/states/idaho/; Richtel, M. (2012, January 3). Teachers resist high-tech push in Idaho schools. *The New York Times.* Retrieved from www.nytimes.com/2012/01/04/technology/idaho-teachers-fight-a-reliance-on-computers.html?pagewanted=all; Wright, M. (2012, May 8). State legislature passes new online graduation requirements. *Valor Dictus.* Retrieved from http://valor-dictus.com/news/2012/05/08/state-legislature-passes-new-online-graduation-requirements/; Florida Legislature. (2011). *The 2011 Florida statutes.* Retrieved from http://leg.state.fl.us/Statutes/index.cfm?App_mode=Display_Statute&Search_String=&URL=1000-1099/1003/Sections/1003.428.html; Legislative Council, State of Michigan. (2009). *The revised school code (excerpt).* Retrieved from www.legislature.mi.gov/%28S%28sacmdc2rrpildsiv1x45cuuo%29%29/mileg.aspx?page=GetObject&objectname=mcl-380-1278a. Regarding the evidence base related to requiring online learning, see: Means, B., & SRI International. (2009). *Evaluation of evidence-based practices in online learning: A meta-analysis and review of online learning studies.* Washington, DC: U.S. Department of Education, Office of Planning, Evaluation and Policy Development, Policy and Program Studies Service; Barbour, M., & National Education Policy Center. (2012). *Review of "Overcoming the governance challenge in K–12 online learning."* Boulder, CO: Great Lakes Center for Education Research and Practice.

10. Hu, W. (2011, December 21). Testing firm faces inquiry on free trips for officials. *The New York Times.* Retrieved from www.nytimes.com/2011/12/22/education/new-york-attorney-general-is-investigating-pearson-education.html.

11. Cochran-Smith, M., Piazza, P., & Power, C. (In press). The politics of accountability: Assessing teacher education in the United States. *The Educational Forum.*

12. National Commission on Teaching and America's Future. (2012). *Evaluation and data: Age and experience by state.* Retrieved from http://nctaf.org/research/evaluation-and-data; Carroll, T. G., Foster, E., & National Commission on Teaching and America's Future. (2010). *Who will teach? Experience matters.* Washington, DC: National Commission on Teaching and America's Future, p. 11.

13. Hargreaves, A., & Goodson, I. (2006). Educational change over time? The sustainability and nonsustainability of three decades of secondary school change and continuity. *Educational Administration Quarterly, 42*(1), 3–41.

14. Giddens, A. (1999). *The Third Way: The renewal of social democracy.* Malden, MA: Blackwell; Giddens, A. (2000). *The Third Way and its critics.* Cambridge, UK: Polity Press; Giddens, A. (Ed.). (2001). *The global Third Way debate.* Cambridge, UK: Polity Press.

15. Sahlberg, P. (2011). *Finnish lessons: What can the world learn from educational change in Finland?* New York: Teachers College Press; Sahlberg, P. (2011). The Fourth Way of Finland. *Journal of Educational Change, 12*(2), 173–185.

16. Hargreaves, A. (2003). *Teaching in the knowledge society: Education in the age of insecurity.* New York: Teachers College Press; Marshall, F. R., & Tucker, M. S. (1992). *Thinking for a living: Education and the wealth of nations*. New York: Basic Books.

17. Weber, M. (1949). *The methodology of the social sciences.* New York: Free Press.

18. Camp, R. C. (1989). *Benchmarking: The search for industry best practices that lead to superior performance*. New York: Quality Resources.

19. Tucker, M. S. (2009). Industrial benchmarking: A research method for education. In A. Hargreaves & M. Fullan (Eds.), *Change wars*. Bloomington, IN: Solution Tree.

20. Tucker, Industrial benchmarking, p. 120.

21. Examples of international benchmarking include: Organisation for Economic Co-operation and Development (OECD). (2011). *PISA 2009 at a glance*. Paris: OECD; National Center for Educational Statistics. (2009). *Trends in International Mathematics and Science Study (TIMSS) 2007 U.S. public-use data file.* Retrieved from http://nces.ed.gov/pubsearch/pubsinfo.asp?pubid=2010024; Mourshed, M., Chijioke, C., Barber, M., & McKinsey & Company. (2010). *How the world's most improved school systems keep getting better*. New York: McKinsey & Company; Barber, M., Mourshed, M., & McKinsey & Company. (2007). *How the world's best-performing school systems come out on top*. New York: McKinsey & Company; Tucker, M. S., & National Center on Education and the Economy. (2011). *Surpassing Shanghai*; Tucker, M. S., (2011). *Standing on the shoulders of giants: An American agenda for education reform*. Washington, DC: National Center on Education and the Economy (NCEE).

22. See Schleicher, A. (2009). Securing quality and equity in education: Lessons from PISA. *Prospects: Quarterly Review of Comparative Education, 39*(3), 251–263; Schleicher, A. (2009). Lessons from the world—In countries where educators are strong leaders, innovative teaching practices thrive. *Educational Leadership, 67*(2), 50.

23. See Lundvall, B-A., & Tomlinson, M. (2002). International benchmarking as a policy learning tool. In B-A. Lundvall & M. A. Rodrigues (Eds.), *The new knowledge economy in Europe: A strategy for international competitiveness and social cohesion*. Cheltenham, UK: E. Elgar.

24. Mourshed, Chijioke, Barber, & McKinsey and Company, *How the world's most improved school systems keep getting better*; Barber, Mourshed, & McKinsey & Company, *How the world's best-performing school systems come out on top*.

25. OECD. (2011). *Strong performers and successful reformers in education: Lessons from PISA for the United States*. Paris: OECD, p. 254.

26. Carnegie Forum on Education and the Economy. (1986). *A nation prepared: Teachers for the 21st century: The report of the Task Force on Teaching as a Profession, Carnegie Forum on Education and the Economy, May 1986*. Washington, DC: The Forum; National Center on Education and the Economy (U.S.). (2007). *Tough choices or tough times: The report of the New Commission on the skills of the American workforce*. San Francisco: John Wiley & Sons.

27. Tucker, *Standing on the shoulders of giants.*

CHAPTER 2

1. Christensen, C. M. (1997). *The innovator's dilemma: When new technologies cause great firms to fail*. New York: Collins.

2. Christensen, *The innovator's dilemma*, p. 24.

3. Christensen, C. M., Horn, M. B., & Johnson, C. W. (2008). *Disrupting class: How disruptive innovation will change the way the world learns*. New York: McGraw-Hill.

4. Christensen, Horn, & Johnson, *Disrupting class*, p. 98.

5. Tyack, D., & Tobin, W. (1994). The "grammar" of schooling: Why has it been so hard to change? *American Educational Research Journal, 31*(3), 453–479.

6. Metz, M. H. (1989). Real school: A universal drama amid disparate experience. *Journal of Education Policy, 4*(5), 75–91.

7. Bernstein, B. B. (1971). *Class, codes and control*. London: Routledge and Kegan Paul; Goodson, I. (1988). *The making of curriculum: Collected essays*. London: Falmer Press; Skerrett, A., & Hargreaves, A. (2008). Student diversity and secondary school change in a context of increasingly standardized reform. *American Educational Research Journal, 45*(4), 913–945; Young, M. F. D. (1971). *Knowledge and control: New directions for the sociology of education*. London: Collier-Macmillan.

8. Fink, D. (2000). *Good schools/real schools: Why school reform doesn't last*. New York: Teachers College Press, p. 162; Gold, B. A., & Miles, M. B. (1981). *Whose school is it, anyway? Parent-teacher conflict over an innovative school*. New York: Praeger; Smith, L. M., & Keith, P. (1971). *Anatomy of educational innovation: An organizational analysis of an elementary school*. New York: Wiley.

9. Giles, C., & Hargreaves, A. (2006). The sustainability of innovative schools as learning organizations and professional learning communities during standardized reform. *Educational Administration Quarterly, 41*(2), 124–156; Hargreaves, *Teaching in the knowledge society.*

10. Cuban, L. (1986). *Teachers and machines: The classroom use of technology since 1920*. New York: Teachers College Press, pp. 60–61.

11. Goldring, E., & Cravens, X. (2006). *Teacher's academic focus for learning in charter and non-charter schools*. Nashville, TN: National Center on School Choice, Vanderbilt University.

12. Drucker, P. F., Dyson, E., Handy, C., Saffo, P., & Senge, P. M. (1997). Looking ahead: Implications of the present. *Harvard Business Review, 75*(5), 18–32.

13. Collins, J., & Hansen, M. T. (2011). *Great by choice: Uncertainty, chaos, and luck: Why some thrive despite them all.* New York: Harper Collins.

14. Collins & Hansen, *Great by choice,* p. 77.

15. Collins & Hansen, *Great by choice*, p. 78.

16. Collins & Hansen, *Great by choice,* p. 21.

17. Leadbeater, C. (2004). *Personalisation through participation: A new script for public services*. London: Demos.

18. Institute of Educational Sciences (NCEE). (2011). *The nations' report card: Findings in brief: Reading and mathematics 2011*. Jessup, MD: National Center for Educational Statistics.

19. Guisbond, L., & National Center for Fair and Open Testing. (2012). *NCLB's lost decade for educational progress: What can we learn from this policy failure?* Jamaica Plain, MA: National Center for Fair and Open Testing.

20. OECD. (2011). *Education at a glance 2011*. Paris: OECD.

21. Zhao, Y. (2012). *World class learners: Educating creative and entrepreneurial students*. Thousand Oaks, CA: Corwin, pp. 25, 133, and 158.

22. Burkhauser, S., Gates, S. M., Hamilton, L. S., Ikemoto, G. S., & RAND Education. (2012). *First-year principals in urban school districts: How actions and working conditions relate to outcomes.* Santa Monica, CA: RAND Corporation; Ronfeldt, M., Lankford, H., Loeb, S., & Wyckoff, J. (2011). *How teacher turnover harms student achievement*. Cambridge, MA: National Bureau of Economic Research.

23. Springer, M. G., Hamilton, L., McCaffrey, D. F., Ballou, D., Le, V-N., Pepper, M., Lockwood, J. R., & Stecher, B. M. (2010). *Teacher pay for performance: Experimental evidence from the Project on Incentives in Teaching.* Nashville, TN: National Center on Performance Incentives, Vanderbilt University.

24. Fullan, M. (2006). *Turnaround leadership*. San Francisco: Jossey-Bass.

25. Center for Research on Education Outcomes, *Multiple choice*; Dynarski, S., Hoxby, C. M., Loveless, T., Schneider, M., Whitehurst, G. J., Witte, J., Croft, M., & Brookings Institution. (2010). *Charter schools: A report on rethinking the federal role in education.* Washington, DC: Brown Center on Education Policy at Brookings.

26. Daly, A. (2009) Rigid response in an age of accountability: The potential of leadership and trust. *Educational Administration Quarterly, 45*(2), 168–216.

27. Tucker, *Standing on the shoulders of giants.*

28. Goldring & Cravens, *Teachers' academic focus on learning in charter and non-charter schools.*

29. Zhao, *World class learners;* Zhao, Y. (2009). *Catching up or leading the way: American education in the age of globalization.* Alexandria, VA: Association for Supervision and Curriculum Development (ASCD).

30. Berliner, D. C. (2006). Our impoverished view of educational research. *Teachers College Record, 108*(6), 949–995.

31. Mourshed, Chijioke, & Barber, *How the world's most improved school systems keep getting better*; OECD. (2010). Ontario, Canada: Reform to support high achievement in a diverse context. *Strong performers and successful reformers in education: Lessons from PISA for the United States.* Paris: OECD; Levin, B., Glaze, A., & Fullan, M. (2008). Results without rancor or ranking: Ontario's success story. *Phi Delta Kappan, 90*(4), 273–280; Fullan, M. (2010). *All systems go.* Thousand Oaks, CA: Corwin.

32. Hargreaves, A., & Braun, H. (2012). *Leading for all: Final report of the review of the development of Essential for Some, Good for All—Ontario's strategy for special education reform devised by the Council of Directors of Education.* Toronto, ON, Canada: Council of Directors of Education. The data concerning Ontario that are cited in this chapter and in Chapter 6, unless otherwise stated, derive from this study, the final report, and the data supporting it. Attributions for the sources of particular quotations or factual claims are included in these endnotes, unless the attributions are obvious in the main body of the text. The study and report were concluded with significant contributions from a large graduate assistant research team at Boston College, whose names are recognized in the earlier acknowledgements.

33. Open-ended survey response which includes the remaining quotations in this paragraph.

34. Focus group interview, District 3.

35. Opening orientation meeting with elementary school principal and staff in District 3.

36. Focus group interview, District 3.

37. Open-ended survey response.

38. This chart was in the principal's office of an elementary school in District 3 above.

39. Focus group interview, District 3.

40. Interview with elementary school teacher in District 8.

41. Open-ended survey response.

42. Interview with anonymized senior ministry official.

43. Interview with another senior ministry official.

44. Interview with the anonymized senior ministry official cited in Note 42.

45. Campbell, D. T. (1975). *Assessing the impact of planned social change.* Paper No. 8, Occasional paper series. Hannover, NH: Public Affairs Center, Dartmouth College, p. 49.

46. Bird, S., Cox, D., Farewell, V. T., Goldstein, H., Holt, T., & Smith, P. C. (2005). Performance indicators: Good, bad, and ugly. *Journal of the Royal Statistical Society, Series A*(168), 1–27.

47. Examples of perverse incentives across a range of sectors are presented in Seddon, J. (2008). Systems thinking in the public sector. Axminster,

UK: Triarchy Press. For perverse incentives in crime: Goebel, P. R., & Harrison, D. M. (2012). *Money to burn: Economic incentives and the incidence of arson*. Emmitsburg, MD: National Emergency Training Center; in health care: Besley, T., Bevan, G., & Burchardi, K. (2009). Naming and shaming: The impacts of different regimes on hospital waiting times in England and Wales (CEPR Discussion Paper No. DP7306). Retrieved from http://papers.ssrn.com/sol3/papers.cfm?abstract_id=1433902; in education: Ryan, J. E. (2004). The perverse incentives of the No Child Left Behind Act. *New York University Law Review, 79*(3), 932.

48. Open-ended survey response, District 6.

49. Boellstorff, T. (2008). *Coming of age in second life: An anthropologist explores the virtually human*. Princeton, NJ: Princeton University Press, p. 21.

50. Cuban, *Teachers and machines*.

51. Shirley, D. (2011). The Fourth Way of technology and change. *Journal of Educational Change*, 12, 187–209.

52. Alberta Education. (2010). *Education Business Plan 2010–13.* Edmonton, AB: Government of Alberta. Retrieved from http://education.alberta.ca/media/1213923/20100122educationbusinessplan.pdf; Alberta Education. (2010). *Inspiring action on education*. Edmonton, AB: Government of Alberta. Retrieved from http://engage.education.alberta.ca/inspiring-action/.

53. Ballou, B. R. (2012, June 6). Haverhill teen convicted in texting-while-driving case. *The Boston Globe*. Retrieved from http://articles.boston.com/2012-06-06/metro/32066554_1_texting-fatal-crash-courtroom

54. Jackson, M. (2008). *Distracted: The erosion of attention and the coming dark age*. Amherst, NY: Prometheus Books.

55. Spitra, J. B. (2011) *Overload! How too much information is hazardous to your organization.* Hoboken, NJ: John Wiley & Sons.

56. Honoré, C. (2004). *In praise of slowness: How a worldwide movement is challenging the cult of speed.* San Francisco: HarperSanFrancisco.

57. Turkle, S. (2011). *Alone together: Why we expect more from technology and less from each other*. New York: Basic Books, p. 18.

58. Turkle, *Alone together*, p. 18.

59. Turkle, *Alone together,* p. 14.

60. Warschauer, M., & Matuchiniak, T. (2010). New technology and digital worlds: Analyzing evidence of equity in access, use, and outcomes. *Review of Research in Education, 34*(1), 179–225.

61. Lowther, D. L., Strahl, J. D., Inan, F. A., & Bates, J. (2007). *Freedom to Learn program: Michigan 2005–2006 evaluation report.* Memphis, TN: Center for Research in Educational Policy; Silvernail, D. L., & Gritter, A. K. (2007). *Maine's middle school laptop program: Creating better writers.* Portland, ME: Center for Educational Policy, Applied Research and Evaluation, University of Southern Maine; Shapley, K., Sheehan, D., Sturges, K., Caranikas-Walker, F., Huntsberger, B., & Maloney, C. (2009). *Evaluation of the Texas Technology Immersion Pilot: Final outcomes for a four-year study (2004–05 to 2007–08).* Austin: Texas Center for Educational Research.

62. Aboujaoude points out that there is a debate raging among psychiatrists today about whether it is scientifically accurate to use the term "Internet addiction," with the majority currently preferring to identify and to treat Internet abuse and dependence instead: Aboujaoude, E. (2011). *Virtually you: The dangerous powers of the e-personality*. New York: W.W. Norton, pp. 214–234.

63. Powers, W. (2010). *Hamlet's Blackberry: A practical philosophy for building a good life in the digital age*. New York: Harper.

64. Powers, *Hamlet's Blackberry,* p. 218.

65. Honoré, C. (2008) *Under pressure: Rescuing our children from the culture of hyper-parenting*. New York: HarperOne, p. 110.

66. Tremblay, M., Barnes, J., Copeland, J., & Esliger, D. (2005). Conquering childhood inactivity: Is the answer in the past? *Medicine and Science in Sports and Exercise, 37*(7), 1187–1194.

67. MacDonald, E., & Shirley, D. (2009) *The mindful teacher.* New York: Teachers College Press; Shirley, The Fourth Way of technology and change.

CHAPTER 3

1. Sahlberg, *Finnish lessons.*

2. World Economic Forum. (2011). *The global competitiveness report 2011–2012.* World Economic Forum, Geneva, Switzerland. Retrieved from http://reports.weforum.org/global-competitiveness-2011–2012/.

3. OECD (2011). Finland: Slow and steady reform for consistently high results. In *Strong performers and successful reformers in education: Lessons from PISA for the United States*. Paris: OECD, pp. 117–136.

4. Mourshed, Chijioke, Barber, & McKinsey & Company, *How the world's most improved school systems keep getting better;* Ruzzi, B. (2005). Finland education report. *National center on education and the economy new commission on the skills of the American workforce.* Washington, DC: National Center on Education and the Economy; OECD, *Strong performers and successful reformers in education.*

5. Compton, R. A., Faust, S. T., Woodard, A., Ellis, B., Wagner, T., New School Films, & True South Studios. (2011). *The Finland phenomenon: Inside the world's most surprising school system.* United States: 2mminutes.com.

6. Taylor, A. (2011). 26 amazing facts about Finland's unorthodox education system. *Business Insider.* Retrieved from www.businessinsider.com/finland-education-school-2011–12?op=1#ixzz1yG0iV56X; Partenen, A. (2011). What American schools keep ignoring about Finland's school success. *The Atlantic.* Retrieved from www.theatlantic.com/national/archive/2011/12/what-americans-keep-ignoring-about-finlands-school-success/250564; Anderson, J. (2011, December 13). From Finland, and intriguing school-reform model. *The New York Times.* Retrieved from www.nytimes.com/2011/12/13/education/from-finland-an-intriguing-school-reform-model.html?_r=1&pagewanted=all.

7. Hargreaves, A., Halasz, G., & Pont, B. (2008). The Finnish approach to system leadership. In Pont, B., Nusche, D., & Hopkins, D. (Eds.), *Improving school leadership, Vol. 2: Case studies on system leadership* (pp. 69–109). Paris: OECD.

8. Grubb, N., Marit Jahr, H., Neumuller, J., & Field, S. (2005). *Equity in education: Thematic review of Finland.* Paris: OECD.

9. Sahlberg, *Finnish lessons.*

10. Hargreaves, A., & Fullan, M. (2012). *Professional capital: Transforming teaching in every school.* New York: Teachers College Press.

11. Adapted from Hargreaves, Halasz, & Pont, *The Finnish approach to system leadership.*

12. Adapted from Hargreaves, Halasz, & Pont, *The Finnish approach to system leadership.*

13. Sabel, S., Saxenian, A., Miettinen, R., Kristensen, P. H., & Hautamäki, J. (2011). *Individualized service provision in the new welfare state: Lessons from special education in Finland.* Helsinki: Sitra.

14. Compton, Faust, Woodard, Ellis, Wagner, New School Films, & True South Studios. *The Finland phenomenon.*

15. Sahlberg, *Finnish lessons,* p. 112.

16. Hargreaves, Halasz, & Pont, *The Finnish approach to system leadership*, p. 81.

17. Sahlberg, *Finnish lessons,* p. 63.

18. Sahlberg, *Finnish lessons.*

19. Sahlberg, *Finnish lessons*, p. 82.

20. Barber, M. (2011). *Re-imagining education governance: An international perspective.* Washington, DC: Center for American Progress.

21. This critique of networks has previously been made by Hadfield, M., & Chapman, C. (2009). *Leading school-based networks.* New York: Routledge.

22. Hill, R., Dunford, J., Parish, N., Rea, S., & Sandals, L. (2012). *The growth of academy chains: Implications for leaders and leadership.* Nottingham, UK: National College for School Leadership.

23. Munby, S. (2012). Chains do more than brace weak links. *Times Educational Supplement.* Retrieved from www.tes.co.uk/article.aspx?storycode=6191841.

24. Hargreaves, Halasz, & Pont, *Finnish approach to system leadership*, p. 85.

25. Hargreaves, Halasz, & Pont, *The Finnish approach to system leadership*, pp. 79, 86.

26. Hargreaves & Shirley, *The Fourth Way,* p. 102.

27. P. Sahlberg, personal communication, January 25, 2011.

28. In announcing a review of Key Stage 2 testing at age 11, UK Education Secretary Michael Gove stated that the review should address "how to avoid, as far as possible, the risk of perverse incentives, over-rehearsal and reduced focus on productive learning". See Department for Education, "Lord Bew to chair external review of testing, News and Press Notices, 5th November, 2010, http://www.education.gov.uk/inthenews/inthenews/a0066609/lord-bew-appointed-to-chair-external-review-of-testing, last accessed, 8/20/2012; Bird, Cox, Farewell, Goldstein, Holt, & Smith, *Performance indicators.*

29. National Association of Head Teachers. (2009). *Active trust and supportive responsibility: A charter for assessment and accountability in England.* Haywards Heath, West Sussex: NAHT. Retrieved from www.naht.org.uk/welcome/resources/key-topics/assessment/naht-presents-charter-for-assessment-and-accountability.

30. Sahlberg, *Finnish lessons.*

31. Hargreaves, Halasz, & Pont, *The Finnish approach to system leadership*, p. 86.

32. Hargreaves, Halasz, & Pont, *The Finnish approach to system leadership*, p. 86.

33. Collins, J., & Hansen, M. T. (2011). *Great by choice: Uncertainty, chaos, and luck : Why some thrive despite them all.* New York: HarperCollins, p. 95.

34. Collins & Hansen, *Great by choice,* p. 21.

35. Castells, M., & Himanen, P. (2002). *The information society and the welfare state: The Finnish model.* Oxford, UK: Oxford University Press, p. 166.

36. Sahlberg, *Finnish lessons,* p. 6.

37. Finland is currently more populous than 29 states in the U.S. See: United States Census Bureau. (2010). Population estimates. Retrieved from www.census.gov/popest/data/state/totals/2011/index.html

38. UNICEF. (2001). *A league table of educational disadvantage in rich nations.* Florence: UNICEF, Innocenti Research Centre.

CHAPTER 4

1. Singapore's GDP per capita is fifth in the world: Index Mundi. (2011). *Country comparison: GDP per capita.* Retrieved from www.indexmundi.com/g/r.aspx?t=10&v=67&1 =en; OECD, *Strong performers and successful reformers in education;* One school in Singapore, the Anglo Chinese School, obtained nine perfect scores, making up almost half of only 20 candidates worldwide with the perfect score of 45: International Baccalaureate. (n.d.). Ng, J. (2008, January 8). ACS(I) among world's best in IB exams. *The Straits Times*. Retrieved from http://www.straitstimes.com/Free/Story/STIStory_193799.html

2. Attenborough, D. (n.d.). *Travels with Sir David Attenborough.* Retrieved from www.warman.demon.co.uk/anna/att_int.html.

3. Yew, L. K. (1998). *The Singapore story: Memoirs of Lee Kuan Yew.* Singapore: Simon & Schuster. For some of the most recent dialogue with Lee Kuan Yew that also refers to the visit of Deng Xiaping, see: Kwang, H. F., Ibrahim, Z., Hoong, C. M., Lim, L., Lin, R., & Chan, R. (2001). *Lee Kuan Yew: Hard truths to keep Singapore going.* Singapore: Straits Times Press. For a summary of data on Singapore's achievements, see: Schulman, M. (2009). *The miracle: The epic story of Asian's quest for wealth.* New York: Harper Business, pp. 55–80.

4. Fullan, M. (2001). *The new meaning of educational change.* New York: Teachers College Press, p. 92.

5. Interview with Cheryl Lim.

6. In Southeast Asia, a shophouse is typically a small shop or store with a residence on the floor above it.

7. Turkle, *Alone together.*

8. Aboujaode, *Virtually you*; Jackson, *Distracted.*

9. Cuban, *Teachers and machines.*

10. Handy, C. (1995). *The age of paradox.* Cambridge, MA, Harvard Business Review Press.

11. Vaish, V., Gopinathan, S., & Liu, Y. (2007). *Language, capital, culture: Critical studies of language and education in Singapore.* Rotterdam: Sense Publishers; Gopinathan, S. (2007). Globalisation: The Singapore developmental state and education policy: A thesis revisited. *Globalisation, Societies and Education, 5*(1), 53–70.

12. Goh, K. S., & Education Study Team Singapore. (1979). *Report on the Ministry of Education, 1978.* Singapore: S.N.

13. "Shaping our future: Thinking schools, Learning nation", Speech by Prime Minister Goh Chok Tong at the opening of the 7th International Conference on Thinking, Monday 2nd June, 1997, Suntec City Convention Centre Ballroom, Singapore, http://www.moe.gov.sg/media/speeches/1997/020697.htm

14. Kwang et al., *Lee Kuan Yew: Hard truths to keep Singapore going.*

15. Ng, P. T. (2003). The Singapore school and the School Excellence Model. *Educational Research for Policy and Practice, 2*(1), 27–39; Ng, P. T., & Chan, D. (2008). A comparative study of Singapore's school excellence model with Hong Kong's school-based management. *International Journal of Educational Management, 22*(6), 488–505; Mok, P. K. H., & Ng, P. T. (2008). *Changing education governance and management in Asia.* Bradford, UK: Emerald Group.

16. Tan, O. S., & Educational Research Association of Singapore. (2007). *Teach less, learn more (TLLM). School-based curriculum innovation: Research reports 2007.* Singapore: Curriculum Policy and Pedagogy Unit, Curriculum Planning and Development Division, Ministry of Education and Educational Research Association of Singapore.

17. Lee, H. L. (2004, August). *Our future of opportunity and promise.* Singapore Government Press Release. Address by Prime Minister Lee Hsien Loong at the 2004 National Day Rally, Singapore.

18. Tharman, S. (2005, September). *Achieving quality: Bottom up initiative, top down support.* Speech by Tharman Shanmugaratnam, minister for education, at the Ministry of Education Work Plan Seminar 2005, Singapore.

19. Zulkifli, M. (2009). Experiences in education reform: The Singapore story. Speech by the Singaporean senior parliamentary secretary, Ministry of Education and Ministry of Home Affairs, at the 1st International Conference on Learning and Teaching, Bangkok, Thailand. Retrieved from www.moe.gov.sg/media/speeches/2009/10/16/thailand-conference-learning-teaching.php

20. Hogan, D., & Gopinathan, S. (2008). Knowledge management, sustainable innovation, and pre-service teacher education in Singapore. *Teachers and Teaching, 14*(4), 369–384; Ng, P. T. (2008). Educational reform in

Singapore: From quantity to quality. *Educational Research for Policy and Practice, 7*(1), 5–15.

21. Ng, E. H. (2008, August). Opening address by the Singaporean minister for education and second minister for defence, at the International Conference on Teaching and Learning with Technology, Singapore. Retrieved from www.moe.gov.sg/media/speeches/2008/08/05/opening-address-by-dr-ng-eng-h-1.php.

22. Bentley, T. (2010). Innovation and diffusion as a theory of change. In Hargreaves, A., et al. (Eds.), *The second international handbook of educational change.* Springer International Handbooks of Education, Volume 23, 29–46. New York: Springer.

23. Tucker, *Surpassing Shanghai.*

24. Thaler, R. H., & Sunstein, C. R. (2008). *Nudge: Improving decisions about health, wealth, and happiness.* New Haven, CT: Yale University Press.

25. Johnson, S. (2010). *Where good ideas come from: The natural history of innovation.* New York: Riverhead Books.

26. Brandenburger, A., & Nalebuff, B. (1996). *Co-opetition.* New York: Doubleday.

27. Interview with Adrian Lim.

28. Keat, H. S. (2011, September). Opening address by Heng Swee Keat, minister for education, at the Ministry of Education Work Plan Seminar, Ngee Ann. Retrieved from www.moe.gov.sg/media/speeches/2011/09/22/work-plan-seminar-2011.php.

29. OECD, *Strong performers and successful reformers in education,* p. 161.

30. OECD, *Strong performers and successful reformers in education.*

31. Mourshed, Chijioke, Barber, & McKinsey & Company, *How the world's most improved school systems keep getting better.*

32. Tucker, *Standing on the shoulders of giants,* p. 33.

CHAPTER 5

1. UNICEF, *Child poverty in perspective;* United Nations Development Programme. (2011). *Human development report 2011.* New York: UNDP; Transparency International—Country Profiles. (n.d.). *Transparency International—the global coalition against corruption.* Retrieved from www.transparency.org/country#CAN; The World Factbook. (n.d.). *Distribution of family income—the Gini Index.* Retrieved from www.cia.gov/library/publications/the-world-factbook/fields/2172.html.

2. OECD 2010, *PISA 2009 results: Executive summary.*

3. Tucker, *Surpassing Shanghai.*

4. Knighton, T., Brochu, P., & Gluszynski, T. (2010). *Measuring up: Canadian results of the OECD PISA study: The performance of Canada's youth in reading, mathematics and science: 2009 first results for Canadians aged 15.* Ottawa: Statistics Canada.

5. Knighton, Brochu, & Gluszynski, *Measuring up.*

6. OECD, *Strong performers and successful reformers in education,* p. 68.

7. OECD, *Strong performers and successful reformers in education,* p. 69.

8. Hancock, D. (2009). *Leading and learning—celebrating the great journey.* Speech presented at the AISI Conference, Calgary, AB, Canada.

9. Hargreaves, A., Crocker, R., Davis, B., McEwen, L., Sahlberg, P., Shirley D., & Sumara, D. (2009). *The learning mosaic: A multiple perspectives review of the Alberta Initiative for School Improvement AISI.* Edmonton, AB: Alberta Education.

10. Hargreaves et al., *The learning mosaic.*

11. Sumara, D., & Davis, B. (2009). Using complexity science to study the impact of AISI on cultures of education in Alberta. In Hargreaves, Crocker, Davis, McEwen, Sahlberg, Shirley, & Sumara. *The learning mosaic*, pp. 34–61.

12. This excerpted account is from an adapted and edited version of the original text in Sumara & Davis, Using complexity science to study the impact of AISI on cultures of education in Alberta.

13. Hargreaves et al., *The learning mosaic.*

14. This supposed truism appears in many places. One authoritative source is Michael Fullan. In *Motion Leadership*, p. 25, Fullan states that "research on attitudinal change has long found that most of us change our behaviors somewhat before we get insights into new beliefs. The implication for approaching new change is clear. . . .give people experiences in relatively nonthreatening circumstances and build on it."

15. The critical perspective of the Alberta Teachers' Association on standardized testing, combined with the organization's dedication to continuing to work with government collaboratively whenever possible, is explained in: Alberta Teachers' Association. (2009). *Real learning first: The teaching profession's view of student assessment, evaluation and accountability for the 21st century.* Edmonton, AB, Canada: Alberta Teachers' Association.

16. Alberta Education. (2012). *Alberta education—10 Point Plan for Education.* Retrieved from www.education.alberta.ca/department/ipr/10ptplan.aspx

CHAPTER 6

1. The population of immigrants in Ontario is taken from the website of the Ontario Ministry of Finance: Sponsor. (2003). *Census 2001 highlights: Factsheet 5: Immigration to Ontario.* Retrieved from www.fin.gov.on.ca/en/economy/demographics/census/cenhi5.html

2. See, for example, Levin, B. (2008). *How to change 5000 schools: A practical and positive approach for leading change at every level.* Cambridge, MA: Harvard Education Press; and Fullan, M. (2010). *All systems go: The change imperative for whole system reform*, Thousand Oaks, CA: Corwin.

3. OECD, *Strong performers and successful reformers in education,* p. 22.

4. Ontario Ministry of Education. (2005). *Education for all: The Report of the Expert Panel of Literacy and Numeracy Instruction for Students with*

Special Education Needs, Kindergarten to Grade 6. Toronto, ON, Canada: Queen's Printer, p. 3.

5. Interview with initial coordinator of the design team for the CODE project and former district director of education.

6. Hargreaves, A., & Braun, H. (2012). *Leading for all.* Council of Directors of Education. Toronto, ON, Canada: Council of Directors of Education. The data cited in this chapter, unless otherwise stated, derive from this study, the final report, and the data supporting it. Attributions for the sources of particular quotations or factual claims are included in these endnotes, unless the attributions are obvious in the main body of the text. The study and report were concluded with significant contributions from a large graduate assistant research team at Boston College, whose names are recognized in the earlier acknowledgements.

7. Hargreaves & Braun, *Leading for all,* EQAO Results Chapter. All the data in this paragraph are drawn from this source.

8 Hargreaves, A., & Fullan, M. (Eds.). (2010). *Change wars*. Bloomington, IN: Solution Tree.

9. Interview with Ben Levin, former deputy minister.

10. Interview with Ben Levin, former deputy minister.

11. Rose, D. H., & Meyer, A. (2002). *Teaching every student in the digital age: Universal design for learning.* Alexandria, VA: ASCD; Hitchcock, C., Meyer, A., Rose, D., & Jackson, R. (2002). Providing new access to the general curriculum: Universal design for learning. *Teaching Exceptional Children, 35*(2), pp. 8–17.

12. Interview with special education superintendent in District 3.

13. Interview with school principal, District 9.

14. Open-ended survey response.

15. Edyburn, D. L. (2000). Assistive technology and students with mild disabilities. *Focus on Exceptional Children, 32*(9), 1.

16. Interview with elementary teacher, District 10.

17. Interview in Learning Center, District 7.

18. Interview in Learning Center, District 7.

19. Interview in Learning Center, District 7.

20. Interview with special education resource teacher, District 8.

21. Open-ended survey response.

22. Interview with teacher, District 3.

23. Interview with the superintendent of District 7, a former teacher of the hearing impaired.

24. Interview with teacher, District 5.

25. Interview with Barry Finlay, director of the Special Education Policy and Programs branch for the Ministry of Education.

26. See, for example, Mourshed, Chijioke, & Barber, *How the world's most improved school systems keep getting better*; OECD, *Ontario, Canada: Reform to support high achievement in a diverse context;* Levin, B., Glaze, A., & Fullan, M. (2008). Results without rancor or ranking. *Phi Delta Kappan, 90*(4), 273–280.

27. Interview with ESGA co-chair and former district superintendent of special education. The leadership structures and responsibilities for initiating and implementing what was first known as the CODE project (the project steered by the Council of Directors of Education), and that then became known as Essential for Some, Good for All are rather complex. So, to clarify the sources that follow, the person who was first responsible for confirming and agreeing the existence of the CODE project with the Ministry of Education was Frank Kelly, CODE executive director. The CODE project that turned into Essential for Some, Good for All, or ESGA, then had an initial project coordinator in the first year. Her cited data are referred to as "Interview with initial coordinator of the CODE project and former district director of education." This coordinator left the position after one year, and the leadership of what was now firmly the ESGA project was undertaken by two co-chairs who were also former superintendents of special education. They are referred to in cited data as "Interview with ESGA co-chair and former district superintendent of special education." Last, other members of the small Steering Team are referred to as Steering Team officials. This designation is sometimes also assigned to the project co-chairs, where the need for anonymity is greater.

28. Interview with high school principal, District 7.

29. Interview with two senior Ministry of Education officials who were leaders in the Special Education Programs Branch at the time of ESGA.

30. Interview with two senior Ministry officials who were leaders in the Special Education Programs Branch at the time of ESGA, as in Note 29.

31. Interviews as per Notes 29 and 30.

32. Thompson, E.P. (1971). The moral economy of the English crowd in the eighteenth century. *Past and Present*, *50*, 76–136.

33. Interview with ESGA co-chair and former district superintendent of special education.

34. Interview with Frank Kelly, CODE executive director.

35. Interview with ESGA Steering Team official.

36. Interview with ESGA Steering Team official.

37. Interview with Frank Kelly, CODE executive director.

38. Interview with initial coordinator of the CODE project and former district director of education.

39. Interview with ESGA co-chair and former district superintendent of special education.

40. Interview with initial coordinator of the CODE project and former district director of education.

41. Interview with ESGA co-chair and former district superintendent of special education.

42. Interview with initial coordinator of the CODE project and former district director of education.

43. Interview with ESGA co-chair and former district superintendent of special education.

44. Interview with ESGA Steering Team official.

45. Interview with two senior Ministry officials who were leaders in the Special Education Programs Branch at the time of ESGA.

46. Interview with ESGA Steering Team official.

47. Interview with CODE co-chair and former district superintendent of special education. The ensuing quotation is also taken from this interview.

48. Interview with ESGA Steering Team official.

49. Interview with Frank Kelly, CODE executive director.

50. Interview with ESGA Steering Team official.

51. Interview with Frank Kelly, CODE executive director.

52. Interview with ESGA Steering Team official.

53. Interview with ESGA Steering Team official.

54. This case and the following three are all district examples drawn from the project.

55. Interview with ESGA co-chair and former district superintendent of special education.

56. Interview with initial coordinator of the CODE project and former district director of education.

57. Interview with ESGA Steering Team official.

58. Interview with initial coordinator of the CODE project and former district director of education.

59. The following case example is based on observations and focus group interviews with a large group of school staff, District 2.

60. Open-ended survey response.

61. Based on analysis of closed-question survey responses.

62. Open-ended survey response.

63. See Sharratt, L., & Fullan, M. (2012). *Putting FACES on the data: What great leaders do.* Thousand Oaks, CA: Corwin.

64. Interview with Frank Kelly, CODE executive director.

65. Interview with initial coordinator of the CODE project and former district director of education.

66. Interview with initial coordinator of the CODE project and former district director of education.

67. Interview with Frank Kelly, CODE executive director.

68. Interview with Frank Kelly, CODE executive director.

69. Interview with Frank Kelly, CODE executive director.

70. Interview with ESGA co-chair and former district superintendent of special education.

71. ESGA is not the only Fourth-Way style initiative already at work in Ontario that is more explicitly focused on innovation and professionally generated change as a priority. Another one of these is the Teacher Learning and Leadership project where, since 2007–08, several thousand Ontario teachers with four or more years of teaching experience have been involved in designing, reviewing, reporting on, and collectively sharing their own school-based innovations. For a report of this project's work, see: Lieberman, A. (2010). Teachers, learners, leaders. *Educational Leadership, 67.*

CHAPTER 7

1. UNICEF, *Child poverty in perspective.*

2. Hargreaves, A., & Harris, A., with Boyle, A., Ghent, K., Goodall, J., Gurn, A., McEwen, L., Reich, M., & Johnson, C. S. (2011). *Performance beyond expectations.* Nottingham, UK: National College for School Leadership. The overall study is of 18 organizations in business, sports, and education that, at the time of the study, performed above expectations in relation to past performance, performance of similar peers, and availability of resources and support. The study of Grange Secondary School, like the other cases, was based on an intensive three-day site visit, with a project team of three, who undertook tape-recorded and transcribed interviews with leaders and members of the organization, observed the organization at work, and collected key archival data about performance and processes. At Grange Secondary School, the interviews were with present and former headteachers (principals); other members of the senior leadership team; and a range of department heads, school governors, and learning mentors. Archival data include school inspection reports, records of examination success reported on national databases, internal reports of attendance rates, and nationally published indicators of social deprivation in the wider community. This chapter is drawn from an extended case study report of over 12,000 words produced for and ethically approved by the school and the participants interviewed within it. Data attributions by name or by role are made in these endnotes unless they are self-evident in the body of the chapter.

3. Department for Communities and Local Government. (n.d.). *Indices of Deprivation 2010—Communities and neighbourhoods—Department for Communities and Local Government.* Retrieved from www.communities.gov.uk/communities/research/indicesdeprivation/deprivation10/

4. Interview with the chair of governors.

5. Interview with Graeme Hollinshead, Grange School's recently retired headteacher.

6. Interview with deputy headteacher.

7. Interview with chair of governors.

8. Interview with deputy head.

9. Interview with Graham Hollinshead.

10. Interview with Graham Hollinshead.

11. Interview with Gillian McMullen, headteacher at the time of the study.

12. Interview with vice governor.

13. Interview with assistant head, the next position below deputy head in the English system.

14. Interview with assistant head.

15. Interview with vice governor.

16. Interview with assistant head.

17. Interview with assistant head.

18. Interview with assistant head.

19. Interview with vice governor.

20. Interview with the school's business manager.

21. Interview with department head.

22. Interview with assistant head.

23. Robinson, K., & Aronica, L. (2008). *The element: How finding your passion changes everything.* New York: Viking.

24. Interview with deputy head.

25. Interview with Gillian McMullen.

26. Johnson, L. (2007). Rethinking successful school leadership in challenging U.S. schools: Culturally responsive practices in school-community relationships. *International studies in Educational Administration, 35*(3), 49–57.

27. Interview with assistant head.

28. Interview with head learning mentor.

29. Interview with Graeme Hollinshead.

30. Interview with assistant head.

31. Interview with business manager.

32. Interview with business manager.

33. Interview with Head of Year.

34. Interview with vice governor.

35. Interview with Graeme Hollinshead.

36. Interview with business manager.

37. Interview with business manager.

38. Interview with Gillian McMullen.

39. Interview with Gillian McMullen.

40. Interview with assistant head.

41. Interview with assistant head.

42. Interview with learning mentor.

43. Interview with head of English Department.

44. Hargreaves & Harris, *Performance beyond expectations.* Also Hargreaves & Shirley, *The Fourth Way.*

45. Interview with assistant head.

46. Interview with head of English Department.

47. Chapman, C., & Harris, A. (2004). Improving schools in difficult and challenging contexts: Strategies for improvement. *Educational Research, 46*(3), 219–228; Harris, A., James, S., Gunraj, J., Clarke, P., & Harris, B. (2004). *Improving schools in exceptionally challenging circumstances.* London: Continuum Press; James, C., Connolly, M., Dunning, G., & Elliott, T. (2006). *How very effective primary schools work.* London: Sage.

48. Interview with Graeme Hollinshead.

49. Interview with Graham Hollinshead.

CHAPTER 8

1. Nicholas, P. (2004, July 18). Gov. criticizes legislators as 'girlie men'. *Los Angeles Times.* Retrieved from http://articles.latimes.com/2004/jul/18/local/me-arnold1.

2. Caroll, S. J., Krop, C., Arkes, J., Morrison, P.A., & Flanagan, A. (2005). *California's K–12 schools: How are they doing?* Santa Monica, CA: RAND, p. xxxiv.

3. Oakes, J., Rogers, J., & Lipton, M. (2006). *Learning power: Organizing for education and justice.* New York: Teachers College Press.

4. Noah, T. (2012). *The great divergence: America's growing inequality crisis and what we can do about it.* New York: Bloomsbury; Reich, R. B. (2010). *Aftershock: The next economy and America's future.* New York: Alfred A. Knopf; Reich, R. B. (2012). *Beyond outrage: What has gone wrong with our economy and our democracy, and how to fix them.* New York: Albert A. Knopf.

5. Innocente Research Center, *Child poverty in perspective: An overview of child well-being in rich countries.*

6. Braun, H. (2010). The black-white achievement gap revisited. *Education Policy Analysis Archives, 18*(2), 1–99.

7. Johnson, S., Dondaldson, M., Munger, M., Papay, J., & Qazilbash, E. (2007). Leading the local: Teachers union presidents speak on change, challenges. *Education Sector,* 1–40.

8. Duffett, A., Farkas, S., Rothertham, A., & Silva, E. (2008). Waiting to be won over: Teachers speak on the profession, unions, and reform. *Education Sector,* 1–32.

9. Sarason, S. B. (1996). *Revisiting "The culture of the school and the problem of change."* New York: Teachers College Press.

10. Hoxby, C. (2000). The effects of class size on student achievement: New evidence from population variation. *The Quarterly Journal of Economics, 115*(4), 1239–1285; Finn, J. (2002). Small classes in American schools: Research, practice, and politics. *Phi Delta Kappan, 83*(7), 551.

11. Nye, B. (2000). The effects of small classes on academic achievement: The results of the Tennessee class size experiment. *American Educational Research Journal, 37*(1), 123–151.

12. Collins & Hansen, *Great by choice,* pp. 76–78.

13. Hargreaves, A. (1994). *Changing teachers, changing times: Teachers' work and culture in the postmodern age.* New York: Teachers College Press.

14. Vygotsky, L. (1978). *Mind in society: The development of higher psychological processes.* Cambridge, MA: Harvard University Press.

15. OECD. (2011). *Building a high quality teaching profession: Lessons from around the world.* Paris: OECD, p. 23.

16. For descriptions of teachers engaging in "mindful data analysis," see MacDonald & Shirley, *The mindful teacher,* pp. 52–56.

17. Rawls, J. (1971). *A theory of justice.* Cambridge, MA: Belknap Press of Harvard University Press.

18. Bryk, A. S., & Schneider, B. L. (2002). *Trust in schools: A core resource for improvement.* New York: Russell Sage Foundation.

19. DuFour, R., & Eaker, R. E. (1998). *Professional learning communities at work: Best practices for enhancing student achievement.* Bloomington, IN: National Education Service.

20. California Department of Education. (2010). *Quality Education Investment Act: Report to the legislature and the governor, first progress report.* Sacramento, CA: California Department of Education.

21. California Department of Education. (2010). *Quality Education Investment Act.*

22. As cited in Malloy, C., & Nee, A. (2010). *Lesson from the classroom: Initial success for at-risk students.* Los Angeles: Vital Research.

23. As cited in Malloy & Nee, *Lessons from the classroom.* Table 8.1 and Table 8.2 below are taken from Figure 1 and Figure 2 of this report on pages 10 and 11 respectively. For an explanation of the research methodology used in this study, go to Malloy & Nee, *Lessons from the classroom*, pages 6–7.

24. Hargreaves, *Changing teachers, changing times.*

25. Rogers, J., Bertrand, M., Freelon, R., & Fanelli S. (2011). *Free fall: Educational opportunities in 2011.* Los Angeles: UCLA Institute for Democracy, Education, and Access.

26. Rogers, Bertrand, Freelon, & Fanelli, *Free fall*, p. 5.

27. Brown, Gov. E. J., Jr. (2011, October 8). Address to the California State Senate, Sacramento, CA.

CHAPTER 9

1. Sampson, A. (1999). *Mandela: The authorized biography.* New York: Knopf.

2. Hargreaves & Shirley, *The Fourth Way.*

3. Boyle, A., & Humphreys, S. (2012). *A revolution in a decade.* London: The Learning Trust.

4. Those who can, do; those who can't, teach. (n.d.). In Idioms, by the *Free Dictionary, Thesaurus and Encyclopedia.* Retrieved from http://idioms.thefreedictionary.com/Those+who+can,+do%3B +those+who+can't,+teach.

5. Conaty, B., & Charan, R. (2010). *The talent masters: Why smart leaders put people before numbers.* New York: Crown Business.

6. As cited in Whicher, S. E. (1957). *Selections from Ralph Waldo Emerson: An organic anthology.* New York: Houghton Mifflin, p. 153.

7. Kets de Vries, M. (2006). *The leader on the couch: A clinical approach to changing people and organizations.* San Francisco: Jossey-Bass.

8. UNESCO. (1996). *Learning: The treasure within.* Paris: International Commission on Education for the 21st Century.

9. Mourshed, Chijioke, & Barber, *How the world's most improved school systems keep getting better.*

10. Sahlberg, *Finnish lessons,* pp. 90–91.

11. Boulay, B., Gamse, B., Checkoway, A., Maree, K., & Fox, L. (2011). *Evaluation of Massachusetts Expanded Learning Time (ELT) initiative: Implementation and outcomes after four years.* Evanston, IL: Society for Research on Educational Effectiveness.

12. Zhao, Y. (2012). *World class learners: Educating creative and entrepreneurial students.* Thousand Oaks, CA: Corwin.

13. Robinson & Aronica, *The element.*

14. Piddocke, S., Magsino, R. F., & Manley-Casimir, M. (1997). *Teachers in trouble: An exploration of the normative character of teaching.* Toronto: University of Toronto Press.

15. Ingersoll, R. (2003). *Who controls teachers' work? Power and accountability in America's schools.* Cambridge, MA: Harvard University Press.

16. Richtel, M. (2011, October 22). A Silicon Valley school that doesn't compute. *New York Times.* Retrieved from www.nytimes.com/2011/10/23/tech nology/at-waldorf-school-in-silicon-valley-technology-can-wait.html?_r=1.

17. Lever. (n.d.). *Dictionary and Thesaurus—Merriam-Webster Online.* Retrieved from www.merriam-webster.com/dictionary/lever.

18. What is driver? (n.d.). *BusinessDictionary.com—Online Business Dictionary.* Retrieved from www.businessdictionary.com/definition/driver.html.

19. Glossary of Generator Terms. (n.d.). *Lawn Mower Parts & Small Engine Parts by Briggs & Stratton.* Retrieved from www5.briggsandstratton .com/eu/en/corp/glossary/generator.aspx.

20. Dynamo (n.d.). *Macmillan Dictionary and Thesaurus: Free English Dictionary Online.* Retrieved from www.macmillandictionary.com//thesaurus/ british/dynamo#dynamo_6.

INDEX